Sexuality, Politics, and
Social Control in Virginia,
1920–1945

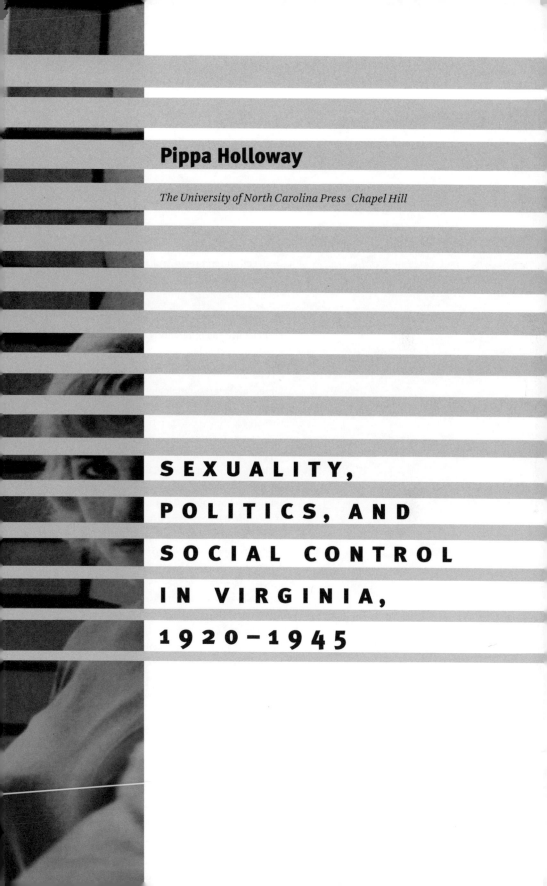

Pippa Holloway

The University of North Carolina Press Chapel Hill

SEXUALITY, POLITICS, AND SOCIAL CONTROL IN VIRGINIA, 1920–1945

Designed and typeset in Arnhem and Meta
by Eric M. Brooks
Manufactured in the United States of America

The paper in this book meets the guidelines for
permanence and durability of the Committee on
Production Guidelines for Book Longevity of the
Council on Library Resources.

Library of Congress Cataloging-in-Publication Data
Holloway, Pippa.
Sexuality, politics, and social control in Virginia,
1920–1945 / Pippa Holloway.
    p. cm.
Includes bibliographical references and index.
ISBN-13: 978-0-8078-3051-2 (cloth: alk. paper)
ISBN-10: 0-8078-3051-8 (cloth: alk. paper)
ISBN-13: 978-0-8078-5764-9 (pbk.: alk. paper)
ISBN-10: 0-8078-5764-5 (pbk.: alk. paper)
1. Sex customs — Virginia — History. 2. African
Americans — Virginia — Sexual behavior. 3. African
Americans — Virginia — Social conditions.
4. Sexually transmitted diseases — Law and
legislation — Virginia — History — 20th century.
5. Working class women — Virginia — Sexual
behavior — History — 20th century. 6. Virginia —
Race relations — History — 20th century. 7. Elite
(Social sciences) — Virginia — History. 8. Virginia —
Politics and government — 1865–1950. I. Title.
HQ18.V8H65   2006
306.7089'009755 — dc22   2006014101

cloth   10 09 08 07 06   5 4 3 2 1
paper   10 09 08 07 06   5 4 3 2 1

For my parents

Contents

Acknowledgments

One of the great joys of finishing this book is the opportunity it gives me to thank the many people who have assisted, encouraged, and inspired me along the way.

I have been grateful to receive financial support for this project from a number of sources. The Sexuality Research Fellowship Program of the Social Science Research Council funded me for a yearlong postdoctoral fellowship that allowed me to focus full-time on finishing this book. This program also offered opportunities to interact with a community of scholars doing research on sexuality. I want to particularly thank SRFP Director Diane di Mauro for her work in support of sexuality research.

I am also grateful to have received grants from the Faculty Research and Creative Activities Committee at Middle Tennessee State University and a Mellon Research Fellowship from the Virginia Historical Society. Ohio State University supported my research with the Presidential Fellowship, the Elizabeth Gee Dissertation Completion Award, the Graduate School Alumni Research Award, and the Ruth Higgins Summer Fellowship.

Brent Tarter and John Kneebone helped lure me into the study of Virginia history, and I am happy to be able to thank them in the pages of this book. Many other fine staff members at the Library of Virginia provided various assistance along the way, and I want to thank the Commonwealth of Virginia for supporting scholarship on Virginia history with such an exceptional institution. Individuals at many other archives have been helpful and patient, and I want to thank the staff at the Norfolk Public Library, the Fisk University Library, the Richmond Public Library, the Norfolk Records Management Division, the University of Virginia Alderman Library, the National Archives in College Park, Maryland, and the National Archives Mid-Atlantic Region in Philadelphia.

My colleagues in the history department at MTSU have worked to support each others' research in countless important ways, and so I owe a lot to them. Thaddeus Smith, chair of the MTSU History Department, and Jan Leone, who served as interim chair, deserve particular thanks. Members of the history department Women's Work Group helped by reading and commenting on a portion of this manuscript.

I have had the great fortune to learn from many wonderful history teachers. In particular, I thank Susan Hartmann, Leila Rupp, Jennifer Terry, and Steve Conn at Ohio State University. When I was a student at UNC-Greensboro, I was privileged to study southern history with two leading historians of the region, Alan Trelease and William A. Link, both of whom deepened my interest in southern history. A number of other historians have befriended me and guided me in important ways, including John D'Emilio, Nan Enstad, Nancy Hewitt, Steven Lawson, Jennifer Terry, and Birgitte Søland.

At the University of North Carolina Press, Chuck Grench lent his knowledge and expertise to this project, and I thank him for that. Many other fine professionals at the Press have also been involved at various stages. The Press also secured three excellent outside readers, all of whom challenged me to make this a better book. Finally, John K. Wilson contributed his copyediting skills. I thank all of these individuals for their time and energy.

I am particularly grateful to a number of individuals who engaged this project by reading chapters, commenting on conference papers, and in some cases working their way through the whole thing: Johanna Schoen, Regina Kunzel, Leisa Meyer, J. Douglas Smith, and Sonya Michel. Phyllis Hall, Nancy J. Rosenbloom, and Johanna Schoen generously shared sources with me that they encountered in their own research. Susan Freeman and Margot Canaday are two friends and colleagues who have provided intellectual engagement in far too many ways to count.

Two individuals stand out for special thanks for their involvement in my career and for enriching my life in many ways. Susan Hartmann was my dissertation director and remains a dear friend, generous with her time, energy, and kindness. Susan Cahn was my mentor for a yearlong postdoctoral fellowship, during which she read my manuscript twice and provided me with valuable feedback. She has been a wonderful friend and teacher.

While beginning this project, I enjoyed Ulpian Toney's amazing cooking, along with conversations about history and politics on a par with any graduate seminar. Betty and Dave Dickey have also been especially caring and encouraging. My step-great-aunt, Aileen "Peaches" Lynn, brought a unique joy to life in Ohio; I was glad she lived long enough to see me get a job at her alma mater, MTSU.

Throughout my life, my family has been a great source of love and inspiration. My brothers, Ken and Greg Holloway, are two of my best friends and trustworthy allies. My stepparents, Tom Lynn and Natalka Kononenko, welcomed me into their lives and have been steady influences for many years now. My father, Peter Holloway, is my biggest cheerleader and my role model for his energy, integrity, and dedication to higher education.

I want to extend a big thank-you to Debra Dickey, who has been with me through the ups and downs of this project for a good long time. She has brightened my days as we enjoyed adventures, good food, and many laughs together. I am very fortunate to share my life with her.

Finally, I want to acknowledge my mother, Caroline Tobia Holloway, who died in 1998 while I was in the first stages of this project. Her sudden and untimely death was a great loss to all those who loved and admired her. I have missed her terribly. My sorrow in her passing is slightly tempered by the honor of acknowledging her here.

*Sexuality, Politics, and
Social Control in Virginia,
1920–1945*

Introduction

Virginia's political leaders paid a striking degree of attention to sexual behavior in the 1920s and 1930s. First, in 1922 the General Assembly created the State Board of Censors, charged with preventing films from being shown in the state that were "obscene, indecent, immoral, inhuman, or . . . of such a character that their exhibition would tend to corrupt morals or incite to crime." With this act, Virginia became the first state in the South to establish a statewide movie censorship board. In 1924 Virginia lawmakers passed the nation's strictest interracial marriage law, forbidding white people to marry anyone besides those who had "no trace whatsoever of any blood other than Caucasian." At the same session, the General Assembly acted to permit the sterilization of "mental defectives," with legislation designed to be a model for other states to emulate. The U.S. Supreme Court later upheld the new sterilization statute in *Buck v. Bell*. In the following decade, Virginia's legislature funded one of the most extensive venereal disease control efforts in the South and passed a law requiring premarital testing for venereal disease.[1]

Such policies that revolved around monitoring and regulating sexual behavior illuminate the architecture of Virginia's state government and important aspects of southern politics. When white elites had a monopoly on political power, as they did in Virginia during this period, they built a state that reflected their commitment to political dominance based on race and class.[2] Though many aspects of the state may reveal the ideology of those who constructed it, sexual regulation offers particular insight into the ideologies of race and class held by southern political leaders. A belief that African Americans and lower-class whites were oversexed and lacked sexual self-restraint had a long tradition in the South and indeed much of the nation.[3] Virginia's history in this period demonstrates how these fears provided the ideological basis for public policies that regulated the sexual behavior of lower-class whites and African Americans in the name of protecting the social order.

The cultural context that constructed these groups as sexually dangerous worked in tandem with the political context that denied them the franchise, offering insight into why white elite rule mattered to the development of southern governments. Foregrounding the relationships of power that structured and facilitated the reach of the state into the realm of the sexual demonstrates how public policy was shaped by the political and ideological context in which public officials operated. As a result, sexual regulation both reflected and sustained the relationships of power operating in Virginia.

An examination of sexual regulation also provides a perspective on how the impact of state authority was differentiated by race and class, in this case showing how African Americans and lower-class whites experienced the discipline of a state that denied them the franchise. These individuals occupied a terrain that was within the accepted realm of state authority because of their tenuous claims to citizenship, and white elites directed the authority of the state at those with the least ability to fight back. Enacting and enforcing policies that were directed primarily at nonvoters posed little political risk, as these individuals had few tools with which to defend their political interests. In this way, limiting access to the franchise tied sexual regulation to the structure of political and economic power.

Once these policies were in place, public health officials targeted African American and lower-class white populations and documented evidence of success in reducing the sexual danger they posed, underscoring the notion that these groups posed a social threat. Economic marginality was important to the continued identification of these groups as sexually dangerous, because employment conditions, poverty, and the need to access state welfare programs left many powerless to reject the demands of those in authority. Cultural understandings of sexual danger were reinscribed by the structure of political and economic power, in turn reinforcing social hierarchies, an undemocratic system of governance, and particular constructions of the state.

The idea that the state—through welfare programs, public health work, and social regulation—reflects and perpetuates systems of political, economic, and social power has been explored in other contexts, perhaps most importantly in the historical literature on the formation of the welfare state.[4] But scholars have paid far less attention to the state in the South during this period, primarily because government authority in this region was quite limited.[5] The idea that "the government that governs least governs best" has been widely held for much of the region's history, and the antagonism toward strong central governments that contributed to the Confederacy's fighting the Civil War survived that war alive and well, growing even stronger during Reconstruction.[6] In the 1920s and 1930s, by all accounts, such attitudes persisted and were central to the ideology of Virginia's most powerful white political leaders. Harry Flood Byrd, Virginia's governor and leader of the state political machine from the late 1920s until the mid-1960s, devoted much of his career to challenging the expansion of government power and responsibility. As a U.S. senator, Byrd articulated his opposition to strong government in 1934 by challenging Roosevelt's policies as attempts to "control the daily activities of our people."[7] However, Virginia's leaders did support some measures that imposed exactly this type of control over those who resided in the state. What could be more coercive than eugenic sterilization, interracial marriage laws, and mandatory venereal disease testing?

Ideological as well as practical considerations did limit the state's power, and white elites did not have a blank check to construct a precise and powerful disciplinary apparatus aimed at the disfranchised masses. Restrictions existed on the reach of state authority despite a consensus among Virginia's governing elites about the kind of danger posed by uncontrolled sexual behavior among African Americans and lower-class whites and a general agreement about how the state should respond to it. A significant factor in the imposition of sexual discipline was a need to contain its cost—a political reality that had the potential to check the extent of government expansion. While legislators demonstrated a willingness to increase governmental authority in some areas, they were far less eager to increase governmental expenditures. Fear that certain state interventions might undermine social hierarchies also curtailed government's reach.

Just because white elites agreed on a general approach to the regulation of sexual behavior did not mean they always agreed on the details. Examining the disagreements among those who constructed sex-related policies and their implications for implementation is critical to understanding the larger meaning of state regulation. Though many plans were approved, others were rejected or revised prior to enactment. Also important to consider are disjunctures between the rhetoric that surrounded calls for legislation and the practice of implementing new laws. Chronicling the formation of public policy with this level of detail shows how the governing class resolved differences in its ranks and demonstrates that in different political contexts different visions of sexual regulation prevailed.

Sexual regulation performed another important function in Virginia that went beyond the actual task of regulating behavior. Those who sought an expanded role for government in the area of sexuality asserted that these policies represented a step toward progress and modernization that would help Virginia's economy. Sexual regulation would demonstrate the existence of modern conceptions of government, medicine, and the law in Virginia. According to this view, modern and progressive governments worked to provide optimum conditions for business growth, including the maintenance of a stable social order and a healthy, docile workforce. This perspective connected sexual behavior and its regulation with Virginia's drive for economic development. Policy makers, as a result, were more willing to enact proposals whose cost was further justified by their long-term economic benefits to the state.

Sexuality, Politics, and the State

This work employs the study of sexual regulation as a methodology to gain insights into southern politics, particularly into the politics of race and class in the South. "Sexual regulation" refers here to both the act of restricting sexual behavior as well as the act of categorizing and describing it. In defining regulation this way, I follow other historians of sexuality in referencing the scholarship of historian Michel Foucault. Foucault criticized traditional interpretations of social regulation (of which sexual regulation is one important type) for limiting the definition of "regulation" to the prohibition of acts. Defining regulation so narrowly overlooks important aspects of power. Foucault's expanded understanding of sexual regulation demonstrates how it has also functioned to classify sexual behavior and organize it along the boundaries of "normal" and "deviant." Regulation not only functions to restrict those behaviors defined as abnormal but to enable those behaviors defined as normal. Sexual regulations, therefore, work to distinguish between normal and deviant sexual behavior and to cast deviant behavior as socially dangerous.[8]

Foucault further contributed to the understanding of sexual regulation by seeking to trace the historical path by which this process of defining and categorizing sexual acts led to the categorization of individuals according to their sexual acts. He argued that in the modern era individuals have become sorted according to their acts, with some individuals being defined as sexually dangerous, or sexually deviant. This development, in turn, joined with historically specific understandings of the relationship of "self" to sexuality, resulting in new conceptions about the importance of one's sexual behavior to selfhood. For example, in defining the "homosexual" as a category of individuals deserving various kinds of oversight, psychiatrists, physicians, and scientists also contributed to the production of "homosexuals" as a self-identified category of individuals.

This recognition of sexual regulation and its productive potential undergirds this study. This is not simply an examination of state prohibitions of certain acts but of state activities aimed at defining sexual acts and the people who undertook them. Looking at sexual regulation this way involves tracing how the state built and enforced a system that divided sexual behavior along the binarism of "safe" and "dangerous" and then used categories of sexual behavior to classify (and perpetuate classifications between) citizens. So, for example, laws aimed at checking the reproduction of particular elements of the population were a kind of sexual regulation. Such laws, which included Virginia's eugenic sterilization policies, did not so much prohibit certain behaviors but defined them and categorized the people who carried out these activities. The sterilization statute gave a categorization to sexual activity by so-called mental defectives that differentiated these acts from the sexual behavior of mentally "normal" people. And the law attached a certain meaning to behaviors and individuals in each classification, labeling the former dangerous and the latter acceptable. A further kind of sexual regulation came about from the sterilization procedure itself. Those whom the state surgically prohibited from reproducing had their sexual behavior defined by the state; sex for them would no longer be procreative. The sterilization statute, then, did not give the state the power to proscribe sex but to describe and circumscribe it. Other sex-related policies enacted in Virginia during this period functioned in similar ways, classifying and defining sexual acts as well as citizens.

In Virginia, a binary organization of sexual behaviors and the individuals who participated in them into "normal" and "abnormal" was built on the existing classifications of race, class, and citizenship. Siobhan Somerville has shown that the policing of racial boundaries informed the construction of categories of sexual identity and vice versa in the late nineteenth and early twentieth centuries. The ideologies of race that constructed a boundary between "black" and "white," she argues, were intertwined with the struggle to define "homosexual" and "heterosexual."[9] Looking at the construction of public policies in Virginia that differentiated between categories of sexual identity shows that ideas about citizenship were similarly intertwined with the establishment of classifications of sexual behavior. The distinction between sexually "normal" and "dangerous" followed and justified the distinction between "citizen" and "noncitizen." Citizens were productive, noncitizens destructive, and sexual behavior was one area where the destructive character of noncitizens could be emphasized and delineated. Labeling certain groups "sexually dangerous" and others "sexually normal" aided in the establishment of a "class that was governed" that was distinct from the "governing class."[10]

Sex-related policies in Virginia during this period demonstrate how dividing citizens by race, class, citizenship, and sexual behavior became a project of the state. White elite leaders believed Virginia needed to regulate the sexuality of lower-class whites and African Americans of all classes. The sexual lives of these nonelite populations were thought to produce political danger for the governing class. In truth, of course, individuals of all classes and races engaged in nonnormative sexual practices that might be considered to have dangerous implications. But white elites believed their own sexual behavior primarily existed in the private sphere and consequently lacked political implications.[11] As the white middle class grew in size and social importance in this period, policy makers struggled with how to contain the sexual behavior of this population with an ideology of the state designed primarily with lower-class whites and African Americans in mind.

Those who controlled the political and economic spheres used the state to construct categories of sexuality and citizenship: Citizens were those who were sexually continent and normal. They controlled their sexual desires, restricting their sexual activity to the private sphere and confining themselves to established standards of sexual morality. Citizens belonged to the class that regulated its own sexual behavior without government involvement. They voted, held office, and influenced government policy. Lower classes — those denied access to the franchise — were unable to control their own sexual urges and were sexually dangerous. Their sexual behavior had public implications and required regulation. As a result, political, class, and sexual divides were interconnected and interdependent.

The political threat posed by these sexualized subjects was dynamic, changing and adapting to the evolving social and political contexts. As Virginia built an increasingly powerful and interventionist state over the course of the Progressive Era, the Great Depression, and the war years, white elites raised the possibility of sexual threats in different ways to define themselves as the class that could use the state to restrict others. They also responded to the changing status of the middle-class population. Sexual regulation was both a flexible tool that could be deployed in diverse ways in changing times and a productive technique that created classes of rulers and subjects. Furthermore, these regulations also helped create a government marked as modern, as the existence of sexually demarcated classifications of citizen-ship was, for Virginia's ruling elite, an indication of progress and advance-ment. Sexual regulation played a role in both creating and populating the state.

Focusing on sexual regulation in the context of Virginia politics connects the theoretical considerations of sexual discipline to the more practical world of politics. Foucault argued against the search for a centralized source of oppression and rejected the idea that power resides in specific locations or individuals. Rather, he suggested that historians look at the process of power, a broad range of operations and relations through which power op-erates. This perspective has helped inspire historical studies that look be-yond the formal state (lawmakers, police, and courts) as the agent of sexual regulation in the modern era. Individuals with access to social power and an interest in perpetuating existing hierarchies of power have participated in such regulation, including doctors, psychiatrists, educators, and the clergy. Together they created a decentralized network of power that expanded the reach of the state into many areas, including sexuality. This network could then regulate sexuality in a much more sophisticated way, not just by pun-ishing behaviors but by shaping the meanings of these behaviors.[12]

The state that undertook the work of regulation in Virginia was a multi-faceted entity that exercised power in disparate areas. State attempts at sexual discipline relied on the combined efforts of government authorities and private individuals, and a network that reached beyond the formal state operated to regulate sexuality in Virginia. While municipal and state gov-ernments enacted and enforced policies concerning sexual behavior, those who supported the state also played a critical role in defining particular be-haviors as dangerous and in implementing public policy.

Virginia is an especially revealing location in which to view this broadly defined state because of its starkly drawn boundaries of race, class, and gen-der. A fairly homogeneous group of white elite males worked to advance a shared economic and political agenda. They sought docile but productive workers, an economic system that perpetuated vast disparities in wealth, and the subordination of African Americans. This class held an extraordi-nary degree of control over the state, science, education, religion, law, and more. So, while sexual regulation here did indeed emerge from a network of disciplinary systems, there was a simplicity to the distribution of power in Virginia that makes possible a relatively precise identification of social and political agendas and the processes that served them.

Formal political power in Virginia was deeply polarized by race and class, as it was to greater or lesser extents across the South. A small class of wealthy whites controlled the agenda of the state, while African Americans and lower-class whites had no voice in politics of any consequence. In 1949 one of the most important scholars of southern political history, V. O. Key, described Virginia's government as a "political museum piece." The statistics on participation in gubernatorial elections demonstrate the extremes of Virginia politics even in relation to its neighbors. A smaller share of potential voters cast ballots in the governor's race in Virginia than in any other state in the South. Key further noted that in midcentury Virginia, 11.5 percent of the eligible population voted in the Democratic primaries, and a similarly small number voted in other state elections. White upper- and middle-class Virginians wielded a disproportionate level of influence in state politics — and thus comprised the vast majority of that 11.5 percent — while black and lower-class white citizens held almost none.[13]

As in other southern states, Virginia's turn-of-the-century suffrage restrictions have been held primarily responsible for low electoral participation. But Virginia stands out, even among southern states, as having granted the rights of citizenship to a particularly narrow group. J. Morgan Kousser has pointed out that a 54 percent decline in voter turnout occurred after the 1902 Virginia constitution made voting contingent on payment of a poll tax, a lengthy residency requirement, and a literacy test. As a result, Kousser writes, "The active electorate was so small that from 1905 to 1948 state employees and office-holders cast approximately one-third of the votes in state elections." Key concludes, "By contrast, Mississippi is a hotbed of democracy."[14]

This polarized political and economic landscape shaped the fate of Virginia's growing middle class. Some members of the white middle class did vote, particularly those employed by the state government. These individuals might best be termed the "upper middle class," and their interests tended to align with the upper class. Upper-middle-class white men and women played a key role in serving the state, and thus protecting elite interests, by working as government bureaucrats, members of the law enforcement and justice systems, social workers, and more.

But the sexual behavior of the middle class remained suspect. White elites demonstrated increasing concern that members of this class would reject upper-class values of sexual containment and fall victim to lower-class licentiousness. The involvement of middle-class whites in the growing culture of public entertainment concerned elites, as middle-class sexual behavior seemed to be tending toward public expression. As a result, some forms of sexual regulation targeted the middle class as well. Virginia's efforts at movie censorship are an example of state discipline of middle-class sexuality as it appeared in the public sphere. Further concern with the public sexual practices of middle-class white women became manifest in the "pickup girl" scare during the Second World War as these women increasingly socialized in bars and other public places. Evidence that the white middle class would follow upper-class reproductive patterns further concerned Virginia's leaders. Some eugenic advocates feared that low levels of reproduction by the middle class — like low levels of reproduction among elites — would degrade the quality of the population.[15]

On the other hand, lower-middle-class whites increasingly aligned with poor and working-class whites in this period, repudiating their loyalty to white elites. Historian J. Douglas Smith finds that lower-class white Virginians began to question the ability of the wealthiest whites to protect their interests in the 1920s. Racial tensions played an important part in provoking changes in class allegiance. African Americans amplified their calls for social and political changes at a time when urban populations of both races began to expand. Threatened by this nascent resistance to white supremacy, lower-middle-class, working-class, and poor whites blamed elites for a failure to manage race relations. These lower-class whites demanded that segregation be strengthened and African Americans be more thoroughly excluded from state services. Under attack from nonelite whites and blacks, elites failed to satisfy either side, and the system of paternalism, by which elite Virginians had managed race relations for decades, began to crumble.[16]

The black community was also stratified by class, and some of the wealthiest African Americans functioned as community representatives or liaisons to white leaders, providing them with a degree of influence in the political arena. A small number of these upper-class African Americans even retained the franchise in Virginia after 1902, primarily members of the upper tier of the professional class. But since the vast majority of African Americans remained disfranchised, this study uses the shorthand "African Americans and lower-class whites" to describe those without access to the ballot.[17]

In Virginia, like the rest of the nation, access to political power was divided by gender as well as by race and class, with men having a disproportionate influence in the establishment and enforcement of public policy. Advocates of sexual regulation sought to appeal to the ideologies of gender held by this predominantly male ruling class, a strategy that consequently inscribed gender ideologies in the kinds of regulations implemented. But white elites of both sexes worked to block attempts to access political power by African Americans and lower-class whites, and both sexes benefited from the political power granted to their class by the status quo.

Gender has historically played an important role in demarcating boundaries of race and class in Western historical contexts. In the South, racial and class differences were constructed in gendered terms, with white elite female respectability providing the standard by which the deviance of lower-class whites and African Americans were judged. Ideas about the sexual purity and restraint of white women, in particular those of the upper class, have served to maintain and naturalize boundaries of race and class, and challenges to the purity of white elite women were seen as challenges to the social dominance of whites. As a result, gender served as a defining feature of sexual normalcy and deviance, with the sexual respectability of upper-class women contrasting with the sexual disrepute of lower-class whites and African Americans, reaffirming the need to regulate the sexual behavior of the lower classes.[18]

While some of the regulation of sexual behavior in Virginia during this era was motivated by a desire to discipline female sexuality, in many cases the project of sexual regulation targeted men as well. The sexual behavior of African American and lower-class white men frequently fell under the gaze of the state. And in some instances, middle- and upper-class white men were suspect as well. The political context of this period of Virginia history made challenges to the class and racial order the primary concern of white elite political leaders, and thus a spectrum of sexual behaviors that seemed to threaten this order demanded discipline. For example, white men who violated the Racial Integrity Act faced punishment, the portrayal of indecent male behavior in films provoked censorship, and middle-class white high school and college students were required to submit to venereal disease tests.

The individuals who wrote and enforced state policy and the electorate to whom state officials and policy makers felt responsible comprised a small, clearly identifiable group with a shared ideology and common agenda. These individuals advanced a program of sexual regulation and reaped diverse benefits from these policies. This is not to say that the political landscape of Virginia was entirely flat and completely lacking in conflict or diversity of interest. To the contrary, policy makers wrestled with competing agendas and priorities throughout this period. But Virginia's leadership class shared a commitment to white elite rule that was rooted in shared beliefs about African American inferiority, sexual danger, and the threat of populist uprisings.

Scholarship on sexuality, most notably scholarship on the role of sexuality in colonial contexts, has demonstrated that an important genesis of sexual danger is the fear of the transgression of boundaries. The ability of sexual behavior to cross, weaken, or blur social distinctions is one of the characteristics that has made sex seem so dangerous. Sexual behavior or even sexual attraction across racial and class boundaries might weaken social distinctions, and interracial sex might undermine racial distinctions through the production of mixed-race offspring. Furthermore, disease might cross social boundaries through sexual contact. In multiple historical contexts, but again perhaps most starkly in that of colonial rule, physical contagion (be it the tainting of whiteness through the production of interracial offspring or the corporal corruption brought by disease) has been thought to cause and be caused by moral and cultural contagion. The converse is also true. Just as sexuality is a point where borders of race and class might be crossed, sexual regulation has historically served as a mechanism to protect these distinctions.[19]

These historical precedents help explain why sexual regulation in particular became a central project of the state in 1920s Virginia. The possibility that white elite control was on the decline contributed to the increased attention to sexual regulation in that decade.[20] Policing the behaviors that might pollute the white race or white bodies would protect the hierarchy that placed white elites at the top of the social and political order. From this perspective, the impact of the policies discussed in this work extended far beyond the people directly affected by them. Though the actual scope of sexual regulations was often narrow, their importance surpassed the actual number of people punished or the cost to the state. Sexual regulation does not have to encompass a sizable part of the government activity in Virginia to be of historical importance. These sex-related policies operated on another level, beyond the extent to which they expanded the coercive powers of the state. Thus, with a growing sense that the established political order was under threat, policy makers turned to sexual regulation as a means of defending it.

The Context of Southern Political History
Southerners had already begun to debate the merits of expanded government in this period. During the Progressive Era, the South began a transition toward the acceptance of a greater degree of governmental power and involvement in daily life. Using the technique of moral crusades, southern progressive reformers promoted new ideas about government and helped

spark a movement for modernization and economic development through improved public education and public health. Nonetheless, a general opposition to the development of strong governments continued, curbing the extent of Progressive Era reform. These attempts to expand governmental power met with resistance from local communities that sought to maintain autonomy and control. Southerners were simply unwilling to sufficiently expand governmental power to create the administrative systems necessary for real changes. In most cases, reform required centralization, but this centralization caused local communities to resist these efforts.[21]

Though many southern leaders had misgivings about expanding the power of state government to institute a broad-ranging progressive agenda, many did agree on a more limited set of reforms often called "business progressivism." Virginia's business progressives, joined by those in other southern states in varying degrees, called for a limited expansion of state government in order to promote economic growth. Harry Byrd, for example, was an exemplary business progressive. In his inaugural address, Byrd proclaimed that under his leadership "the manifold activities of the state [would be] systematized and directed with the great efficiency of a business corporation."[22] Business progressives in Virginia worked to modernize state government, reorganize tax systems, and expand state services. In particular, Governor Byrd turned the attention of state government to expanding the state's highway system as a means to economic advancement. Municipal leaders in Richmond embraced business progressivism before many other cities in the region. Motivated by the hope that the city would emerge as a regional leader, they promoted the expansion of public initiatives as early as 1900. Good government could generate economic growth, and Richmond's middle and upper classes embraced the politics of reform. This approach to government enabled reformers to counter those who called for low taxes and minimal public services.[23]

Roads and taxes were at the heart of the business progressives' agenda, but policies that focused on sexual behavior were also entwined with Virginia's drive for economic development and progressive government. Those who sought an expanded role for government in the area of sexuality used the rhetoric of economic progress to justify their proposals. But sexual regulation was not the only area in which the agenda of business progressivism proved expansive. In fact, during this period a number of reforms, some of which had only a tenuous connection to business growth, were touted as having economic benefits. The Commission on Interracial Cooperation (CIC) sought to improve relations between the races in the region, stem racial violence, and better the lives of African Americans. Though members of the CIC certainly had a commitment to social justice, the desire for greater social order and its accompanying brand of economic progress also played a motivating role.[24] The antilynching campaigns of the 1920s and 1930s shared similar impulses, moral, political, and economic. Antilynching efforts in Virginia gained invaluable support from white elites who called attention to the role of lower-class whites in committing these racist attacks. Elites consolidated their power by reigning in lower-class whites whose unchecked racism, combined with their populist sentiments, posed a threat to Virginia's nearly oligarchic rule. Racial tension might produce social instability, diverting the state from the path of business growth, and so progressive governments should work to keep such antagonisms to a minimum.[25]

Those advocating new sexual regulations between 1920 and 1945 framed their plans primarily in terms of public health and economic efficiency, although their efforts did have some continuity with those of the previous generation of moral reformers. State involvement in moral issues had won support during the drive for Prohibition, laying the groundwork for the support of a wider range of policies directed at sexual morality. Moral standards that had been established and enforced by churches, families, and communities gave way to governmental surveillance of the population and state constraints on individual behavior in this period.[26]

Joining moral reform with business progressivism served to unite the ruling class in Virginia, which in this era was comprised of the elite manufacturing interests, agricultural families, and a growing urban upper-middle class.[27] The policy makers who proposed the various schemes at regulating sexual behavior under discussion here succeeded in gaining the support of all parts of the electoral class by emphasizing both their moral and economic benefits, while making sure they did not upset the racial order. Industrialists, of course, stood to gain from the economic rewards these policies could bring the state. However, the urban middle classes — those likely to be more sympathetic to progressive reform and suffrage — were more apt to find the moral aspects persuasive. This is not to say that southern industrialists opposed moral reform or that urban progressives resisted economic growth but rather that these policies had multiple facets upon which different groups could affix their focus. The final element of the New South political alliance, the planters, demanded that blacks remain at the bottom of the social scale. Their interests were met in the process of drafting legislation, as they underscored the importance of preserving the racial status quo in any new government undertakings.

With the onset of the Great Depression, the local and national political contexts changed. Historians have suggested that though the New Deal did transform attitudes toward government in the South, its impact on Virginia was smaller than in other southern states, and opposition to expanding government authority remained strong in Virginia throughout this era. The economic depression generated support in the South for more governmental power, even for the federal government, whose influence southerners had long rejected. As a result, southerners began to imagine a changed relationship between individuals and the state as increased numbers of people relied on the government for relief. Also transformed in this era was the relationship between the states and the federal government, as state resources for relief work (actual or perceived) soon met their limit, necessitating federal intervention. As a result, the region experienced political centralization and bureaucratization. Further changes in this period came from developments in agriculture and industry that increased the size of the industrial workforce, often concentrated in cities, and decreased the need for farm labor. Cities grew, and municipal and state governments expanded, taking on new roles and responsibilities.[28] Most historical accounts of southern governments in this period assume that the impulse to expand the state usually came from outside the region—that is, federal pressure—or absolute necessity.[29] Virginia's history of sexual regulation, however, suggests that some of the expanded state efforts of the 1930s and 1940s were "homegrown" and had roots in the statewide drive for sexual discipline in the 1920s as well.

The New Deal changed Virginia less than it did other states, including its southern neighbors, because the Depression had a comparatively minor effect on the Old Dominion. Though Virginians certainly experienced an economic downturn, the relatively diversified industry and conservative fiscal policies dampened its impact. Furthermore, two regions of the state—Hampton Roads and northern Virginia—had economies that relied heavily on federal money, buffering them from the worst effects of the Depression and helping them bounce back more quickly. Finally, as was true of other southern states, economic fluctuations had a lesser effect on poor Virginians who relied heavily on subsistence agriculture; they could not get much poorer than they already were. As a result, Virginia had less need for federal assistance and resisted many of the changes that such federal intervention brought other states.[30]

The relative prosperity in Virginia helped set the stage for vitriolic attacks on Roosevelt's policies by two Virginia political leaders, Senators Carter Glass and Harry Byrd. Governor John Pollard appointed Byrd to fill a vacated seat in the U.S. Senate in 1933. Glass, a former secretary of the treasury under Woodrow Wilson and eight-term member of the U.S. House of Representatives, served in the Senate from 1920 until 1946. Virginia's senators became two of the most outspoken conservative critics of the New Deal in the Congress.[31] Glass began his offensive in the early days of the Roosevelt administration, when even Byrd supported the president's plans, warning, "Roosevelt is driving this country to destruction faster than it has ever moved before. Congress is giving this inexperienced man greater power than that experienced by Mussolini and Stalin, put together."[32] Byrd's attacks began in Roosevelt's second year, when he publicized his disagreements with the administration's farm policies. Echoing Glass's earlier comparison between Roosevelt and authoritarian foreign leaders, Byrd called the Agricultural Adjustment Act the "Hitler of American Agriculture."[33] His campaign against the New Deal continued on a variety of fronts, including opposition to the Federal Emergency Relief Administration, an attempt to reduce the size of the Works Progress Administration's allocation, and a vote, with Glass and four other senators, against the Social Security Act.[34]

Though the views of Byrd and Glass toward government were not, of course, reflective of all other Virginia politicians at the time, the tight grip Byrd held on the state's political machine through his governorship and career in the U.S. Senate meant that many Virginia officials shared his views on most issues. Historian Ronald Heinemann's biography of Byrd illustrates the level of control the former governor held, describing the process by which the machine selected its gubernatorial candidate, an activity labeled in those years "giving the nod." Byrd and other "Organization" stalwarts met with prospective nominees and weighed their merits. Byrd led the group to a consensus around one candidate. The individual selected would be the machine's nominee for the primary; he would be virtually guaranteed victory in that race and then would be certainly guaranteed victory in the partisan election. While Byrd did tolerate some independence among Organization candidates, they all had to share his general political philosophy. Machine members did not control all elected seats in the state and did not win all they ran for, but the control by Byrd's machine was as near to complete as anywhere in the nation.[35]

State and municipal efforts to command more authority over sexual behavior, already expanding in the 1930s, grew greater still during the Second World War as the level of danger certain activities posed seemed to increase. The expanded military presence in Virginia brought more federal money and influence to the region. The South housed a disproportionate number—over 60 percent—of new army camps and received 40 percent of federal expenditures on new military and naval stations in this period.[36] A concomitant nationwide venereal disease control effort connected national security to individual surveillance, and local officials in Richmond and Norfolk worked to control venereal disease by monitoring sexual behavior between unmarried heterosexuals.

Traditional hostility to high taxes, growing bureaucracies, and federal power remained strong and factored into decisions about policies in urban Virginia. Despite the fact that the war brought significant transformations to the state, the vision of government realized in the earlier decades persisted in this era. Leaders in Richmond and Norfolk were wary of building the broad system of sexual surveillance and discipline envisioned by federal leaders, though the two cities approached the issue differently.

Changes in the political economy during the Second World War had important implications for the construction of sexual deviance. The venereal disease control campaign threatened to upset the traditional southern focus on the sexual pathology of lower-class whites and African Americans with its insistence on the sexual danger of white women from a range of classes. Political and economic considerations prompted a new emphasis on white female sexual danger, but the public policies local governments produced were shaped by ideologies of race, class, and gender and a consensus about the role of the state. Evidence from the 1940s further illuminates how sexual regulations were produced by both ideological and political circumstances.

The varied attempts to regulate sexual behavior in Virginia investigated in this book offer a new perspective on the development of the state in the South. Heinemann describes Harry Byrd's conception of government this way: "He desired for himself and for Virginia an environment with maximum opportunity and minimum limitations for the individual. Government's role in creating this environment was to be helpful and unobtrusive, a government that was 'lean and mean,' economical and efficient, with low taxes, few regulations, and competent services."[37] Virginia's history of sexual regulation suggests a different story. These policies demonstrated that the state took on a variety of tasks that limited the individual, ranging from establishing stringent regulations on marriage, to disabling the reproductive capacity of some of its citizens, and to monitoring the content of movies in minute detail. Such policies do not evoke a government that is "lean and mean" or that offers "maximum opportunity" to its citizens, but rather one that disciplined one class on the behalf of another. A "lean" state governed the white elite, but those on the margins of political power faced the scrutiny of a "mean" state.

Chapter 1 of this work looks at the process of rallying Virginia's elite to support three new laws passed in the 1920s that legalized eugenic sterilization, provided for the censorship of films by the state government, and tightened restrictions on interracial marriage. The chapter focuses on the process of drafting these laws, bolstering support for them, and passing them. The passage of these three laws in two successive legislative sessions suggests that they sprang from a similar motivation and sought similar ends.

Chapter 2 examines how these laws were enforced in the 1920s and 1930s. It interrogates the rhetoric that surrounded calls for legislation and compares these rationales with actual implementation of the new laws. Although the activities of the Board of Censors continued until 1965, its work is most significant in these early decades, during which the board came to terms with its mission and developed its standards. The chapter also examines the nature of the disciplinary state constructed in Virginia, exploring the structures of race, class, and gender that facilitated the reach of public officials into private sexual behavior. Finally, the chapter looks at the extent of and limitations on governmental power in regulating sexual behavior. One such limitation was financial, due to the high degree of resistance to increased taxes. Policy makers were presented the task of implementing new programs with little or no new money, and most of the policies under discussion here produced remarkably few new expenses for the state.

The third chapter investigates the venereal disease control program established in Virginia in the 1930s. To avoid opposition and secure support from the legislature, advocates of venereal disease control designed a program that carefully avoided any impact on elite Virginians. The new policies targeted particular segments of the population—domestics, cooks, industrial workers, and people arrested for sex-related crimes—for surveillance and mandatory treatment. These individuals were primarily members of disfranchised groups: African Americans and lower-class whites. By documenting the categorization of these populations as sexually dangerous, this chapter shows how constructions of race, class, and sexual danger were tied to the distribution of political power. The chapter also considers the relationship between Virginia and the federal government in this decade of expanding federal power and responsibility.

The fourth chapter locates another side of Virginia politics and venereal disease control in the Depression years by identifying contested elements of these policies. Three examples receive particular attention. The first is the controversy generated by federal funding for a venereal disease clinic in Norfolk run by African Americans. A second example is the "barber bill," which would have allowed the state to regulate the health, hygiene, and moral standing of barbers through a licensing board. This bill was aimed at putting African American barbers out of business, and its failure reveals a limit to what the state might do in the name of public health, even to African Americans. Premarital venereal disease testing legislation proposed in 1938 is the final example of policy debate. Unlike the other measures that only affected people on the margins, mandatory premarital testing would affect Virginians of all races and classes. The plan provoked outrage and angry testimony from citizens concerned about the extent of government intervention in their private lives.

Chapter 5 documents the history of efforts for and against birth control in Virginia in the 1920s and 1930s. Opponents and supporters of contraception drew on the same arguments about sexual regulation and progress that proponents of the other three sex-related laws of the 1920s had advanced. In fact, individuals on both sides of the birth control debate had been involved in these other campaigns as well. But important differences separated birth control from the other measures explored in this work.

Chapter 6 is the first of two chapters that shift the focus from state to municipal efforts at controlling sexual behavior. During the Second World War, Richmond officials began a campaign to stop prostitution and combat venereal disease by increasing mandatory venereal disease testing and requiring treatment in some cases. City officials also widened their attention from an exclusive focus on professional prostitutes toward the more difficult problem of general female sexual promiscuity, embodied in the supposedly new phenomenon of "pickup girls." Concern about increasing governmental power and financial considerations checked the expansion of state power over these populations.

The seventh chapter looks at Norfolk and the Hampton Roads region during the war. This part of the state experienced a massive influx of people in this period, bringing significant challenges to those who sought to impose any kind of order on the population. The city's reputation for vice contributed to its being labeled America's "worst war town" in 1943, and two federal investigating committees visited the region in an attempt to sort out its problems. Steadfast resistance to regulation and discipline by servicemen (and their female acquaintances) rendered carefully planned interventions by bureaucrats ineffective. The chapter concludes that at the heart of the city's troubles were the conflicting agendas of local and state governments, federal health officials, and the military.

The epilogue examines the legacy of venereal disease control efforts and prostitution regulation in the immediate postwar period and briefly surveys the fate of the other policies considered in this work though the 1970s.

In the years between 1920 and 1945, the confluence of ideas about eugenics, progress, and modern government led the white elites of Virginia to find sexual regulation a promising area that would help protect the existing social and political order. Though sexuality functioned as a means to an end for those with political power in Virginia, enacting policies regulating sexual behavior was more than just another way to keep citizens in line. Rather, sexuality was an important site where elites could assert their authority by underscoring the wisdom and naturalness of their rule while simultaneously defending against challenges to it.

This history demonstrates the contingent relationship between political power and constructions of sexual deviance. As policy makers articulated and developed the logic behind expanding sexual regulations, worked to mobilize support for these policies in the legislature and among medical and other professionals, and publicized the benefits such regulations would bring the state, they also were working to justify and defend government by white elites in Virginia. The process of expanding sexual regulation helped create a distinction between citizen and noncitizen that paralleled the distinction between agent of the state and target of the state. In doing so, Virginia's elites reinforced the importance of excluding some from citizenship. The absurdity of giving the franchise to those whose wanton behavior could damage Virginia—weakening the economy and moral order in various ways—was reinforced by highlighting the dangers of this behavior. As a result, the structure of political power reinscribed the pathology and deviance of those on the margins.

All this serves to further outline the impact of disfranchisement and the denial of full citizenship to African Americans and lower-class whites for roughly a century of southern history. Denial of citizenship was more than a denial of the right to vote, more than an unjust distribution of public services, and more than the inability to influence elected officials. Rather, government by white elites had significant implications for the formation of the state, the construction of sexual danger, and the maintenance of hierarchies of class, race, and gender. Constructions of race, sexuality, and citizenship in Virginia were neither neutral nor preordained but were instead shaped by the fact of elite government. This approach to governing and regulation — the idea that government discipline should be aimed at "others" but not at "us" — has a history that extends far beyond midcentury Virginia. Virginia's white leaders were neither the first nor the last to suggest that "we" should govern "them," but they did it with a degree of aplomb that makes its parameters and significance particularly clear.

A Decade of New Legislation

At the 1922 and 1924 sessions of the Virginia General Assembly, legislators approved several important bills aimed at regulating sexual behavior. First, in March 1922 the Assembly passed "an act to regulate motion picture films and reels." Any film shown in the commonwealth would henceforth be previewed by the newly created Virginia State Board of Censors. The board would license films for popular viewing only if they were free of "obscene, indecent, immoral, inhuman" depictions and if the censors agreed that the films would not "tend to corrupt morals or incite to crime."[1]

At the next session of the General Assembly, in 1924, lawmakers passed "an act to preserve racial integrity." This new law forbade whites from marrying nonwhites — individuals who were black, Asian, American Indian, "Malay," or members of any other "non-Caucasic strains." But what made this law noteworthy was its strict definition of whiteness. Even though the Assembly had tightened the definition of "colored" just fourteen years earlier to include anyone with one-sixteenth or more of "negro" blood, this new Racial Integrity Act was even more restrictive, defining "white persons" as those with "no trace whatsoever of any blood other than Caucasian." After 1924, having a single black ancestor, regardless of how remote, would make one ineligible to marry a white person. The new law also increased the punishment for attempting interracial marriage to a possible jail sentence of two to five years.[2]

At the same 1924 session, the General Assembly also passed the Virginia Sterilization Statute, permitting the sterilization of any resident of the state's four mental institutions or the Lynchburg State Colony for Epileptics and the Feeble-Minded who was "affected with hereditary forms of insanity, idiocy, imbecility, feeble-mindedness, or epilepsy." The text of this law explained that the propagation of the mentally ill was a "menace," highlighted the benefits of sterilization to both the individual patient and society, and emphasized the fact that sterilization would facilitate the release of many in institutions. It also rigorously defined the process physicians had to complete before undertaking the surgery by providing for hearings before a hospital board, the appointment of guardians in some cases, and the right of representation by counsel in court appeals.[3]

Virginia's leaders demonstrated with these new laws a conviction that certain kinds of sexual behavior were dangerous, and their passage represented both a local manifestation of enthusiasm for eugenics and a growing belief in the need for state regulation of sexual behavior. The ideology of eugenics provided the foundation for the sterilization and racial integrity campaigns, but policy makers seeking to use the state to promote eugenics made choices that were embedded in the specific political context of white elite rule. Focusing sexual regulation on the politically marginal, white elites used eugenics to produce sexual regulations that reinscribed and maintained traditional relations of race and class while also building on social constructions of gender.

Laws motivated by eugenics built on the political and cultural ideologies of Virginia's white elites, including understandings of sexual danger and a belief in the need for state sexual regulation. Promoters of eugenics in the South appealed to convictions that white southerners already held, specifically the idea that uncontrolled sex went hand in hand with social disorder and threats to elite rule. These white elites found the converse notion — that efforts to regulate sexual behavior would strengthen their social control — similarly persuasive. Movie censorship sprang, then, from the same framework that made eugenics so appealing. The general notion of sexual danger that made eugenics plausible in Virginia inspired support for censoring the sexual and racial content of movies as well. Eugenics-based public policy won credibility in Virginia in part due to the authority often granted to scientific knowledge. But scientific ideology was also valorized by its connection to sexual ideologies, facilitating the transformation of eugenic theories into public policy.

Neither the idea that sex was dangerous nor the appeal of expanding state responsibility in certain areas was new to the 1920s. The possibility that certain sexual behaviors could harm American society was as old as the nation itself, and during the Progressive Era concerned citizens and leaders across the country had viewed prostitution and venereal disease as interrelated threats.[4] Progressivism had ushered in increased demand for government involvement in improving the lives of its citizens in the name of economic and social development. One of the most popular manifestations of Progressivism in the South was public health work, and public health efforts encouraged southern leaders to connect individual health and personal conduct to the well-being of the larger society. States across the South and the nation had expanded their health and welfare programs in the Progressive Era, and Virginia was as enmeshed in hookworm eradication, tuberculosis prevention, and more as any other southern state.[5]

While other historians have observed that Virginia's Racial Integrity Act and sterilization policies stemmed from similar agendas, they have reached this conclusion by examining the intellectual framework behind them and the arguments made by their most vocal proponents.[6] It is true that the two plans shared a common genesis in eugenics, but it is equally important to look at the legislative process that produced their passage and the ways a broadly defined state enforced them.[7] This expanded context enables an exploration of the role of sexual regulation in the construction of a disciplinary state and demonstrates the importance of racial and sexual ideologies to the maintenance of social and political hierarchies. Furthermore, this perspective allows for the consideration of how fears of sexual danger connected eugenics-related policies and movie censorship. This chapter focuses on the process that led to the passage of these three laws, while the following chapter explores how state bureaucrats interpreted and enforced them.

Virginia had been a leader in caring for the mentally disabled ever since the nation's first hospital for the insane opened in the state. The Publick Hospital for Persons of Insane and Disordered Mind opened in 1773 in Williamsburg; no other state would open such a facility for almost fifty years. By 1884 Virginia had four institutions for those labeled insane. In 1910 the state opened the Virginia State Colony for Epileptics in Lynchburg, the same year the legislature established the Board of Charities and Corrections and charged it with overseeing the state's expanded welfare programs.[8]

Soon after the Lynchburg colony's establishment, members of the new Board of Charities and Corrections began to pressure the state to expand the facility's mission to include the "feeble-minded," a population that would later be termed "mentally defective" and still later "mentally handicapped."[9] This proposed expansion was rooted in the shifting popular view of such persons, a change, according to historian James Trent, from considering them a burden to society to seeing them as a threat.[10] Most menacing were the highest functioning of this group, those who could care for themselves, hold jobs, and perhaps even appear normal to the untrained eye. In these individuals lurked dangerous weaknesses, in particular moral weakness. Mental health leaders in this era considered moral degeneracy, defined most often as "loose" sexual behavior, a sign of mental degeneracy. Thus, lack of moral restraint was believed to be an important indicator of "feeble-mindedness."[11]

The Board of Charities and Corrections sought to demonstrate the sexual danger feebleminded people posed in order to justify an increased state commitment to institutionalization. A survey of white and black children in Virginia's welfare and penal institutions had already found nearly half to be feebleminded. Board members hired social worker Elizabeth Wells to explore the connection between prostitution and feeblemindedness. Wells surveyed prostitutes in Richmond, concluding that more than half were feebleminded. Armed with this evidence, lobbyists persuaded the legislature to approve the admittance of feebleminded women to the colony, admitting men two years later. In 1919 the board changed the Lynchburg facility's name to the State Colony for Epileptics and the Feeble-Minded, making it the first such facility in the South.[12]

Historian Steven Noll finds that southerners sought the construction of these institutions to provide both protection for the feebleminded and protection from them. Supposedly high rates of reproduction in this population and the tendency of feebleminded individuals, according to the dominant belief of the time, to give birth to similarly defective children made them particularly perilous to the state. Unchecked, they were comprising a growing segment of the population. The military's revelation of a high incidence of feeblemindedness in young men examined for the draft during the "Great War" accelerated calls for a solution. Casting about for an answer, the Virginia General Assembly passed a law in 1918 prohibiting the marriage of individuals who were criminals, mentally retarded, epileptic, insane, or infected with venereal disease. However, the law made no provision for enforcement—the legislature set up no mechanism to certify people as free of or afflicted by any of these characteristics. Clerks of courts who issued marriage licenses could simply deny the license to individuals they believed met any of these criteria.[13]

With calls for protection from the menace of the feebleminded becoming increasingly strident and institutions filled to capacity, the idea of eugenic sterilization seemed a logical solution. Drawing inspiration from the eugenics movement, public health leaders seized on sterilization as a way to curb the menace of the mentally defective. This procedure—surgery to remove or disable an individual's reproductive organs (in women, closing or severing the fallopian tube, and in men, performing a vasectomy)—would stop these individuals from producing further generations of feebleminded individuals.

Doctors in Virginia began sterilizing feebleminded women in state institutions soon after the state opened the Lynchburg facility in 1916. By all accounts, a large number of surgeries were performed there, though an exact number is difficult to come by. The superintendent in Lynchburg, Albert S. Priddy, admitted to surgically sterilizing approximately eighty women between 1916 and 1917. It is not completely clear how many surgeries were performed exclusively for the purpose of sterilizing the patient. Priddy suggested that in many cases surgery was initiated to treat gynecological problems and that sterilization occurred as a result of these procedures. But as he was a staunch advocate of sterilization, it is likely that his definition of "medical necessity" was flexible and that his diagnosis of "pelvic disease" often served as an excuse for sterilizing patients.[14]

In these early years, there was no existing legislative sanction for sterilization, and soon Priddy faced a lawsuit brought by a white man named George Mallory. Mallory claimed that Priddy had sterilized his wife, Willie, and daughter Jessie without consent. The family's trouble stemmed from a 1916 raid by the police on the Mallory family's home in Richmond. George Mallory was away and two male friends were visiting when the police came and charged Mrs. Mallory with running a brothel. They arrested her along with her children and the male visitors. The young children were put in the care of a charitable society, but their mother and two eldest daughters, Jessie and Nannie, were held at the city detention home. After a few weeks, they were judged to be feebleminded and sent to the Lynchburg colony. Several months later Priddy sterilized Willie and Jessie Mallory and ordered them discharged. An angry George Mallory wrote to Priddy threatening trouble unless Nannie was released unharmed. Priddy wrote back saying that the surgery had been performed at the request of the two women as treatment for pelvic disease. He also told Mallory that he would have him arrested and sent to the Lynchburg institution if Mallory threatened him again.[15]

Priddy's response angered George Mallory, who responded with a lawsuit. Though in March 1918 a jury found Priddy not guilty in *Mallory v. Priddy*, the lawsuit frustrated and angered him. More important, it prompted him to begin a campaign for the legal sanction of sterilization.[16] In the 1919 annual report of the Lynchburg hospital, Priddy called for judicial immunity for doctors who performed sterilizations. His friend and colleague Dr. Joseph DeJarnette, director of the Western State Hospital, echoed Priddy's appeal in his institution's annual report. Soon they had enlisted the support of Aubrey

Strode, an attorney and member of the General Assembly. Strode drafted the bill that became the sterilization statute, modeling it on the "Model Eugenical Sterilization Law" written by Harry Laughlin.[17]

The connections between Priddy, DeJarnette, and Strode, their shared intellectual grounding in eugenics, and the specific content of the sterilization statute have been documented by others and need not be reiterated here. Gregory Dorr's work looks at the intellectual legacy of a group of eugenics-minded professors at the University of Virginia, arguing that the "liberal sowing of eugenics ideology" in Virginia "began to bear legislative fruit" with the passage of the sterilization statute and the Racial Integrity Act.[18] Priddy, DeJarnette, and Strode demonstrated their roots in this intellectual tradition by arguing that "mental defectives," particularly those identified as "feeble-minded," tended to reproduce their own kind. Without governmental intervention, the state would soon be overflowing with moral and intellectual degenerates, whose (alleged) laziness, inability, and need for state welfare services would ravage the state's economy. Sterilizing such individuals could break the cycle and improve the fitness of the overall state population.[19]

Receptivity among legislators to the ideas of eugenics clearly played an important role in the passage of the eugenic sterilization law, but supporters of this law also appealed to other principles held by legislators as well. Furthering the allure of sterilization were claims of its economic benefits. Sterilization would save the state money, because many individuals who had been institutionalized could be discharged or paroled following sterilization since they no longer could produce children. Not only would the state avoid the cost of lifelong institutionalization, but some of these individuals might become productive, self-supporting workers. These ideas were written into the text of the sterilization statute:

> Whereas, the Commonwealth has in custodial care and is now supporting in various State institutions many defective persons who if now discharged or paroled would likely become by propagation of their kind a menace to society but who if incapable of procreating might be discharged or paroled and become self-supporting with benefit both to themselves and to society.[20]

In a letter to Strode, DeJarnette estimated the economic benefits of sterilization would save Virginia $400 million over one hundred years if the sterilization statute passed.[21]

Calls for eugenic sterilization also featured appeals to popular understandings of gender and, in particular, ideas about female sexual danger. The *Mallory* case and Priddy's descriptions of other sterilizations performed prior to 1924 reveal the extent to which the drive for eugenic sterilization was motivated in part by a desire to control disorderly women. The connection mental health leaders made between moral and mental degeneracy meant that women who had multiple sexual partners or who were sexually active outside of marriage could be categorized as "feeble-minded," even if they gave no other indication of being so. Feebleminded women were easy targets for state discipline through the mental health system. Fear of uncontrolled female sexual behavior and a desire to reign in this population was a major motivation in the long battle to legalize sterilization in Virginia.[22]

For Superintendent Priddy, the primary threat posed by feebleminded women was their sexual deviance. When asked who at his institution would benefit from the new policy of sterilization, he replied, "I should think from 75 to 100 women. The men have other anti-social tendencies just as glaring as child-bearing, and we would have to keep them there [in the institution]—they rank below the tramps and hoboes."[23] Sexual deviance was what made women threatening. Men, though, might be dangerous in any number of ways, including promiscuity, crime, vagrancy, and more. Therefore, sterilizing women would bring the most benefits.

John H. Bell, Priddy's successor in Lynchburg, held similar views on the unique threat of female sexuality, going so far as to argue that "if all mentally defective women were sterilized, there would be but little reproduction of feeble-minded persons." Bell reasoned that the "female defective" was more dangerous than the male because she could be preyed upon by sexually aggressive men of all mental levels. Furthermore, feebleminded men were less dangerous since "the feeble-minded male cannot enter into serious competition with the normal male for the affections of the feeble-minded female."[24] These complicated formulations led to the same conclusion: sterilize women.[25]

Armed with the argument that eugenic sterilization was vital to the state's economic well-being and appealing to fears of female sexual danger, advocates of the procedure began their effort to obtain legal approval for sterilization in Virginia. In 1924 they achieved their goal. The legislature passed the Virginia Sterilization Statute with no opposition in the Senate and only two votes against it in the House of Delegates. Governor E. Lee Trinkle signed the bill into law on 20 March.[26]

The law's authors crafted the statute carefully and planned for it to be a national model for such legislation. The conditions that had to be met before surgery could occur were meant to circumvent judicial objections that had befallen laws in other states.[27] With similar care and planning, Priddy chose the first person to be sterilized under the new law, an eighteen-year-old white woman named Carrie Buck, with the intention of bringing a "friendly suit" to prove the new law's constitutionality. Buck fit the bill perfectly in Priddy's eyes, because her case involved hereditary mental retardation (doctors testified that her mother, sister, and seven-month-old daughter were retarded) and sexual immorality, as her daughter, Vivian, was born out of wedlock.[28] Further evidence that the Buck family's (alleged) problems were due to heredity rather than environment came from the fact that Buck was adopted when she was four years old by respectable, and thus presumably mentally normal, parents. Mrs. J. T. Dobbs raised Carrie in Charlottesville "until her moral delinquencies culminated in the illegitimate birth of a child." Nothing could help the Buck family, but eugenic sterilization could save the state from further damage from this dangerous clan.[29]

The trial of *Buck v. Priddy* in the Circuit Court of Amherst County reveals the extent to which those involved with promoting Carrie Buck's sterilization focused on controlling female sexuality, in particular through this surgery. The case shows the complex ways in which physical sexual differences became interpreted through a cultural framework that saw women as pathological, dangerous, and in need of control. The fact that women, not men, give birth to babies meant that the maternity of a child was more certain and easily ascertained than the paternity. There was no question that Carrie Buck was unmarried and pregnant, and therefore there was no question in the minds of these observers of her moral and mental degeneracy. Carrie Buck could not escape the responsibility for her pregnancy nor the fact of its illegitimacy, while the baby's father could and did. Buck later said that the baby's father was a nephew in the Dobbs family and that she became pregnant after he raped her. He was never accused of being feebleminded, morally or mentally deficient, or sexually dangerous, because his identity was never officially demonstrated. And, of course, he was never surgically sterilized.[30]

Biological and cultural circumstances also led Priddy to chose a female inmate, Carrie Buck, as the test case rather than a man. Priddy already had experience with sterilizing women in the years before Buck's case came to trial. As the case of the Mallory family illustrates, Priddy surgically sterilized numerous women, explaining the need for such surgery with a diagnosis of pelvic disease or other unspecified health problems. Women were thought to be more fragile and prone to reproductive problems, and thus various kinds of unspecified surgical procedures were to be expected. Patients and their families would have been reluctant to engage the doctor in discussions of female anatomy, and most either trusted his judgment in performing such procedures or felt powerless to question him. On the other hand, male anatomy and health did not have same the tradition of silence and air of mystery. And doctors rarely, if ever, performed surgery on men that might have sterilization as an unintended side effect. Given his vast experience sterilizing women in the course of "normal" medical care, Priddy was fully prepared to defend the benefits of performing the procedure on women. Selecting a woman as the test subject for the trial was an obvious choice for him.

Another easy choice for Priddy was the selection of a white person for the test case. Those pushing for sterilization in Virginia made no particular mention of African Americans, and indeed the campaign to legalize sterilization implicitly focused on the white population. There were several reasons for this focus. The patients that Bell, DeJarnette, and Priddy oversaw were all white, and thus in seeking authority to sterilize their patients, these physicians had whites in mind for the surgery since their hospitals only served white patients. In addition, advocates of eugenic sterilization were primarily concerned with "purifying" the Caucasian race (or, more specifically, those of western and northern European ancestry) and were thus less interested in sterilizing African Americans, who they would have considered largely unredeemable.[31] Finally, this focus on whites was part of the larger context of southern government in the age of Jim Crow. States provided far more services for whites than for African Americans, a bias that extended to a preference for Progressive Era reforms aimed at uplifting the white population.[32] Eugenic sterilization fit into this tradition, as those campaigning for its legalization appealed to this history of white-oriented reform.

The term "friendly suit" describes *Buck v. Priddy* rather well, since the attorneys on both sides of the suit supported the statute and had long-standing social relationships. Aubrey Strode, who served as the attorney for the state, had drafted the sterilization statute. Priddy had performed gynecological examinations on Strode's second wife prior to their marriage. Carrie Buck's attorney, Irving Whitehead, had been a friend and business associate of Strode's since childhood and had served on the board of the Lynchburg colony that had voted to support sterilizations in the past. Shortly after the case was heard in the Amherst Circuit Court, Priddy sent Whitehead a check for $250 as payment for representing Carrie Buck.[33]

Priddy died of Hodgkin's disease in January 1925 while the case was still on appeal, and John H. Bell replaced him as director of the hospital and as the defendant in the lawsuit. When *Buck v. Bell* was argued before the Supreme Court, it marked the first time the high court heard arguments on a sterilization law.[34] On 2 May 1927 the Court delivered an eight-to-one opinion upholding the statute. Writing for the majority, Justice Oliver Wendell Holmes commented, "We have seen more than once that the State may call upon the best of its citizens for their lives; it would be strange indeed if it could not call upon those who already sap the strength of the State. . . . Three generations of imbeciles is enough."[35] The Virginia statute did, as hoped, prove to be an inspiration for other legislation, and in the aftermath of *Buck v. Bell*, thirteen states enacted sterilization laws.[36]

Medical professionals across the state reacted with approval to the Supreme Court's decision. Many believed Virginia would reap economic benefits from increased sterilizations and considered sterilization to be an element of progressive social policy. Sterilization, it was believed, benefited the patient because it decreased the rate of institutionalization, a claim explored further in the next chapter. Furthermore, doctors who advocated sterilization saw themselves as participating in a new era of sexual frankness, rejecting "silence, shame, and sham" in favor of honest discussions of sexual issues in society.[37] All in all, many welcomed this procedure as part of a trend toward modernization and progress.

Behind this progressive and paternalistic exterior lay another motive that can be discerned by looking more closely at who led the fight for sterilization in Virginia. The men who put the state in the forefront of sterilization also ran the mental institutions, in particular Drs. Priddy and DeJarnette. Though they sought to protect Virginia's feebleminded citizens and promote economic growth, these were not their only concerns. These men were also motivated by issues relevant to their positions as directors of institutions, motivations that came into play in a number of ways. First and most obviously, Priddy sought legal sanction to run his institution the way he felt was best (for the state and for his patients). Resentful that his decision to sterilize patients had resulted in a lawsuit, he sought legal protection for his actions. The sterilization statute would give him the power to do what he wished in his institution. Second, sterilizing patients gave Priddy and others more control over the population of their facilities. Sterilizing and then releasing the patients most likely to survive well on their own — the feebleminded — allowed the facilities to reduce overcrowding and focus their limited resources on those with more severe handicaps.[38]

Finally, publicizing the threat that mentally retarded people posed through their unchecked reproduction only served to make the job of caring for these people — the job held by those leading the charge for eugenic sterilization — that much more important. The legislation significantly enhanced the stature of those who directed these institutions; they were now in charge of protecting the entire population from degradation. Virginia's mental health professionals could save the state from ruin now that the legislature had freed them from restraint and liability.

Looking at the multiple reasons for legally sanctioning sterilization, then, offers a more nuanced understanding of the statute. A belief in eugenics coupled with personal and professional concerns led mental health leaders to pursue the sterilization statute. Then they framed the case for sterilization in ways sure to persuade legislators, appealing to several core convictions held by these white elite men. Members of the General Assembly were familiar with eugenic theories and found them convincing and suggestive of progress. But advocates of eugenics also succeeded in connecting eugenic theories to existing ideas about race, class, gender, and politics to construct public policies. Arguments about the economic well-being of the state had widespread appeal to legislators sympathetic to business progressivism and convinced of the role of the state in promoting economic growth. Sterilization would mitigate female sexual danger and protect the white race; this too was familiar ground for these legislators.

Did this expansion of state power cause any concern among Virginia's citizens? Other scholars have looked for objections to the expanded authority granted to government under sterilization laws and found few such complaints prior to 1945. While some launched criticism of the scientific validity of eugenic theories and others (particularly the leaders of the Catholic Church) opposed the procedure on moral grounds, the possibility that the rights of citizens were violated by the procedure failed to cause much concern.[39]

The only objection to surgical sterilization in Virginia that I have been able to locate occurred in the 1910s, when Charles V. Carrington, the surgeon to the Virginia State Penitentiary, sought legislation to require the sterilization of "habitual criminals." Supporters introduced a bill mandating surgery "for the prevention of procreation" in these individuals. The Senate passed the proposal, but the House of Delegates rejected it. The *Virginia Medical Semi-Monthly* attributed the bill's failure to a misunderstanding of the bill and "blind sentiment." This is not much of an explanation. A better reason may be found in the burden the proposal put on state institutions, as

Carrington would have forced all state institutions (not just prisons) to perform mental exams on all inmates and patients. Those who ran such facilities would have been reluctant to have such requirements imposed.[40]

Steven Noll has argued that the drive for eugenic sterilization was at times blocked by "wider concerns over the role of the state." Specifically, Noll says that southern conservatives "viewed it as another example of encroaching state power over the rights and prerogatives of individuals." Noll's evidence is weak on this particular point, and the evidence and the state's history suggest that, at least in the case of Virginia, opposition to state power was rooted in an aversion to higher taxes and expanded costs of government, not threats to democratic values, which already were pretty tenuous there.[41]

Soon after dispensing with the issue of eugenic sterilization, the Virginia General Assembly turned its attention to what many believed to be a related question — interracial marriage. Bans on marriage between individuals of African and European ancestry had existed since almost the beginning of the Virginia colony. Soon after Virginia began importing African slaves, in the early seventeenth century, laws restricting the behavior of slaves and defining relationships between races were passed, including prohibitions on sex and marriage between blacks and whites. Following independence, the General Assembly revised the statute, keeping the restrictions on marriage intact and in 1787 defining "mulatto" for the first time. In the Reconstruction era, the revised code eliminated the term "mulatto" and instead defined "colored" as people having more than one-fourth "negro" blood, and then in 1910 the legislature changed this definition to one-sixteenth or more.[42]

In 1924 the General Assembly strengthened restrictions on interracial marriage by passing the Racial Integrity Act. Arguing that the existing statute permitting persons with less than one-sixteenth "negro blood" to claim whiteness allowed for racial mixing to occur, proponents of the Racial Integrity Act stressed the importance of absolute racial purity to the future of civilization and to social order. For purposes of marriage, whites in Virginia now had to be 100 percent white, with no nonwhite ancestors. One exception was permitted under the new law, an exception that would prove controversial. If an individual had only white and American Indian blood, he or she could still marry a white person: "persons who have one-sixteenth or less of the blood of the American Indian and have no other non-Caucasic blood shall be deemed to be white persons."[43] The logic behind this was carefully planned. This "Pocohontas exception" protected descendants of Pocohontas and John Rolfe — whose numbers included some of Virginia's elite families — ensuring they could still be classified as white.[44]

The timing of the Racial Integrity Act, contemporaneous with the passage of the eugenic sterilization law, was far from coincidental. Together these laws underscored the support for eugenics in the state and legislature. The shared intellectual roots of these laws and the connections between their backers are explored in other works, most comprehensively by Gregory Dorr. The present work builds on Dorr's study by looking at the policymaking process and legislative history of these acts to demonstrate that, with these measures and related proposals, Virginia's leaders articulated a vision not only of race and class but also of governance.[45]

The most obvious similarity between these laws is the manner in which support for their passage was organized and planned. In both cases, a small number of people with a personal interest in the matter, as well as a strong belief in eugenics, convinced legislators of the potential degradation of the population, a degradation that would bring disorder and economic ruin to the state. Earnest Sevier Cox and John Powell formed the Anglo-Saxon Clubs of America (ASCOA), a Virginia-based group that worked for racial purity, including the passage of the Racial Integrity Act.[46] Walter Plecker, another key player in the campaign who served as the director of the state's Bureau of Vital Statistics, worked to rally support across the state and in the General Assembly. Just as hospital directors had used the sterilization law to strengthen their professional authority, Plecker, too, successfully expanded the power of the Bureau of Vital Statistics following the Racial Integrity Act's passage. Cox, an anthropologist and ethnologist, provided intellectual inspiration to Plecker. Cox held views on eugenics and race that were then at odds with most leaders of his profession, but his involvement with this successful campaign bolstered his local reputation.[47]

Like proponents of eugenic sterilization, promoters of the Racial Integrity Act appealed to long-standing notions about female sexual danger. An article by Lisa Lindquist Dorr notes that Powell's published investigations of interracial sexual activity focused almost exclusively on illicit relations between white women and African American men. Powell hoped that fears of white women crossing racial boundaries would rally support for the proposed law. Legislators would agree that the state should play a role in containing white women who dared challenge established traditions in this way (as well as, of course, punishing their black male companions). This further linked the drive to protect the racial order with the preservation of normative constructions of gender and sexuality.[48]

Supporters of the Racial Integrity Act also connected appeals to eugenic ideology with a concern about the well-being of the state's social and eco-

nomic order. In public addresses, Powell and Cox, the ASCOA's most prominent spokesmen, cited many examples of uncontrolled, uncensured interracial mixing across the state. Local newspapers, most prominently the
Richmond Times-Dispatch and the *Richmond News Leader*, published articles
that outlined the ideas and agenda of the ASCOA, providing their movement
with important publicity. Powell and Cox contended that racial mixing produced an inferior type of individual in which the superior characteristics of
Anglo-Saxons were destroyed by the introduction of inferior African genes.
If racially mixed individuals dominated Virginia's population, higher civilization would be destroyed and the state ruined. Unless some kind of order
was imposed on this situation, they warned, the state would be dominated
by degenerate "mongrels." Furthermore, they claimed that the current lax-
ness of racial standards left the state chaotic and disorderly.[49]

The implications of racial degradation of the population for the state's
economic future seemed obvious. Physically and mentally degenerate individuals made poor workers, and so the population of these individuals
should be curbed. Whites were mentally and physically superior, so they
made for more productive workers. The Racial Integrity Act would enhance
the white share of the population and thereby increase the quality of the
labor force. This reasoning fit squarely into the rhetoric of southern progressives, who had made a convincing case for the importance of improving and
protecting the labor supply.[50] Framing arguments for interracial marriage
and eugenic sterilization in terms of promoting economic growth made
these ideas particularly persuasive to policy makers in Virginia. Supporters overcame traditional reluctance to spend state money by convincing the
legislature that, though the policies would cost money to implement, they
would eventually produce savings for the state.

The suggestion that checking the reproduction of the lower classes
would produce better workers and more economic growth, of course, had
been articulated by leaders of the national eugenics movement. Those who
advocated and voted for eugenic policies in Virginia clearly were influenced
by these theories. But a belief in eugenics was far from sufficient to spur governmental action in 1920s Virginia. Rather, eugenic theories enabled those
long suspicious of the lower classes to articulate the danger these individuals posed in more concrete terms, the popular and persuasive vocabulary of
economic progress, and to construct a state to contain these dangers.[51]

The approach policy makers took to the legislative process illuminates
the intersection of political ideologies with racial and eugenic theories. At
first glance, the sterilization statute and Racial Integrity Act seem to repre-

sent different visions of state power, as eugenic sterilization was a procedure that might only affect a small fraction of the population, while protecting racial purity involved the state in the marital decisions of all Virginians. In fact, however, the potentially broad impact of the Racial Integrity Act proved its most contentious aspect, producing a series of debates over how far state authority should reach.

The first matter for legislative deliberation involved the verification of race prior to marriage. Those empowered to issue marriage licenses had to be sure of the accuracy of the applicant's stated color. Verifying race, however, was no easy task. One initial version of the Racial Integrity Act contained a provision for the registration of the racial identity of everyone born before 1912 — that is, those whose births occurred before the Bureau of Vital Statistics existed and whose racial backgrounds were thus not on file. While still not a perfect solution, this approach would have generated more data on racial backgrounds and allowed for more sophisticated efforts at proving racial identity.[52]

In the final draft of the bill, its authors eliminated the compulsory registration requirement and replaced it with the stipulation that people who wished to register their race with the state could do so voluntarily.[53] Although this revision eliminated the one provision of the racial integrity bill that probably would have resulted in some additional expense, the evidence suggests that it was a desire to limit governmental authority, not financial concerns, that led to this amendment. Debate in the Virginia Senate over the bill revealed opposition to the registration provision in particular, with Senator Holman Willis of Roanoke calling that clause an "insult to the white people of the state" and Senator Henry T. Wickham of Richmond speaking out similarly.[54]

Though conceding that registration of race would be voluntary, not mandatory, legislators did successfully strengthen the hand of the state in proving racial background. The legislature provided that the state's Bureau of Vital Statistics could issue statements certifying an individual's racial composition for these verification purposes.[55] Walter Plecker and his successors would be the final arbiter of doubtful cases. Plecker would use this authority to its fullest extent, seeking legislative sanction to extend his reach even further in the coming years.

The Racial Integrity Act provoked differing reactions from black and white newspapers in the immediate aftermath of its passage. The white-run *Norfolk Virginian-Pilot* agreed in principle with efforts to maintain racial integrity but warned that local registrars could easily be bribed into registering someone's race incorrectly. Even if registrars were infallible, the *Virginian-Pilot*'s editors argued, most miscegenation occurred among unmarried couples, which the law, of course, would not prevent.[56]

The reaction of the African American press in 1924 suggests the difficulties black leaders faced in challenging the Racial Integrity Act—a challenge that could easily have been interpreted as a defense of interracial sex and marriage and thus a dangerous position for a black newspaper to take. The *Norfolk Journal and Guide* allowed John Powell to express his views at length in a series of three interviews in 1926, an attempt by Powell to reproduce in Virginia the kind of alliance some black nationalists and white supremacists enjoyed nationally. In the interviews, Powell cited examples of uncontrolled, uncensured interracial mixing across the state.[57] Powell also appealed to black Virginians to protect the purity of their race, saying that they should be just as concerned with intermixing as whites were. He found a sympathetic audience among some African Americans to the extent that his position represented a veiled denunciation of white men's sexual advances toward African American women. Powell also found some allies among black nationalists affiliated with Marcus Garvey's Universal Negro Improvement Association, though many other blacks recoiled at this affiliation.[58]

Another African American newspaper, the *Richmond Planet*, offered a mixed assessment of the new racial integrity law. On the one hand, the paper made a case for the law's irrelevance. "Well-thinking" African Americans did not seek interracial marriage, and thus the law "did not concern any Negro in this state." But the campaign for racial integrity was nonetheless dangerous. Those making an issue of racial integrity in the legislature would ultimately harm race relations, the paper predicted.[59] The *Norfolk Journal and Guide* took a similar approach in citing the new law's potential to harm race relations: "With the sanction and seal of the great State of Virginia upon his utterances, Dr. Plecker . . . is industriously engaged in sowing the seeds of bitterest racial discord, from one end of the country to the other."[60] Showing the same caution their colleagues at the *Richmond Planet* had exhibited, the *Journal and Guide* writers were careful not to be seen as supporting racial mixing. "The racial integrity law is a belated move to afford the white race the sort of protection that should have been given both races many generations ago. It is difficult to see any good which can come out of Virginia's Racial Integrity Law."[61] The passage of Virginia's new law was barely noted by the African American press nationally, though the subsequent attempts to revise the law did receive national attention.[62]

Soon after the passage of the 1924 act, Plecker found that a significant ambiguity had been left in the law. A case involving a young woman who claimed the right to marry a white person despite the "colored" designation on her birth certificate demonstrated that the Pocohontas exception could allow individuals to claim Indian, not African, ancestry and thus evade legal restrictions.[63] Though the Pocohontas exception aimed to protect Virginia's finest families and Native Americans from being legally defined as non-white, it also allowed certain individuals to assert that they were Indian, not "colored," and therefore permitted to marry whites. Plecker believed that many, if not all, those who called themselves Indians did, in fact, have some African American ancestors. In addition, he alleged that people who were really black were claiming to be Indian, not only so they could marry inter-racially but also so they could attend white schools and live without the re-strictions African Americans faced. Plecker used his position in the Bureau of Vital Statistics to compile evidence that there were no Indians in the state who were not of mixed blood. In 1925 Plecker produced a list of three thou-sand Indians in Virginia who he claimed were "Negroid" and sent the list to an Indian-run journal called *Indian Truth*.[64] A few months later representa-tives from the Bureau of Vital Statistics testified in a Richmond court that a man who identified himself as Indian was in violation of the Racial Integ-rity Act for marrying a white woman. The court rejected the bureau's claim that the man was colored and permitted him to marry his white fiancée, and this case deepened Plecker's resolve to stop these "self-styled Indians" from being classified as white.[65]

At the next session of the General Assembly, in 1926, Plecker and his allies sought to close what was now clearly a loophole. They proposed an amendment to the Racial Integrity Act that would legally categorize all non-white people as "colored," thereby eliminating the Pocohontas exception. The only exceptions would be those with Native American ancestors who married whites before 1619 (the descendants of Pocohontas and Rolfe) and members of the "civilized tribes" of Oklahoma and Texas who had become Virginia citizens. Defining most, if not all, of Virginia's Native American population as "Negro" or "colored" would give the Bureau of Vital Statistics the authority to reject any claims from Indians that they were of the Indian race, with no African American ancestors.[66]

The proposal was debated in the 1926, 1928, and 1930 sessions of the General Assembly but never passed.[67] Unlike the 1924 Racial Integrity Act, this plan met with vehement opposition on a number of fronts. News of the proposed revision and the debates it generated circulated throughout the state and in the national black press.

The question of Indian racial identity gave voice to a group rarely heard in modern Virginia politics, Virginia's Native Americans. Many Indians viewed Plecker's actions as an attack on their very existence — it would have stripped the racial category "Indian" of its unique status. Several testified before a Senate committee, demanding their right to be identified as Indians, not colored. The dramatic testimony of these individuals — many of them dressed in what the press called "tribal regalia" — riveted those present at the General Assembly committee hearing in 1926. "Will you palefaces blot out with the stroke of a pen a nation?" asked Chief Sachem Wa-hun-sun-a-cook of the Pamunkey tribe. "I am before you not as a first family of Virginia, but as a first family of America, and I defy any man to say to the contrary."[68] At another committee hearing two years later, the chief pointedly rejected any affiliation with African Americans and demanded the state respect his Indian identity. "I will tie a stone around my neck and jump into the James River rather than be classed as a Negro. It would be finer to perish in the waters of this stream than suffer such indignity," he announced.[69]

A number of white Virginia men spoke in praise of the state's Indians, citing their bravery in defending the early colonists against enemy tribes, in an attempt to convince legislators that Indians should be accorded a separate racial status. One was Senator Williams C. Wickham from Hanover, who described a battle where Pamunkeys and colonists joined against an enemy tribe. "There were but seven braves left of all the Pemunkeys [sic] after the battle and these men, the friends of our ancestors — descendants of our forefathers' friends and defenders — shall we by law sever the hand that has been extended to them in fellowship? Shall we make Negroes out of them?"[70] Further seeking to underscore the distinction between Indians and African Americans, other whites commented on the integration of Virginia's Indians into the white world — specifically their attendance at white churches. One white speaker noted that Native Americans were far superior to the "dirty negro."[71]

The rallying of white support for Native Americans, coupled with the racist rhetoric of those supporters, provoked a response in the black-run *Richmond Planet*. In an article on the editorial page published as a letter to the editor, R. A. Cephas gave his thoughts on the testimony of the Pamunkey chief and his supporters. He expressed frustration that praise of Indians was followed by insults to African Americans. "To compare our cleanliness or dirt with that of the Indian is simply astounding. If the bunch of Indians that I saw huddled up there represent cleanliness, then God forbid that any such cleanliness shall ever befall me or any of my race." Though far from complimentary toward Indians, Cephas believed that the whites who testified on behalf of the Indians were the most insulting. "It was left to Virginia white men (our so-called best friends) to vilify a race of people who took no part in the proceedings, had not friend at court, and did not oppose the passage of the pending bill."[72]

Concern for the Indians might not have defeated the bill, but concern for its impact on white citizens did. Defining anyone with Indian blood (aside from those exceptions noted above) would, it was said, lead many prominent white families in the state to become classified as colored. In an article headlined "Bill Brands 63 'First Families' of VA. 'Colored,'" the *Richmond News Leader* cited unnamed "genealogists" as saying that among those who might soon become colored were "two United States senators, a United States ambassador to France, two secretaries of war, two presidents of the United States, five generals, three of the most distinguished of living Southern novelists, three governors of Virginia, a speaker of the house of representatives, two bishops, three congressmen, one rear-admiral, two judges of the Virginia Supreme Court, and many of the foremost officers of the Confederate army."[73] The paper spoke out directly against the proposal in its editorial page: "To classify these people as 'colored,' because their Indian blood is readily 'ascertainable' from established genealogies, is preposterous and insulting."[74] J. Shelton Horsley, one of the state's most prominent physicians, opposed the bill as well. Horsley testified before a Senate committee in 1930, suggesting a commission of biologists and sociologists study the issue and report back in 1932. Implicit in Horsley's recommendation was the notion that Plecker's endorsement was not sufficient to convince him of the plan's virtue.[75]

Black newspapers across the nation followed suit in decrying the folly of this newly proposed racial categorization. The *Baltimore Afro-American*, for example, noted the absurdity of recategorizing white families as black, detailing how some white high schools expelled students on the verge of graduation when they were discovered to be black. The *Kansas City Call* sarcastically referred to arguments for racial integrity as the ranting of the "Caucasian intelligentsia."[76] Back in Virginia, the *Norfolk Journal and Guide* noted how the racial integrity issue "manages to bring succeeding legislatures into well-placed ridicule" and concluded that the discussions of racial integrity "scarcely do more than give the impression to outsiders that Virginia is in the throes of race amalgamation which it is not."[77]

At a 1928 hearing on the proposal, John Powell made a passionate defense of categorizing the majority of the state's Indians as African Americans. First, he noted that if Indians really had no African American blood then they would not be concerned about the proposal. But if their race was in fact intermixed, then the state was right to target them. As for the assertion that white families might soon find themselves on the wrong side of the color line, Powell responded, "I am indignant that a Virginian should charge that many of our white people have a trace of negro blood. That is an aspersion of a northerner, not a Virginian. I am amazed also that another Virginian, and a preacher, should admit that Indians with negro blood are admitted to white churches on a basis of equality. The admissions of my opponents show why this bill should be passed. Fifty-thousand near-white mixed breeds are pressing down on the color line and if we let down the bars, our civilization is doomed."[78]

The plan to count most Native Americans as African Americans did find some support in Virginia's press. The *Richmond Times-Dispatch* observed that if people really believed that the white and black races should not intermix under any circumstances, then they should support the strictest racial integrity laws. Those who opposed the amendment must admit to opposing full racial purity.[79]

The plan to amend the Racial Integrity Act never passed, but the debate it generated functioned in some notable and revealing ways. First, the debate split Plecker from many of the Racial Integrity Act's original supporters. Individuals who opposed the revision because of its impact on the white community joined forces with allies of the state's Native Americans to defeat the measure. Second, it provided African Americans an opportunity to speak out against racist policies without taking the extreme (at the time) position of supporting racial mixing. Black newspapers in Virginia and across the nation minced no words in denouncing the ridiculousness of the proposal. Virginia appeared perverse, not progressive, to African American journalists across the country.

Though some of Plecker's plans to defend the purity of the white race in Virginia failed, he and his allies did win other notable victories. In 1926, as the General Assembly was weighing the proposal to include the state's Native Americans in the "colored" population, a move to tighten racial segregation was also afoot. The Public Assemblages Act (often referred to as the "Massenburg bill" in reference to its author, Delegate Alvin Massenburg) would forbid integrated groups in any public setting, even when the integration was fully voluntary. So, for example, all audiences would have to be separated with designated white and nonwhite areas. Several of the leaders of the fight for the Racial Integrity Act backed this bill as well. Their primary focus was Hampton Institute, where mixed audiences occasionally congregated in the school's auditorium. Some whites joined with African Americans to oppose the measure, but many of Virginia's white leaders supported it.[80]

A key element of white criticism of the Public Assemblages Act was its impact on Chinese and Japanese students at Virginia universities. Since the bill would classify Asians as nonwhite, they would have to sit with African Americans in segregated settings. Universities, churches, and the foreign mission board of the Southern Baptist Convention opposed the proposal. Echoing the Baptists' fear, the *Richmond News Leader* expressed concern that news would travel abroad that Virginians discriminated against Asians, and the work of these missionaries would be hampered.[81]

Writing in the *Norfolk Journal and Guide*, Norfolk's African American newspaper, J. A. Rogers recoiled at the hypocrisy of white liberals who exhibited more concern for Asian immigrants than African Americans. Opponents of the bill, he said, "really seemed so alarmed over the Chinese and the Japanese that one would have thought that they were the citizens and the Negro the alien. Well, the Japanese have battleships and the colored folks—well."[82] Massenburg and his supporters were able to rally sufficient support for their plan, and it passed by votes of sixty-three to three in the House and thirty to five in the Senate. Governor Harry F. Byrd's misgivings about the plan prompted him to allow it to become law without his signature.[83]

Four years later racial purity advocates succeeded in strengthening legislative enforcement of racial purity and segregation. Since the original Racial Integrity Act had only applied to marriage, the old one-sixteenth definition applied to all other areas of racial classification, including schools, cemeteries, restaurants, and other areas of public accommodation. For example, a person with any African American heritage could not marry a white person, but as long as he or she was less than one-sixteenth African American, he or she could still attend white schools and use white accommodations. This plan to apply the "one drop" measure to all areas of racial segregation passed the legislature during the 1930 session.[84]

Eliminating the Pocahontas exception and passing the Public Assemblages Act were important to Plecker, and they underscore the connection he saw between racial purity and segregation. Weakness in racial purity could undermine segregation, as mixed-race individuals pressed for admittance to the white world. At the same time, failure to maintain strict segregation could undermine racial purity. He described this possibility in the bureau's 1928 annual report: "If near-white children are allowed to attend white schools, sympathy is aroused, attachments are formed, public sentiment is weakened, and ultimate marriage either in their home counties or elsewhere naturally follows."[85]

Segregation for Plecker was, of course, more than a system of preventing affectional and sexual relations across racial lines. Rather, he believed that the nation had to choose between separation and amalgamation. Only complete separation could stop amalgamation.[86] Even dead bodies had to be watched to make sure they were not crossing racial lines. Plecker's office monitored cemeteries, and on at least one occasion he warned an all-white cemetery in the state that a man buried there was a mulatto.[87]

Plecker's primary focus was on preserving a social order of white dominance, and he saw racial purity and segregation as parts of a whole. Plecker probably would have been the first to admit that in fact he sought more to "re-create" than "preserve" a segregated social order, as the campaigners for the Racial Integrity Act relied heavily on evidence of contemporary racial mixing to bolster their arguments.[88] On some level, he was right — many African Americans were vigilant in looking for weaknesses in the system of white rule, and the demands by African Americans for racial equality would soon be too loud to ignore. He was also right that racial purity no longer existed — though he harkened back to a racially pure South that had only existed briefly hundreds of years earlier. He used all the weapons he could to halt these changes, but he would finally fail.

Historian Peggy Pascoe has argued that while many have assumed that interracial marriage laws sought to stop interracial sex, it was marriage, not sex, that was the fundamental focus in many state legislatures. Pascoe suggests that because marriage to a white person conferred respectability and economic benefits to nonwhite individuals, marriage concerned legislators far more than interracial sex did.[89] While this may have been the case for some in the Virginia General Assembly, Plecker was a true believer in the dangers of all things interracial, whether or not marriage was involved. Plecker even denounced the common but unacknowledged liaisons between white men and African American women that had been quietly accepted by most whites as part of the South's racial and sexual order. In a pamphlet distributed across the state, Plecker reminded white men that they had to avoid sexual liaisons with African American women. "Let the young men who read this realize that the future purity of our race is in their keeping, and that the joining of themselves to females of a lower race and fathering children who shall be a curse and menace to our State and civilization is a crime against society, and against the purity and integrity of their future homes and the happiness of their future loved ones and themselves." Plecker also faulted white men for fathering "mulatto" children, saying they lacked self-respect and had failed their race.[90]

Popular movements produced neither the Racial Integrity Act nor the Virginia Sterilization Statute. A handful of close allies among the white elite were behind the introduction of the Racial Integrity Act (and its subsequent revisions) as well as the eugenic sterilization proposals. These men were able to rally support in the legislature and across the state for plans that were rooted in the tenets of economic growth and eugenics. Like eugenic sterilization, racial integrity would also, they hoped, make Virginia a leader in progressive legislation. Plecker demonstrated pride in this progress when he noted that "the 1924 Virginia legislature led the world in its passage of the Racial Integrity law."[91] Though the world did not follow, Georgia and Alabama did, soon passing equally rigorous definitions of whiteness.[92] Similarly minded experts also convinced the U.S. Congress that year that immigration quotas based on race and nationality were needed to protect the nation from the influx of inferior genes, leading to the passage of the 1924 Immigration Act.[93]

Supporters of racial integrity and eugenic sterilization in Virginia articulated a vision of government that monitored and regulated sexual behavior to protect the racial and economic interests of the state. Uniting their commitment to eugenics with progressive visions of government and economic growth, they built a coalition of support among legislators, physicians, newspaper editors, and other leading white citizens for certain kinds of state intervention in sexuality. While these two eugenic measures offer the most useful source for weighing how ideas about sexuality intersected with understandings of the role of the state, a contemporaneous plan in Virginia for censoring movies offers the opportunity to further explore some of these issues.

Movie censorship first came before the Virginia General Assembly in 1918, backed by Senator G. Walter Mapp from Accomac and an alliance of Virginia women's groups. Legislators held a public hearing on the proposal, and among those opposing movie censorship was D. W. Griffith, the director of the landmark film *Birth of a Nation*. Thomas Dixon, author of *The Clansman*, upon which Griffith had based his film, also expressed his opposition to censorship in a letter to the governor. Legislators voted the proposal down.[94]

Two years later, Mary Gray Peck, a representative from the National Board of Review, visited Virginia in an effort to thwart passage of state censorship legislation. Peck found that "reform elements, chiefly thru women's organizations," were behind the censorship effort. She also observed, "most of the women interested in the subject [of censorship] were prominent suffragists." On 22 January Peck met with a group in Richmond at the Parish House of the Centenary Methodist Church that included members of the Southern Conference of the Methodist Episcopal Church, the Richmond Parent Teacher Association, the Woman's Christian Temperance Union, representatives from the Juvenile Court, and Senator Mapp. Senator Mapp, according to Peck, sought to dominate the proceedings and "pronounce an oration of his own." Peck responded by telling him "diplomatically" that "the only way for him to *get* information was to stop talking long enough for his questions to be answered." After that rejoinder, Peck found Mapp to be a "Virginia Gentleman . . . consideration and attention personified."[95]

Peck sought to convince Mapp and the other supporters of state censorship to drop their plan in favor of "cooperative censorship" — essentially, voluntary cooperation between local theaters and a local censorship committee. Under this plan, theater managers would submit films to this committee before they showed them in local theaters. One option Peck promoted was that the theaters across the state should agree to conform to decisions made by a Richmond-based committee.[96]

When Peck left the state, she was cautiously optimistic that, if theater owners and city leaders worked together as she had suggested, "the censorship problem for the present is solved in the state of Virginia."[97] But this was not the case, and Mapp and his allies tried again in 1922 to pass statewide legislation. At another public hearing in late February, nationally known leaders on both sides of the issue staged a debate. The Reverend William Sheafe Chase, a clergyman from New York's Christ Episcopal Church who had promoted federal censorship legislation, spoke in favor of the plan, citing the dangers posed across the country by the growing movie industry, which held "tyrannical control" over American cinema. A local Baptist minister, the Reverend George S. McDaniel, concurred with Chase and also claimed the support of the majority of Virginians for the measure.[98]

Thomas Dixon came to Virginia to testify at the hearing and condemned censorship as "undemocratic and un-American." Trying to discredit McDaniel, Dixon contended that the clergyman was a hypocrite because his family had fled censorship in the "Old World" in coming to the United States.[99] While the *Richmond Times-Dispatch* did not report any direct references in the course of the debate to the possible implications of censorship for Dixon's own work, an editorial published the same week commented on

Dixon's anticensorship efforts and warned that protecting morals was but a "flimsy pretense" for censorship. Rather, the *Times-Dispatch* argued, some people sought to censor so that they could reject "any picture that presented a political or historical view contrary to [their] own"—presumably, a reference to potential threats that censorship boards would pose to films like *Birth of a Nation.*[100]

Individuals on both sides of the debate raised the example of Prohibition. One proponent of movie censorship, Mrs. Howard M. Hodge, president of the Virginia branch of the Woman's Christian Temperance Union, argued that just as the state had prohibited the sale of alcohol to protect the home against immorality, it should also undertake the censoring of movies. In contrast, opponents of censorship offered Prohibition as an example of the failure of government intervention in the moral sphere.[101]

Newspapers in both Richmond and Norfolk argued against censorship in their editorial pages, with the *Richmond Times-Dispatch* warning that censorship of the press and other kinds of public speech could soon follow movie censorship. In another editorial, the paper rejected "morals by legislation," suggesting instead that individuals needed to fight their own internal moral battles, rather than expect the law to attempt to make moral decisions for them. The paper also compared the General Assembly's threats to freedom and progress to those in the medieval, pre-Enlightenment days.[102]

The *Norfolk Virginian-Pilot*'s comments reflected more concern with governmental corruption and the ability of state officials to do a good job of censoring. Noting that the state was notorious for the "payment of substantial salaries out of the public taxes to public officials who perform no useful public service," the editorial's author declared that a censorship board would either renege on its duty and pass all films or acquire a "dull, ungiving censoriousness." In any case, the paper exhibited little alarm over the potential loss of civil liberties, focusing primarily on wasted money and, somewhat oddly, expressing sympathy for the censors with this conclusion: "To be forced to sit through all the movies, not to be able to depart by the front door when the affair begins to pall, not to be able to call it a night when things become banal—what fortune in all of Dante's inferno can match this in cruel refinement?"[103] In the *Norfolk Ledger-Dispatch*, the city's other main newspaper, an editorial on the new law did not mention issues of morality or public order at all, commenting only that though movies in poor taste might "annoy and irritate persons of intelligence," the public's enjoyment of such entertainment was simply a fact of life.[104]

Clergy could be found both supporting and opposing the creation of a state censorship board, though the newspaper accounts of their remarks suggest that some made paradoxical arguments. While Chase and McDaniel argued for the measure, Rabbi Edward Calisch of Richmond opposed it, telling his congregation, "It is part of an effort by self-appointed reformers and uplifters and sectarian organizations to place the manners and morals of the American people under the control of their own particular viewpoint." Though on the one hand, Calisch opposed governmental intervention in an area that he felt should be under the purview of families, on the other hand, he also compared censorship to Prohibition, saying that the ban on alcohol would have been beneficial if it had been enforced properly.[105] The Reverend Ken G. Broughton, pastor of Richmond's Grove Avenue Baptist Church, also spoke in a somewhat convoluted way against the measure. "The surest way to make a race of moral weaklings is to make too many laws — so many that man will not have to work out his salvation, but simply live within the law. . . . There may be danger of soul sensitiveness being lost by the transference of responsibility from the individual to the state." However, Broughton's remarks later in the same sermon indicate he favored some kind of censorship. He declared that state-run censorship would be complicated and inefficient and suggested a national censorship program should be implemented instead, presumably by the federal government.[106]

Common to all these debates over censorship was an understanding that issues of morality would be the focus of the proposed censorship board. Movies, censorship's supporters held, portrayed immoral behavior and thus promoted it. A series of scandals in the early 1920s furthered suspicions of the immorality of the whole film industry. The most prominent of these came in 1921 and involved the well-known comedian Roscoe "Fatty" Arbuckle, who was tried for the murder of a young woman in a drunken hotel-room party, and two Hollywood stars, Mabel Normand and Mary Miles Minter, who were investigated — though never indicted — for the murder of director William Desmond Taylor.[107]

Sexuality was an important element in defining conduct as immoral, and the prevention of sexual immorality was a key motivation for those seeking censorship. One vocal supporter of censorship in Virginia, the Reverend William S. Golden of Westminster Presbyterian Church in Richmond, articulated the connections he saw between sexual morality and film in a Sunday morning sermon shortly before the legislature voted on the censorship bill. Golden spoke out against the rise in divorce rates, blaming this rise on a growing moral decline. Immorality and "jazz marriages" were due to "indecent dressing and dancing, liquor parties, wild rides and absence of decent restraints." But the ultimate blame lay with movies. "Improper movies, exhibited before millions daily, are bearing their logical fruit."[108]

Those opposing censorship found an ally in Senator Robert F. Leedy, who represented Clarke, Page, and Warren Counties. Leedy tried to kill the censorship plan with a filibuster, though his effort failed. He then attempted to water down the proposal by affiliating the state board with the National Board of Review and allowing the national board to be the first judge of which movies to ban in Virginia. A state board would have still been created, but if it chose to censor any films other than those selected by the national board, Virginia's censors would have to defend their actions before the judge of the Circuit Court of the City of Richmond, who would be the final decision maker. The legislature rejected Leedy's plan.[109]

Though the opponents of censorship did capture headlines and picked up some allies in the General Assembly, they failed to derail the bill. In March 1922 the legislature passed "an act to regulate motion picture films and reels; providing a system of examination, approval and regulation thereof, and of the banners, posters and other like advertising matter used in connection therewith; creating the board of censors; and providing penalties for the violation of this act." To oversee the censoring of films, the Assembly created the State Board of Censors.[110]

Legislators did agree in the course of the 1922 debates to one important check being placed on the new board's authority. Senator C. O'Conor Goolrick from Fredericksburg objected to the inclusion of "sacrilegious" films among those that could be censored. Legislators removed that language as part of the compromise that secured the bill's passage.[111]

The creation of Virginia's movie censorship division made the state a leader in this area. Chicago had approved the nation's first municipal movie censorship ordinance in 1907; soon after, Pennsylvania, Ohio, and Kansas enacted the nation's first statewide censorship laws. A Supreme Court decision, *Mutual Film Corporation v. Industrial Commission of Ohio*, upheld these laws in 1915, but no additional states passed such laws until 1921. After the Arbuckle trial and a few smaller scandals, legislatures in thirty-two states responded by debating movie censorship legislation, but only three passed new laws: New York, Florida, and Virginia.[112]

The willingness of the Virginia General Assembly to take on statewide movie censorship in advance of most other states is part of a pattern common to the three efforts at sexual regulation considered here. In each case, Virginia led the nation or region in enacting them. In censoring movies, banning marriage between whites and mixed-race individuals, and performing surgical sterilizations, state leaders either went further than most other states in involving government in the sexual behavior of its citizens or made Virginia among the first states to inaugurate such policies. Promoters of each of these regulatory efforts claimed to be helping to fashion a progressive government in the state, and advocates hoped such policies would reinforce the image of the state as a leader of reform and modern governance in the South.

The success of the movie censorship plan indicates that while eugenics played an important role in provoking state regulation of sexual behavior, an acknowledgment of sexual danger more generally also motivated this expansion of the state. Virginia's legislators acted in the belief that sexuality was a potentially dangerous force that, uncontrolled, could undermine racial traditions, economic stability, and the marital bond. Legislators believed, then, that sexual regulation represented a legitimate objective for government expansion, but they also formulated a set of rules and parameters that defined the extent of this regulation. Faced with multiple policy options, Virginia's leaders made decisions about what to support and what to reject, and these choices offer important insight into how they envisioned the role of the government in sexual discipline.

An important pattern emerges from this legislative history. Laws restricting civil liberties raised no red flags when they affected "marginal" elements of the population — people who were poor and working class and/or nonwhite. But when the government reached into the lives of a broader segment of the population, a segment that included the state's elites, governmental authority was contested and limited.

Compare, for example, the controversy and complaint generated by the movie censorship act with the relative silence surrounding the sterilization statute. On one level, the two proposals were similar. They both asked for expanded governmental power to protect the state from those who might be tempted into immorality. People might want to watch offensive movies, but the state could ban these films. The mentally ill might engage in immoral behavior, but the government could prevent their reproduction from dragging down the state. But the proposal to censor movies raised questions in the press and for the general public. Citizens packed public hearings, public leaders voiced opinions, and a serious opposition in the legislature threatened to derail the plan. Was government power overreaching its limits? Should morals be taught by the family or the state? Would other forms of censorship follow? Movie censorship was important to those who spoke out against it because the plan could affect them and people like them.

The two proposals impacted different populations and thus provoked different reactions. Movie censorship, which could affect all Virginians, generated debate and public discussion, whereas the sterilization statute did not. Though censorship was aimed at those who were too morally weak to reject obscene movies on their own accord, all Virginians could have their freedom of speech threatened by a censorship board. In short, movie censorship's impact went well beyond the lower classes and brought the power of the state into regulating the cultural consumption of the middle and upper classes as well.

Sterilization, however, would only touch those on the margins and therefore provoked little discussion and no serious opposition. It affected people only in state-run institutions. The populations of these facilities in Virginia and the rest of the nation were closely correlated to class.[113] Feebleminded people in state institutions were, according to Lynchburg colony superintendent Priddy, "the shiftless, ignorant, and worthless class of anti-social whites in the South."[114] One of Priddy's successors, G. B. Arnold, also suggested the correlation between class and institutionalization: "Our opinion is that just about 5 percent of the families in Virginia furnish some 90 percent of the inmates of this State's mental and penal institutions!"[115] Those 5 percent of families were among the state's poorest. Opposition to governmental power and authority, then, faded away when officials wielded it only over those on the margins.

Limiting those eligible for sterilization to people in institutions reduced the likelihood of the procedure being performed involuntarily on ostensibly normal, upper- or middle-class white people. This restriction raised the possibility that the courts would object to the law, as they had to others, as "class legislation" because it targeted only particular groups of citizens.[116] But advocates chose to risk potential constitutional objections to counter possible opposition in the legislature.

Further evidence that freedom was only worth protecting when it was the freedom of the upper class can be found in Plecker's legislative agenda. The Racial Integrity Act passed, but the legislature rejected the compulsory registration provision. The general principle behind the Racial Integrity Act did not meet criticism, only the parts of it that could touch a broad section of the population—the provision that would force everyone to present their racial credentials to the state, as if all Virginians were equally suspect. The pattern repeated itself in the rest of Plecker's agenda. Eliminating the Pocohontas exception, a plan that could have had a significant impact on white elites, also failed.[117] The Public Assemblages Act, a law that would restrict the behavior of African Americans and the white racial liberals who wanted to attend integrated functions, passed but provoked opposition. Misgivings about the plan, including its effect on visiting Asians and white missionaries, concerned Governor Byrd enough that he refused to sign the law.[118]

Plecker's views on state intervention set him apart from other leading Virginians. His vision of the state was more expansive, and he promoted policies that would have given the state (and not coincidentally himself, as an agent of the state) greater power to surveil and enforce separation of the races. Plecker's ideas about gender, specifically his willingness to intervene in white men's sexual liaisons with black women, also indicate his broader vision. While John Powell focused almost exclusively on the transgressions of white women, Plecker extended his critique to white men as well. While Powell condemned lower-class white women who failed to live up to the ideals of the southern lady, Plecker extended this condemnation to upper-class white men who failed to live up to the ideals of the southern gentleman. While other advocates of eugenic sterilization and racial integrity agreed to limit the power of the state, Plecker fought to broaden state power against their opposition.

The insistence by most of Virginia's leaders, except Walter Plecker, that state authority must carefully focus on the politically marginal underscores the importance of the distribution of political power in Virginia to the construction of sexual regulation. The stark polarization of wealth and access to the franchise along lines of race and class allowed policy makers to imagine clean divisions in the citizenry. One part of the society made the laws; another clearly identifiable group would obey them. Those whom the state targeted had few, if any, resources with which to fight back.

The two eugenics-related policies helped justify the class-based division among whites with regard to access to the franchise. Lower-class whites might undermine the social order, damage the economy by reproducing inferior genes, and undermine the white race by giving birth to mixed-race offspring. White elites, the governing class whose wisdom brought them to support eugenics, would protect the state. Thus, eugenics in Virginia reaffirmed the rights of certain white men to rule other whites.

The fact that Virginia's elites felt no qualms about passing laws that restricted the lives of the nonvoting classes still does not explain why legislators decided to focus their attention on this particular kind of legislation — laws regulating sexual behavior. The answer is that sexual regulation, economic growth, and progressive visions of the state all went hand in hand, because eugenics connected sexual regulation to a progressive agenda and underscored the danger of unrestrained sexuality. Progressive and modern governments, Virginia's leaders believed, had to monitor and regulate sexuality on-screen and off. The rhetoric of sexual danger became a tool policy makers used to articulate and realize their particular vision of the state.

Taken as a whole, then, policies that sought to monitor and regulate sexual behavior offer important insight into the nature of Virginia's government in the 1920s. Those with political power in Virginia had a vision of an expanded state government that would promote economic growth. Tied up in this vision was a belief in a particular kind of modernization, one that involved controlling the disorderly elements of the state by regulating their sexuality. The idea that reproduction of the unfit and an expanding class of racial "mongrels" would, over time, result in the degradation of the entire population became part of the progressive agenda in Virginia as eugenic advocates made the connection between "fit" citizens and a healthy economy. Such modern ideas would make the state a leader in the South. Drafting the Virginia Sterilization Statute, Racial Integrity Act, and statewide movie censorship offered models for other states to follow, further enhancing Virginia's progressive image.

Looking at the state apparatus that Virginia's elites tried to build reveals their agenda, one in which economic motives were tied to sexual regulation. They planned for an expanded state that would manage the lower classes and take away their threat to economic prosperity. Individuals with a stake in particular changes sold their proposals to the legislature by tying them to this progressive agenda. Economic growth would be fueled by control over the disorderly elements of the population, a group whose behavior became particularly dangerous when it involved sexual matters. Gone was the emphasis on moral purity that marked earlier decades of sexual regulation as a more pragmatic approach to governance and economic progress took hold.

Disciplining Sexual Behavior

The Racial Integrity Act, the sterilization statute, and movie censorship were passed by a legislature caught up in speculation about the threat of sexual danger and a belief in the promise of sexual discipline. Sex had stimulated support for legislation expanding Virginia's government, but once state officials were granted this new authority, they would use this power to diverse and sometimes personal ends. The way the state developed in the aftermath of this new legislation was not predetermined, and the implementation of new regulations was not always in accord with the principles that motivated them. In the years following the enactment of these new laws, ideas about sexual danger intersected with other ideologies and existing structures of political power to shape methods of governance.

This chapter asks how sexuality functioned in the world of public policy by looking at the enforcement of the sex-related legislation passed by the Virginia legislature in 1922 and 1924. It looks for and seeks to explain disjunctures between the rhetoric that surrounded calls for legislation and the practice of implementing new laws. This chapter also examines the kind of disciplinary state Virginia's leaders went about constructing when they had the legal tools to do so, identifying the circumstances that facilitated the reach of public officials into the realm of the sexual and locating the conditions that constrained it.

The focus here is on the details of implementing public policy over the course of the 1920s and 1930s, with an eye toward understanding how that process was shaped by the political economy in which public officials operated. Central to Virginia politics was the fact that white elite men held most of the political and economic power. Differences of race, class, and gender influenced how individuals experienced state discipline of their sexual behavior. Another significant element that shaped the imposition of sexual discipline was a need to restrict costs, and at times such concerns constrained the state's reach. Increasing governmental authority was more popular than increasing governmental expenditures. Policy makers proved to be masters of cheap government in this era, implementing new programs with little or no new money.

Though advocates of these policies promised that each would bring various benefits to the state, supporters of sterilization made the grandest claims. Hundreds of millions of dollars could be saved by preventing the reproduction of undesirables, they argued, but for sterilization to produce these gains, doctors had to perform the surgery as often as possible. It stood to reason that the more sterilizations were carried out, the greater the rewards would be.

With the blessing of the Supreme Court and promises of future gains, medical leaders in Virginia stepped up their pace after 1924 and performed more sterilization operations than ever before in the state. The Lynchburg State Colony performed the largest number of surgeries, with Western State Hospital in second place. Doctors at Eastern State Hospital, Central State Hospital, Southwestern State Hospital, and the Petersburg State Colony also undertook these procedures. Between 1924 and 1949, Virginia physicians sterilized approximately 5,366 individuals. This represented about 11 percent of the approximately 49,000 people sterilized nationally. Virginia ranked second in the United States, behind California, in total number of sterilizations performed in this period. Even after the Second World War, when the policies of Nazi Germany turned many in the United States against eugenic theories, Virginia's doctors persisted—sterilizing 1,877 people between 1949 and 1979.[1]

Virginia's medical community—in particular, the Medical Society of Virginia (MSV), a statewide group of white physicians—worked to promote sterilization and build support for the procedure in the decade after *Buck v. Bell*. Frequent public addresses and articles in the *Virginia Medical Monthly* (which were often reprints of lectures given by physicians and health officials) explained the rationale for sterilization, underscored its benefits, and described the procedure.[2] For example, in a speech given before the South Piedmont Medical Society in Danville, a local physician, R. W. Garnett, noted that in the six years since *Buck v. Bell* "only" 1,333 sterilizations had been performed in the state, representing just a fraction of the state's "defective" population. Garnett warned his colleagues that their work must be accelerated to protect the state from "biologic degeneration."[3]

Given the fact that the only doctors who could legally perform the surgery in Virginia were those who worked at state mental hospitals, why did individuals such as Garnett bother to spend time talking up sterilization to private physicians? And why did the *Virginia Medical Monthly*, the journal of the MSV, devote so much space to the topic? One reason was that such talks reminded doctors of their important social role — a role that the MSV could help them achieve. In other words, reminding doctors that organized, "forward-thinking" physicians could help the state would likely strengthen their commitment to their professional organization, thus boosting the MSV.

More important, however, is the fact that eugenic sterilization depended on a degree of community support and participation to be implemented successfully. Judges were responsible for signing orders of commitment, and they did so following a review of the case by at least two physicians. Thus, the support of local physicians — specifically, their willingness to recommend the commitment of candidates for sterilization — was essential. Support from local professionals and civil servants was important, too. Social workers were often involved in overseeing cases, transporting patients, and mediating between the family and the state. Local law enforcement usually initiated the commitment proceedings, and they would also apprehend and hold the individual until the court decided his or her fate.[4]

Family members were frequently contributors to the chain of events that led to an individual's commitment and eventual sterilization. Carrie Buck was the first of many who found themselves in this situation; in her case, her adoptive family sought her commitment. Raymond Hudlow was sent to the Lynchburg State Colony and sterilized in 1942 after his father told a welfare officer that his son had run away from home repeatedly, thrown tantrums, and engaged in unspecified acts of sexual perversion.[5] Sallie Ann Johnson Wilcher became pregnant at age sixteen by her brother-in-law in 1929. When her father became ill two years later, Wilcher was accused by her grandmother of immoral behavior. Soon social workers brought her to the Lynchburg facility, where doctors sterilized her, too. Jesse Frank Meadows's father and stepmother accused him of setting a forest fire and had him sent to Lynchburg, where he was sterilized in 1940.[6]

The professionals who assisted the state in carrying out eugenic sterilization were members of the middle and upper classes. In contrast, those who underwent sterilization were nearly all working class or poor. Raymond Hudlow's family lived in Covington, Virginia, surviving on father Luther Hudlow's meager wages as a farmhand and on food they raised themselves. Wilcher was from the Natural Bridge area, where her father worked in a brickyard. Meadows grew up in a lower-class Madison County family; many of his relatives were among the sharecroppers and subsistence farmers displaced by the construction of the Shenandoah National Park.[7] All three of these individuals were white and from lower-class families.

Advocates of eugenic sterilization in Virginia openly articulated the class bias in sterilization procedures. When asked in 1931 how to tell the difference between "normal" individuals and those who should be sterilized, John H. Bell, the superintendent of the Lynchburg State Colony, wrote that one indicator of "normalcy" was "a male and female whose two preceding generations had not produced a single socially or economically inadequate person."[8] A study by Bell's successor at the state colony, G. B. Arnold, showed that Bell's idea that sterilization should be aimed at the poor was reflected in the demographics of their patients. Arnold found that of the first 1,000 individuals sterilized in the state after 1927, 812 "came from families of the definitely low class — and by 'low class' we mean families whose heads are barely eking out an existence." He identified 139 patients as being from "middle-class families," though many, if not most, of these would today be considered lower middle class or perhaps working class, those just above desperate poverty. Only 8 of the 1,000 were from "families whose financial circumstances were definitely superior."[9] Upper-class whites ran the state and enforced its policies, taking on the task of expanding the state's power and reach into the lives of the poor and working class.

Members of the lower classes who experienced state discipline in the form of eugenic sterilization were both white and African American, although there is no evidence that advocates of sterilization in Virginia had planned on targeting African Americans in particular, if at all, prior to 1924. But once hospitals across the state began to perform sterilizing surgery, African Americans underwent the procedure as well. Since fewer state-run institutions for African Americans meant fewer African American residents of such facilities, and laws permitted the sterilization of only those individuals who resided in state institutions, African Americans were less likely to be sterilized. Nonetheless, Virginia's mental health leaders did perform a significant number of sterilization procedures on African Americans between 1929 and 1972. In fact, of the more than 7,000 individuals sterilized in Virginia, approximately 1,800 of them were African American.[10]

Mental health leaders sought the sterilization of African Americans for the same reasons they sterilized whites. Sterilization offered the same institutional benefits at Central State Hospital and at the Petersburg State Colony as it did at the white facilities. Dr. Hugh Henry, the superintendent at Central State between 1924 and 1938, embraced sterilization and began authorizing surgeries as soon as the state won *Buck v. Bell.* In addition, some eugenic advocates believed that any race could be improved by controlling the reproduction of those with weaker minds. Walter Plecker espoused this position in a 1925 speech on racial improvement that he made before the MSV.[11] Finally, some white Virginians felt that mentally unfit African Americans were especially likely to be sexually promiscuous and engage in interracial sex. Thus, they reasoned that this population was more likely to pollute the white race and should be sterilized.[12]

Why did Virginia sterilize more African Americans than other southern states? The answer to this question must be somewhat speculative, but a number of factors likely came into play. The presence of eugenic advocates at the University of Virginia helped establish a climate of support for sterilization and an appreciation of the connections between racial improvement and sterilization. This intellectual environment likely influenced Superintendent Henry and inspired him to pursue the surgery aggressively at Central State.[13] Also important was the existence of an infrastructure in Virginia that allowed for the institutionalization of African Americans. States without hospitals for African Americans as large and (relatively) well-funded as Central State could not hope to sterilize this group in significant numbers.

Black and white individuals who underwent sterilization in Virginia were often young, in adolescence or on the brink of it. Meadows was committed and sterilized when he was seventeen; Wilcher was around eighteen; Hudlow was sixteen.[14] At Central State Hospital in 1940, forty-nine of the eighty-seven African American individuals sterilized were under the age of nineteen, with the youngest being a nine-year-old boy.[15] Young people would, of course, find it difficult to resist the power of their family allied with the authority of the state. Both these parties — the family and the government — used the other to gain dominion over youth. Families seeking to divest themselves of troublesome young persons could call on the state to remove and discipline them. The state, with its mission to sterilize as many people as possible, used the power families had over young people to force the surgery on them. Sterilization required the permission of a parent or guardian if the person was young or mentally deficient, and those seeking to step up the pace of sterilization would have found it most convenient to sterilize young people who were already at odds with their families.[16]

The fact that parents or other family members called on authorities to reign in youths they perceived to be wayward should not be interpreted as demonstrating proof that such relatives encouraged or consented to the sterilization of these youths. In many instances, families may not have understood that alerting authorities could result in sterilization. And although the sterilization law required parental consent to perform the surgery on minors, in many situations informed consent may have been difficult or impossible to obtain, given the disparities of education, income, and power between parents and officials. Parents might not have grasped the full implications of the procedure or felt unable to dispute the recommendation of a medical professional. In these cases, families clearly ended up serving the state; whether the state in turn served families is open to question.[17]

The rhetoric of the campaign for the sterilization statute diverged from its implementation after 1927 in terms of the gender of those sterilized. In Virginia, as in many other states, women were sterilized at higher rates than men, with women representing almost 60 percent of the people whom physicians sterilized in Virginia between 1928 and 1940. This percentage was close to the national average.[18] On one level, the fact that women were more likely to be sterilized than men did match the rhetoric of those who sought the law's passage. The preceding chapter shows the extent to which the desire to sterilize women in particular motivated those who lobbied for the new law.

This preference to sterilize women persisted despite the fact that performing the procedure on women was medically much more difficult than on men. In fact, there were instances in which women in Virginia and California died while being sterilized, but there were no such reports of men.[19] However, this gendered disproportion makes sense in light of the prevailing attitudes toward female sexual danger that motivated the sterilization statute. Those who had lobbied for the procedure prior to 1924 became those who performed the procedure after 1927, and they had clear convictions about female sexual danger.

Another factor in the gender disparity may have been the attitudes of the patients themselves about the procedure. While consent by the individual or family was not required for sterilization, it was taken into account. Moya Woodside's 1950 study of sterilization in North Carolina presents data suggesting that men were more likely to oppose the surgery than women and that patients were likely to believe that vasectomies resulted in loss of male sexual potency.[20] While individuals or families were not the only ones making the decision for sterilization, if they objected strenuously, physicians would have at times called off the surgery. On the other hand, there is evidence that, far from resisting sterilization, some women sought it. Sterilization would have offered some kind of contraception to people for whom access to birth control was limited or nonexistent.[21]

Though more women than men were sterilized in Virginia, the fact that doctors there sterilized men in 40 percent of the procedures they performed runs counter to the rhetoric that preceded the sterilization statute's passage.[22] Sterilizing women was a procedure with which Priddy and others were familiar, and the sexual danger posed by feebleminded women was an easy selling point to the legislature. Once the General Assembly legally sanctioned the surgery, men (who, evidence suggests, were rarely, if ever, sterilized prior to 1924) now faced the prospect of sterilization as well, though not quite as often as women. Recognition of women's sexual danger did not preclude the possibility of male sexual danger as well.

Why the sudden increase in male sterilizations after 1924? The most obvious explanation is that doctors no longer had to make excuses for sterilizing patients. While women might have been "accidentally" sterilized during the course of some other procedure, men rarely, if ever, faced this situation. Now that doctors could sterilize any inmate, they operated on men as well. As eugenicists, these physicians recognized that feebleminded men were as dangerous to the gene pool as women.

A preference for sterilizing women over men was not uniform in public institutions throughout the state. While most Virginia hospitals sterilized more women than men, Western State Hospital, near Staunton, sterilized more men than women between 1928 and 1948. Of the 1,287 people sterilized there, 686 were men and 601 were women.[23] For much of this period, Dr. Joseph DeJarnette, who had been closely involved with the effort to legalize sterilization, served as the hospital's director. Though we can not be sure why DeJarnette oversaw the sterilization of more men than women, it was likely connected to his deep conviction in the benefits of eugenics. DeJarnette's commitment to racial purity was legendary. His poetry lauding eugenic sterilization had led to his being nicknamed "Sterilization DeJarnette."

> Oh, you wise men take up the burden,
> And make this your loudest creed,
> Sterilize the misfits promptly—
> All not fit to breed.[24]

Curbing the reproduction of the "feeble-minded" brought about benefits whether men or women were involved, and if the surgery could be performed on men quickly and cheaply, then "Sterilization DeJarnette" was happy to see this done.

Gender variations such as this occurred across the nation, as a 1933 survey by the Human Betterment Foundation demonstrated. In California, for example, 52 percent of sterilizations were done on men. A similar situation existed in Alabama and Kansas, where men represented 58 percent and 52 percent of those sterilized, respectively. In the remainder of the states that performed the procedure, women were its primary targets.[25] A variety of factors shaped the way different states and institutions implemented sterilization laws. A national and international movement had inspired eugenic laws, but their implementation was a product of local conditions. Sometimes a firm belief in female sexual danger meant that more women were sterilized, but in other instances, faith in the efficacy of eugenics combined with the comparative ease of sterilizing men trumped this. Local racial attitudes and racial demographics might lead to targeting particular parts of the population, as might the concerns of particular institutions.[26]

White Virginians faced sterilization in greater numbers as growing appropriations for institutional construction brought about increased patient capacity. Virginia built the State Farm for Defective Misdemeanants in 1926 and the State Industrial Farm for Women in 1932, both of which housed a large number of people defined as mentally defective and thus candidates for sterilization.[27] Other new state bureaucracies targeted children and families more directly. In 1928 the newly established Bureau of Mental Hygiene, charged with promoting mental health and preventing mental illness, opened a clinic to give mental examinations to all children who were wards of the Department of Public Welfare.[28] In 1934 the General Assembly mandated the establishment of Juvenile and Domestic Relations Courts in all counties of the state; until this time, these courts had existed only in cities with over fifty thousand inhabitants.[29]

These expansions in the state welfare apparatus meant that more judges, social workers, and other state employees could involve themselves more in monitoring individual behavior and looking for candidates for sterilization. For example, in 1942 Arthur James, the commissioner of public welfare, explained that welfare workers and court officials assisted with locating candidates for sterilization. "Where the judges have information regarding patients which would be valuable to the superintendents [of state mental hospitals] in determining whether or not the persons should be sterilized they may write the superintendents and advise them."[30] This sector of middle- and upper-class professionals were agents of the state, and sexual regulation became one of their tasks.

Those committed to enforcing the Racial Integrity Act recognized a need to harness this growing bureaucracy for the identification and prosecution of interracial couples. "Miscegenation" had, of course, been illegal in Virginia prior to 1924, but the "one drop rule" expanded the number of individuals who could be defined as "colored" and thus prohibited from marrying a white person. Enforcing this new standard posed a significant challenge. Visual inspection had never been a fail-safe means of ascertaining an individual's race, as demonstrated by the number of individuals who successfully "passed" as white, but enforcing this new, stricter law required more sophisticated techniques.

The state's ability to keep tabs on each individual's racial background was restricted by the vastness of the project, the inexact nature of categorizing the population by race, and the limited state apparatus directed toward the effort. But help came from private citizens, people who could and did add an additional level of surveillance, free of charge. Occurrences of Virginians monitoring the behavior of others and exposing violations of the interracial marriage laws were frequent. In fact, private surveillance seems to have played a significant role in this act's enforcement. In much of the state, most particularly the rural areas and small towns where most of the population lived, people often knew their neighbors' families and personal histories. Though a visual inspection might not reveal a "colored" background, knowledge of an individual's parents and other family members could help establish that information, and this could lead to reports of violations of the Racial Integrity Act.

The result was prosecutions such as that of Samuel C. Branaham and Grace Markler in Fincastle, Virginia, in 1938. The couple had been married for thirteen days when allegations surfaced that Branaham was colored. According to newspaper reports, Branaham was working as a supervisor at the Glasgow Rug Factory when one of his employees raised the allegation. "Gossiping neighbors" fueled the speculation, prompting the couple's arrest. This case demonstrates that sexual surveillance was not always directed at the lower classes. Here, workers used reports of interracial marriage to harass their supervisor. Both Samuel and Grace Branaham testified that they did not know Samuel was colored. Prosecutors, aided by the State Bureau of Vital Statistics, produced evidence dating back to 1858 that both of his parents had black ancestors but had "passed" as whites in 1896 when they registered for marriage in Amherst County. This marriage certificate enabled them and their children to live as whites until Samuel ran into trouble. Judge Benjamin Harden ordered the young couple separated and specified that the two were forbidden from living together for thirty years. The judge also told Branaham he could not marry or live with any other white women during this period, or he would be sentenced to prison. The incident might have also cost Branaham his job; many would have considered it inappropriate or perhaps even illegal for an African American to supervise white employees. Branaham offered to resign from the factory, and newspaper accounts reported that the couple ultimately decided to leave the state.[31]

The same year, rumors circulated in a York County community about a newly married couple. Though the two had claimed to be white, many whispered that the groom, twenty-year-old Paul Dickinson, was in fact "colored." Perhaps the fact that Dickinson and his fiancée, Lilian Fannie Lark, had gone to Newport News to be married, where no one knew their family backgrounds, encouraged this speculation. When the police heard the story, they arrested him and charged him with violating the Racial Integrity Act. Prosecutors contacted officials in Dungannon, Virginia (presumably Dickinson's hometown), and procured a copy of Dickinson's birth certificate, which indicated he was indeed "a Negro." The last newspaper accounts of the story reported that charges against the wife had been dropped and that Dickinson was in jail awaiting trial on charges of miscegenation and perjury.[32]

In other instances, the individual filing the complaint (an act that amounted to reporting on other citizens) had a personal involvement in the allegedly interracial relationship. In what the *Norfolk Journal and Guide* labeled as the first case brought to court under the 1924 law, William Dove and his wife, Mary Grove Dove, were accused of violating the Racial Integrity Act by William's brother, Charles. Charles alleged that William, a white man, had married Mary, who, though appearing white, was actually "colored." The case was complicated by the fact that the couple had been married outside the state, in Maryland. Newspaper accounts suggested that a dispute over property between Charles and William motivated the allegation of miscegenation.[33]

Though the complainant in the Dove case was the brother of the groom, on occasion mothers reported their daughters' marriages as interracial, possibly when they did not approve of the match. William Purcell of Richmond was accused of miscegenation by his mother-in-law, Ada Rhoton, in 1949. Purcell had been married to Rhoton's daughter, Stella May, for a few months when she made this charge. Charges were ultimately dismissed against the pair.[34] The following month, in Salem, Virginia, the parents of Florence (Hammond) Hamilton succeeded in persuading a judge that their daughter's husband was African American. The defendant, Clark Council Hamilton, pleaded guilty, received a three-year suspended sentence, and immediately left the state for Baltimore.[35]

In other cases, individuals seeking a divorce used the charge that their spouse was of a different race as a means to nullify the marriage. In 1925 Maude Monahan accused her husband, James Wilson, of being "colored" after she left him and moved to Richmond from Washington, D.C. She reported that he followed her to Richmond and attacked her one afternoon as she was leaving work and returning to the YWCA, where she roomed. Monahan charged Wilson with assault but also told police that their marriage should be nullified because it was interracial. Thirty years later, in a case that went to the U.S. Supreme Court, Ruby Elaine Naim sought to use the same method to end her marriage to Ham Say Naim.[36]

Another case illustrates the complex ways charges of miscegenation found their way into personal and professional conflicts in the lives of Virginians. In 1929 two residents of Phoebus, Virginia, went to Brooklyn, New York, to be married. Since the groom, Emil Umlauf, was white, and the bride, Lizzie Whitehead, was African American, they traveled outside the state to a location where they could be legally married. The two were said to be old friends, as Whitehead lived in the house adjoining Umlauf's, a residence he shared with his aging mother. While they were gone, Umlauf's mother charged that Whitehead had beaten her two months earlier. Police secured a warrant for Whitehead's arrest, and when she returned home to Phoebus, they arrested her. Umlauf, who was the local chief of police, went to the station to seek the release of his new wife and speak to her through the jail window. Police officers witnessing the unfolding events tried to convince Umlauf to sever ties with Whitehead and let her be quietly tried, but Umlauf refused the offer, insisting on his right to defend his wife and his entitlement to marry whomever he wanted. With the white chief of police standing at a jail window loudly proclaiming his marriage to an African American woman, other police officers felt they had no choice but to arrest their boss and charge him with miscegenation. Though the couple was acquitted, the judge asked them to leave the area immediately.[37]

Taken together these cases indicate that some Virginia residents willingly undertook the task of uncovering interracial marriages, and the new Racial Integrity Act encouraged individuals to act as agents of the state in this way. Though at times reports were motivated by racial and class-based fears, in other instances everyday frictions and disputes among families and neighbors brought couples who violated the law to the attention of officials. While African American men who married white women were often the target, prosecutions of white men for marrying African American women also underwent public and legal scrutiny. Regardless of what prompted such surveillance, it always aided the goals of public policy initiatives by extending the reach of the state. Also important for Virginia's frugal political leaders was the fact that voluntary surveillance of this kind lowered the cost of enforcing the new law.[38]

The Racial Integrity Act also provided Walter Plecker, the director of the Bureau of Vital Statistics, the opportunity to extend the power of his office and relentlessly pursue Virginians who threatened to transgress the racial boundaries. Plecker's involvement in policing the color line does much to explain the act's passage as well as its ultimate impact. Indeed, Plecker played a key role in making this law significant. Interracial marriage had been illegal in Virginia long before 1924, and social sanctions against such crossings of racial boundaries were just as old. The fact was that interracial marriages between individuals with discernible racial backgrounds were extremely rare, even before the legislature passed the Racial Integrity Act. But Plecker succeeded in transforming what might have been a fairly meaningless statute into one that changed the lives of hundreds of Virginians.

Plecker recognized that racial categories were very difficult to neatly demarcate and that race could not always be ascertained by visual observation. Furthermore, Virginians, like those in other southern states, had a long history of transgressing racial boundaries in both social and sexual relations. Nonetheless, Plecker insisted that racial boundaries could be established and enforced, and he sought allies across the state who would help him with this surveillance. Reports from private individuals helped, but Plecker also tried to enlist the assistance of a broad range of government employees. Deputy registrars of the Bureau of Vital Statistics watched for "suspicious" marriage records and birth certificates on the local level, and they alerted Plecker to those individuals who attempted to pass as white. Plecker also asked teachers and school administrators to monitor the families of their students and report possible violators to his office. Plecker instructed these officials to scrutinize in particular children registered as "colored" who had older siblings listed as white — siblings who had earlier slipped through cracks in the system. The bureau sent threatening letters to the parties involved and asked local officials to assist with enforcement.[39]

Plecker's efforts continued into the 1940s. As the nation drafted young men to serve in the military, Plecker wrote to voter registrars, health care workers, school superintendents, and clerks of the court across the state reiterating the need for constant vigilance. African Americans, he told them, had successfully slipped into the white world by registering for marriage as Indians and then marrying white people. Plecker helpfully attached a list of "mixed families" to his letter—that is, families with some African American members but with others who had registered with the Bureau of Vital Statistics as Indian. A new problem arose during registration for the military draft. Some blacks were registering for the draft as Indians, thus taking the first step, in Plecker's view, toward passing into the white world. Plecker concluded, "One hundred and fifty thousand mulattos in Virginia are watching eagerly the attempt of their pseudo-Indian brethren, ready to follow in a rush when the first have made a break in the dike."[40]

Plecker believed medical professionals to be his allies—some of the upper-middle-class white men who ran hospitals and schools or held government appointments had even been educated by the eugenics-minded professors at the University of Virginia.[41] The semirespectful tone of Plecker's letter of 1943 (which began, "Dear Co-Workers") stands in contrast to his correspondence with Virginia's mothers and midwives. In a 1924 letter to a Lynchburg midwife, Plecker took a threatening and intimidating approach: "This is to notify you that it is a penitentiary offense to willfully state that a child is white when it is colored. You have made yourself liable to very serious trouble by doing this thing. What have you got to say about it?"[42] Plecker considered midwives (generally lower-class women of both races with little or no formal education) to be adversaries, not professionals and not worthy of his respect. He demonstrated similar contempt for the Lynchburg parents who had employed the midwife:

> This is to give you warning that this is a mulatto child and you cannot pass it off as white.
>
> A new law passed by the last Legislature says that if a child has one drop of negro blood in it, it cannot be counted as white.
>
> You will have to do something about this matter and see that this child is not allowed to mix with white children. It cannot go to white schools and can never marry a white person in Virginia.
>
> It is an awful thing.[43]

The class-based allegiances demonstrated in these contrasting approaches underscored Plecker's political agenda. He sought alliances with members of the upper classes to oversee the behavior of the lower classes. Protecting the social order by policing individuals had political implications. He observed in 1925 that "mulattoes or near whites . . . constitute a strong political faction."[44] Were this population to continue to expand, they might succeed in acquiring the rights of citizenship that white southerners had sought so hard to deny African Americans. Upper-class whites had to work together to preserve their place in society. Physical contamination of the white race had to be averted lest it bring about political vulnerability.

Plecker used his office to extend his authority as much as possible, but significant checks on his power remained, checks that suggested, if not disagreement with his positions, a definite reluctance to commit the state fully to his racial vision. In fact, when Plecker resigned from office in 1946, shortly after his eighty-fifth birthday, he had spent much of his career frustrated by weaknesses that he believed remained at all levels of state government, executive, judicial, and legislative. These weaknesses undermined his mission of protecting the white race.

First was the issue of enforcement. In the years following the Racial Integrity Act's passage, Plecker's calls for cooperation and help with implementation too often, in his view, went unheeded. Local registrars were either unable or unwilling to monitor citizens with the kind of precision Plecker had expected, despite his constant efforts to impose his strict definition of whiteness. Plecker complained that one of the logistical challenges was due to the fact that local deputy registrars would issue marriage licenses to individuals about whom they did not have complete information. Thus, if one member of a couple was from a different county, the registrar in the county issuing the license was supposed to contact the registrar in the home county of the other partner and check his or her race. Reluctant to spend so much time and effort on checking individuals' backgrounds, many country registrars issued licenses without making these contacts.[45] Plecker even resorted to intimidation, threatening these deputy registrars with a yearlong jail sentence if they registered nonwhite individuals as white.[46]

Just as frustrating for Plecker were conflicts between the Bureau of Vital Statistics and the judicial system. A 1924 case, one of the first tried under the new act, illustrated for Plecker this obstacle in the path of racial purity. Robert Painter of Staunton, Virginia, sought to marry Atha Sorrells. The deputy registrar of Vital Statistics for the county searched the records for the ancestry of Sorrells and discovered that her grandmother, born in 1856, was registered as a free person of color. The registrar refused to grant a marriage license. The couple took the case to court, where Sorrells maintained that she was white, with a distant Indian ancestor. Judge Henry Holt rejected the assumption that individuals should be required to demonstrate the whiteness of every ancestor, observing "In twenty five generations one has thirty-two millions of grandfathers, not to speak of grandmothers." Rather, Holt asserted, since Sorrells looked white, she was white. Though Holt conceded that she may have had an Indian ancestor, he rejected Plecker's demand to thus classify her as nonwhite (Plecker would have insisted that all Virginia Indians were "colored"). Ignoring Plecker's opposition, Holt issued the license, and the couple wed.[47]

Reluctant juries compounded Plecker's problems. Juries, he claimed, often refused to convict people of violating the act because of its severe penalty: time in prison. By 1931, desperate to find more people guilty of racial intermixing, he went so far as to suggest that the legislature consider modifying the act, lessening the punishment so that more convictions could be secured.[48]

Finally, support in the legislature was tepid at best. Plecker was unable to realize his dreams of a vast effort to improve the white race by using "propaganda and intensive education" to educate the public about eugenics. Numerous requests from Plecker to expand the bureau's budget so that he could do more to enforce racial purity were ignored. The governor and General Assembly had failed to support key parts of his legislative agenda, and they also failed to give Plecker help enforcing the law. On a number of occasions, he pleaded for an expansion of the bureau's budget so he could hire more staff.[49] In the bureau's 1929 annual report, Plecker warned, "If the State is really intent upon preserving the racial purity of the white population it will be necessary to employ one or more officials whose duty it is to see that the racial integrity law is enforced."[50] Plecker also complained that a local commonwealth's attorney paid insufficient attention to promoting racial integrity, failing to prosecute some of those whom Plecker pointed out as marrying interracially. Though newspapers gave Plecker's complaints publicity, neither the legislature nor the governor acted to help.[51] The abiding commitment to the theory of racial purity claimed by Virginia's white leaders in 1924 turned out in subsequent years to be tempered with ambivalence and concern about Plecker's growing power.

The explanation for why enthusiasm for Plecker's work faded so quickly is rooted in the conflicting views of government first exposed during the legislative campaign. Plecker had earlier clashed with other white leaders over whether legislation should target white elites as well as the poor and working classes, and now he continued his insistence on regulating elite behavior, even seeking to discipline those in authority who refused to help him enforce his view of whiteness. His response to Judge Holt's decision in the Sorrells case showed how far he would go to punish those who disagreed with him. In the aftermath of Holt's decision that Sorrells could marry a white man, Plecker publicly denounced Holt and rejected the judge's standard for defining whiteness. As the controversy played out in the local press,

Plecker even went so far as to obliquely question Holt's racial background, suggesting that some individuals opposed racial integrity for "personal reasons of intimate and delicate nature."[52] Other prominent Virginians and Richmond's two white newspapers responded immediately to defend Holt. Judge Holt's brother-in-law was J. Shelton Horsley, a leading physician in the state, and Plecker's attack on the judge provoked Horsley's ire.[53] A few years later, Horsley testified before a Senate committee against eliminating the Pocohontas exception, publicly breaking rank with Plecker on this issue.[54]

Plecker sought strict enforcement of racial purity laws and proved willing to use the state to discipline anyone who challenged the law or his authority. Some of his associates, however, lost trust in Plecker, fearing that he would undermine the status of white elites by turning the discipline of the state on them as well. Plecker's willingness to betray other white elites in the name of racial integrity had been demonstrated many times, perhaps most conspicuously in his attack on Judge Holt. Many who clashed with Plecker agreed with his eugenic ideology but disagreed with his political sensibilities. Leading Virginians who supported eugenics were perfectly willing to employ it as a way to defend the social and political hierarchy, but these individuals ultimately wanted to preserve the status quo and their place in it. Plecker, in contrast, wanted a change in government and a state with more authority to enforce racial purity. Plecker had no misgivings about increasing state power, because he *was* the state when it came to racial integrity. He sought to expand the state and his own personal power but would not be permitted to do so. Other white Virginia leaders were willing to support government initiatives that promoted eugenics as long as they corresponded with their more limited view of government.[55]

Disagreements between Plecker and other leading Virginians over the implementation of racial purity laws were minor in comparison with the broad agreement among Virginia's ruling elite that dangerous sexual behaviors could threaten racial and political stability. The extent of this agreement can be seen in the activities of the State Board of Censors during its first two decades of existence. A look at the censors' work demonstrates that their efforts stemmed from the same mix of sexual and political ideologies and the related desire to preserve the hierarchies of race, class, and gender that produced and sustained the campaigns for eugenic sterilization and racial integrity.

Governor Trinkle named the initial members to the Board of Censors in 1922. First selected was Evan Chesterman, a writer and former secretary of the State Board of Education.[56] Two more appointments filled out the board:

R. C. L. Moncure of Falmouth (about thirty miles north of Richmond), a former businessman and tax collector; and Emma Speed Sampson, an artist and writer from south Richmond.[57]

Although Virginia's state and local governments in this period were heavily structured around the system of political patronage, and thus appointments to many positions were political rewards that involved little responsibility, the job of serving on the Board of Censors was quite a demanding position. Before a film could be shown in the state, its producer or distributor had to send a copy to the board, along with payment of a license fee. The censors would view the film and write a report on it. If they judged it suitable for showing, they would affix a seal to the film case, plus the cases of all copies circulating in the state. The state instructed movie houses that they could not show a film unless it bore that seal. If the censors determined the film unsuitable, they had two choices. Films that, in the minds of the censors, could be made acceptable by cutting objectionable portions were returned to the director with instructions as to which parts should be excised. Directors who chose to make these cuts could then resubmit the film to the board. But if the censors felt the film was completely unredeemable, they rejected it for display in the state.[58] In the three-member board's forty-three-year existence, the censors examined over 52,000 films, an average of over 1,200 per year. They rejected 157 films, 38 of which they subsequently approved after the cutting of some sections.[59]

The legislation authorizing the censorship board had focused on issues of "morality" and the "incitement of crime" as criteria for rejecting films. In enforcing the former, the board devoted considerable attention to censoring what they considered immoral films, and the moral issues that concerned them often revolved around sexuality. The board censored dramas that depicted sexual situations as well as a number of documentary-type nonfiction films. Though most of these documentaries claimed to be for educational purposes, their promoters sought to show them in regular, mass-market theaters, hoping that their sexual content would bring viewers. Examples of such films included *Girls of the Underworld*, a venereal disease education film about prostitutes, and *The Miracle of Life*, a depiction of conception, fetal development, and birth. The censors rejected both of these films "*in toto*," condemning *The Miracle of Life* as "offensive" and likely to "embarrass people of modest sensibilities." On occasion, as in the case of *The Miracle of Life*, the censors would seek the opinion of the state health commissioner or the state commissioner of public welfare, who joined them in viewing and discussing the film.[60]

The censors did not ban all sex-related documentaries from the state. They approved some that they felt had educational value, deciding apparently that a "truly" educational film was not immoral. In some cases, theaters restricted admission to sex-related films to persons above a certain age and scheduled women-only and men-only screenings. These sex-segregated screenings were motivated as much by profit as by modesty, since restricting audiences in this way suggested particularly salacious content and therefore attracted viewers.

A larger number of films that censors banned or required be cut were dramas or comedies with sexual themes. The major characters of these films were white, and they depicted men and women in sexually charged situations. The reports written by the censors on these films give a sense of the kinds of behaviors they found offensive. For example, in 1924 the censors rejected a film titled *The Last Man on Earth* because it showed "women of various ages contending in the most shameless fashion for the possession of a young man." Furthermore, "little if any attempt is made to conceal the fact that they are impelled by sex impulse." Compounding the problem of *The Last Man on Earth* was the volume of "salacious or smutty sub-titles" throughout the film. After the board's rejection, the filmmakers cut several scenes and resubmitted it. The board reconsidered the film but rejected it a second time.[61]

Censors ordered cuts in scenes depicting all kinds of bawdy behavior. For example, the makers of *Odor in the Court* had to "eliminate the tom cat noise made by Blodgett when girl passes on street."[62] Among the scenes that had to be cut from *The Pace That Kills* before it could be shown in Virginia were those depicting a "girl dancing on a table while men watch and fondle" and "two girls while fighting disrobe each other."[63] Problematic table dancing also had to be cut from *After Bedtime*, which showed "pictures of girls indulging in high kicking and dancing on tables."[64] But the work of the censors did not focus exclusively on policing portrayals of female sexuality. Certain immoral behaviors by men had to be censored as well, as the board indicated after they reviewed the film *The New Aunt*. This film caused objections because "an attempt is made to attain comedy through the antics of a newly married farmer of the burlesque type whom frequently appears in his night shirt and indulges in many suggestive gestures."[65]

Racial issues proved to be an important focus for the censors as well, and here they acted on both their charges to protect morality and to stop the "incitement of crime." J. Douglas Smith's study of movie censorship in Virginia underscores the importance of the board's racial mission, concluding that "although the act did not mention racial content, Virginia's censors clearly understood that their mandate demanded the prohibition of films which portrayed blacks in ways that did not comport with the prevailing standards of acceptance." Films that portrayed interracial sex attracted considerable attention from the censors, and the board found any depictions of interracial socializing, sexual or not, problematic. They also censored films that negatively portrayed the white race or ones that showed interracial tensions.[66]

The board's censorship of the work of the renowned African American filmmaker Oscar Micheaux exemplifies the members' understanding of racial danger as well as the ways censors connected sexual and racial issues. Micheaux sought to show his films in the state on several occasions and ran into conflicts with the Board of Censors over his work. In 1924 the board rejected Micheaux's film *A Son of Satan* because it "touch[ed] unpleasantly on miscegenation," depicting an "intermingling of the two races which would prove offensive to Southern ladies." The censors asserted that the fact that the villain in the film was mulatto "would prove irritating — if not hurtful — alike to quadroons, octoroons, half-breeds and those of pure African descent." Finally, depictions of racial riots in the film might also have a particularly dangerous effect on African American audiences. "Riot scenes of any sort are calculated to arouse the passions, and even the mildest presentation of race conflict or friction is inflammatory material of the most dangerous sort for treatment on the screen. The scenes in 'A Son of Satan' smack far too much of realism and race hatred to be classified as mild, and in the opinion of this Board might lead to serious results." All this led the censors to conclude that Micheaux's film could not be shown in the state because it might "tend to corrupt morals or incite to crime."[67]

Some films intended for white audiences also met with scrutiny from the censors because of their mix of sexual and racial issues. The censors rejected *White Cargo*, a drama about white Englishmen living in Africa that depicted an interracial sexual relationship and marriage, because it was "well calculated to cause friction between the two races now living in amity in the commonwealth." It was unclear whether the censors feared the films might tempt blacks into interracial sex or inspire whites to violence against blacks. Most likely, both possibilities led the censors to conclude that "miscegenation, at best, is an unwholesome theme for motion pictures, and in a State like Virginia, where the intermarriage of blacks and whites constitutes a felony, such plot material, in our opinion, excites a universal sense of revulsion." In the aftermath of the Racial Integrity Act, depicting miscegenation *was* depicting a crime, and two members of the board considered such depiction tantamount to incitement. Board member Moncure did not fully agree, perhaps indicating some misgivings about the new law. Moncure argued that cutting out the sexual scenes between the male protagonist and the African woman ("which show the negress putting forth her meretricious efforts to 'vamp' the white man") would have remedied the film's faults. But his colleagues Chesterman and Sampson, apparently more committed to the vision of racial purity, disagreed, noting that the film's "most disgustingly offensive feature" was the scene depicting the couple's marriage.[68]

Moncure also split with the board's majority over the film *Cracked Wedding Bells*. According to the censors' report, the film depicts a white reporter in blackface attending an African American wedding. The ceremony is halted with the announcement that the groom has been killed, but the bride-to-be, determined to marry someone, picks out the disguised reporter to wed instead. Before the ceremony is completed, "a wagon full of chickens is upset in front of the house and the negroes all rush out to capture the fowls which are their favorite article of diet." Chesterman and Sampson explained that since a state law barred interracial marriage, the film posed a threat by undermining the law. "To ridicule any law is to lessen its effectiveness if not indirectly bring it into disrepute." Moncure disagreed in a separate opinion. "Colored people" might object because the film projected them as ignorant and capricious, but he did not believe that anything in the film was "prejudicial." As for the question of interracial marriage, Moncure pointed out that no interracial marriage actually occurred in the film because all of the characters were "white people blacked up." Furthermore, Moncure wrote, "The wedding ceremony is never consummated." In the copy of the report filed in the archives at the Library of Virginia, someone has crossed out "consummated" and written "completed."[69]

The disagreement between Moncure, Chesterman, and Sampson over *White Cargo* suggest contrary interpretations of the board's mission. Moncure understood the mandate to censor immoral or incendiary films to be somewhat restricted. He agreed that the board should eliminate depictions or intimations of interracial sex. But suggestions of interracial marriage might at times be acceptable. The other board members felt that portrayals of interracial marriages under any circumstance (even when such marriages were accidental and contained no sexual suggestion) were in themselves immoral — because they presumed marriage would be followed by sexual intercourse. Such films were also incendiary because they depicted violations of Virginia's racial purity law, even if no such law existed in the location of the film's setting, as in the case of *White Cargo*.

That two of the censors insisted that violations of the Racial Integrity Act not be shown on films in Virginia demonstrates the particular significance given to sexuality in this era. Films, of course, depicted many crimes — robberies, murders, assaults, and more. There was no insistence that movies should cease depicting such crimes nor any requirement that all crimes committed in films must be punished. But the majority of the Board of Censors demanded that interracial marriages must not appear on screen in Virginia under any circumstance. Sexuality, particularly interracial sexuality, was by their standard exceptionally dangerous and especially contagious, and depictions of this particular crime had to be kept from the public view.

The work of the movie censorship board illustrates the convergence of issues of race, class, and gender in sexual regulation. Though the debates around the bill's passage focused on issues of sex and morality, the actual work of the censorship board soon encompassed policing racial boundaries as well. This shift was not coincidental but demonstrates the extent to which white elite Virginians identified dangers at the intersection of race and sex. Depictions of interracial marriage made racial issues sexual ones, but even interracial socializing was viewed through a sexual lens. Simply depicting interracial mingling, as in the case of *A Son of Satan*, would have to be censored lest it offend "well-bred" southerners or inspire African Americans. Movie censors recognized that policing racial and sexual boundaries were related activities and that both came under the framework of protecting morality. All of this built on an intellectual framework in which eugenics played a significant role. Eugenics confirmed that moral and sexual degeneracy could produce racial degeneracy. Thus, protecting public morals by censoring the sexual aspects of films was a racial as well as a moral mission.

The activities of the Board of Censors also demonstrate the convergence of gender and class in policing sexuality, underscoring the importance of class-based constructions of gender to protecting the social order. Movies posed a challenge to long-held beliefs in the sexual purity of white women when they depicted a growing world of popular culture where women exhibited sexual agency and desire. Several of the scenes that offended the censors showed upper- and middle-class white women abandoning sexual respectability when they socialized with individuals from the lower classes. For example, censors found *The Primrose Path* offensive for depicting the fall of the white teenage daughter of a "respectable policeman." The young woman falls in with a "fast" crowd and is soon found at "automobile necking parties," "wild drinking and dancing parties," and finally a "bawdy house." A similar fall from white upper-class virtue offended the censors in

Three Women. In this film, a "rich widow" falls under the spell of a "money-hunting roue" who later seduces her daughter as well. In each of these films, cross-class socializing produced sexual transgressions, as upper- and middle-class women fall from sexual purity into degeneracy. Censors found both of these films wholly irredeemable; they did not suggest the elimination of particular scenes but rather banned the films entirely from the state.[70]

By policing the boundaries of gender and sexuality, then, censors also policed the boundaries of class. The growing consumer culture and rising middle class brought a new challenge to class boundaries in Virginia. The rising popularity of movies meant that ideas, values, and images from outside the state had a growing influence on its citizens. The audience for movies included middle- and upper-middle-class white citizens, and the project of censorship indicated a recognition that films might tempt these upper classes into sexual immorality. This new medium introduced the latest ideas and images to the minds of the Virginians at an unprecedented rate, and the establishment of the movie censorship board was a way for the ruling elites to assert a measure of authority in this new realm. By regulating depictions of sexually dangerous behavior, censors hoped to prevent the actual behavior, a connection between observation and conduct underscored in the charge that films were likely to "corrupt the morals of the young." Sexual containment distinguished the upper from the lower classes; if the morals of upper-class youth were "corrupted," a key indicator of class would be lost. Movie censorship offered elites a way to manage and organize images and, by extension, behaviors, both of which might challenge the traditional system of class and racial boundaries.

The three policies discussed in this chapter were part of the larger political project of protecting white elite rule. Racial contaminations were dangerous because they would produce political vulnerability. Sexual and moral degeneracy could undermine whiteness, white political authority, and the purity of white womanhood. White elite Virginians believed that maintaining a pure culture, free of racial or sexual decay, was important to political and economic stability. Eugenics provided the framework for this belief, and Virginia's leaders embraced this connection between the sexual and the political.

This enthusiasm for state regulation continued to be tempered by a desire to keep the cost of governance low. Legislators must have been delighted to learn that, far from costing the state, movie censorship actually brought money into the government. While the establishment of the Board of Censors expanded the government's activities, its creation did not require locating any new sources of revenue because of the profits generated by charges for permits, licensing fees, and occasional fines. For example, in the 1928–29 fiscal year, the board cost the state $18,949.01 and took in receipts of $29,394.50. That year, the board's annual report commented that although censorship was "never designed as a paying proposition," it had proved to be a "definite source of revenue."[71] In its forty-two-year existence, the board added over half a million dollars to the state's coffers.[72]

Despite the fact that the Board of Censors actually expanded the state's earnings, the legislature kept the board's expenditures to a minimum. Throughout the board's existence, its only real expense came from the salaries of the board members and a small clerical staff. The limited budget frustrated the censors, especially since their operations generated profits that they were not authorized to spend. At times they publicly expressed this frustration, as in this example from the annual report for 1929–30:

> As things now stand, the Division works under an inflexible budget appropriation — $20,734.50 a year — which greatly restricts the efforts of the censors. No matter what their profits may be or what occasion may arise for extraordinary expenses, they are held fast by the limited annuity allowed them. This appropriation, invariable [sic] smaller than asked for, in recent years has barely sufficed to keep the office running. It has compelled the censors to veer from strict economy to absolute parsimony in the purchase of their postage, stationery, furniture and office supplies. Furthermore, it has left barely enough to provide for extra clerical help in cases of sickness or where the vacations authorized by law have been allowed employes of the office.[73]

Perhaps even more ludicrous, it took several years of requests by the board before the legislature authorized it to buy a movie projector that allowed members to view "talkies." This meant that for a period of time in the late 1920s they could not view many of pictures sent to them and could not hear the dialogue in those they could view. The censors concluded, "With such handicaps as these the censors of course found their usefulness materially impaired, in fact, reduced to almost nothingness."[74]

Though the censors did eventually get a new movie projector, the legislature never gave them the additional money needed to establish a system of enforcement and inspection in the state's movie houses. As a result, the censors had no means by which to monitor or enforce their directives; they relied on local police and theater owners themselves to report violations.[75] At times members of the Board of Censors became quite creative in their attempts to surveil activities in theaters across the state despite the absence of paid staff. In 1924 Evan Chesterman enlisted the help of his nephew, Davis Lee, to find out whether an unauthorized film was showing at the Attucks Theater in Norfolk. Lee wrote back that the picture was not showing and noted that "This [theater] is a colored place so there was some little trouble in getting in. Not that the management was not agreeable but the question was naturally raised in his (P. C. Collin's) mind as to the cause of my visit."[76]

The support of local law enforcement, sympathetic citizens, and even family members enabled the Board of Censors to perform their duties despite their limited budget. The commitment of the censors themselves to their work is also evident, particularly in light of the substandard pay they received. Though the General Assembly originally planned to pay censors $3,000 per year, a last-minute amendment to the bill cut the salaries to $2,400, a move motivated by the legislators' desires to reduce state expenditures and silence accusations that membership on the board was another way to reward political supporters with government jobs.[77] Despite this significant salary reduction, the commonwealth suffered from no shortage of applicants for the board, though the first three members of the Board of Censors all had outside incomes to supplement their modest state salaries.[78]

Individual dedication helped make enforcing the new Racial Integrity Act a similarly low-cost endeavor. The state relied on the fanatical devotion of Walter Plecker, who used the existing infrastructure of the Bureau of Vital Statistics for the act's implementation. The General Assembly had established the bureau in 1912 as part of the State Board of Health with the mission of recording births and deaths in the state.[79] Virginia's birth records included information on the race of the parents of all children, and as a result, the state had data on the racial background of everyone born since 1912. In 1918 legislators expanded the bureau's work to mandate that all marriages be reported to it, a change that also had little impact on the bureau's cost.[80] The report of the state auditor indicates that enforcing racial integrity laws cost the state almost nothing. In the fiscal year ending in June 1921, the expenses of the Bureau of Vital Statistics were reported to be $22,387.85. Five years later, after the Racial Integrity Act had been in effect for two years, the bureau's expenses came to $23,721.12.[81]

Lack of funds plagued all these efforts at sexual regulation in the 1920s and 1930s, and these policies were implemented imperfectly, even haphazardly. Plecker's frustration with lack of financial support for his work was echoed by movie censors who clamored for more money with which to perform their duties. Virginia's doctors performed a relatively large number of sterilizations, enough to make the state a leader in this regard, but many remained dissatisfied at the slow pace of surgeries. Disappointment with the low output of the sterilization program led W. I. Prichard, the superintendent of the Petersburg State Colony, to call for a vast expansion of the effort in 1949.[82]

Parsimony and hesitancy to build a larger disciplinary state complemented each other in 1920s Virginia, making sexual discipline a subtle process, not a blunt force. Virginia's leaders built a flexible state that allowed for significant disciplinary authority without forcing the state to embark on undertakings that would be financially or politically costly. Film censorship had to proceed within strict financial confines. The racial integrity law was flexible enough to allow Plecker to implement much of his agenda, while allowing those who questioned his radical views and their value as public policy to keep him in check. Eugenic sterilization would be permitted within the institutionalized population. The boundaries of that population could be somewhat flexible, but despite broad support, sterilization never occurred at the kind of pace that some had imagined.

Those who performed the regulation of sexual behavior were not limited to government employees but were instead a larger group of individuals and institutions who acted as agents of the state. Nearly always white and upper class, those who helped extend the reach of government included members of private organizations (in particular, the MSV), social workers, the press, doctors and other medical professionals, and the clergy, among others. Cooperation between the state and these professionals enabled the state to expand and enforce new policy efforts. Even when individuals outside the upper class aided the state's surveillance and discipline for purely personal reasons, entwining the state in family quarrels and personal vendettas, the result still abetted the preservation of elite rule. Sexual regulations built upon existing power relations, and this relationship aided the construction of particular individuals and groups as dangerous and contributed to the effectiveness of the policies under discussion here.

This broadly defined state shared a political goal — preserving white elite rule. With faith that the state would act in their interests, white elites supported the state's efforts at sexual discipline. Government would protect the social order from sexual, racial, and political threats while, as an added bonus, promoting economic growth. Sexual regulation cemented these relationships between sex, race, class, and government in the 1920s, reinforcing to elites that the state was their agent, acting to protect them from internal and external threats.

Diagnosis and Treatment

Venereal Disease as a Social Problem

Support for state sponsored venereal disease control efforts reached a low point in Virginia in the 1920s. Like other states, Virginia saw federal money for venereal disease control decline and then cease in the aftermath of the First World War, ending completely in 1926. The Virginia General Assembly increased state appropriations slightly in response to federal cuts, but not enough to continue the program. The director of venereal disease control resigned in 1920, and the state did not hire a replacement. Subsequently, the state changed the name of the Division of Venereal Disease Control to the Bureau of Social Hygiene and discontinued most of the division's venereal disease efforts.[1]

Public health leaders failed to convince the Virginia legislature to save venereal disease control programs, and in fact two of the state's most powerful health officials rejected such measures. Ennion Williams, the director of the Department of Health, vocally opposed government-sponsored venereal disease control and actively participated in the dismantling of venereal disease education efforts in the state. Walter Plecker, the director of the Bureau of Vital Statistics, also opposed such work, fearing venereal disease control would divert money and attention from eugenic programs.

Despite the decline in support for state venereal disease programs during the 1920s, a decade later Virginia policy makers would not only revive but significantly expand them. The numbers are impressive. Virginia's Department of Health performed approximately 25,000 examinations for syphilis in 1928. Ten years later the annual rate had risen to over 170,000 and would continue to grow. In 1930 the state spent $2,500 on venereal disease control programs, a figure that would increase to $118,312 in 1940.[2] By 1941 the state had established 108 subsidized clinics to test for and treat venereal disease. It had, in addition, passed and implemented a law mandating premarital testing for syphilis, hired public health nurses to trace the partners of infected state residents, employed educators who gave lectures and showed films on venereal disease, and much more.[3]

This chapter explains why some doctors in Virginia lobbied for venereal disease control and examines how they convinced state health officials and political leaders to implement such a program. Specifically, I explore how these doctors drew on prejudices of race, gender, and class to convince white elite male policy makers that many of those suffering with venereal disease were dangerous and irresponsible. Finally, this chapter demonstrates how health leaders aimed venereal disease control efforts at specific parts of the population — African Americans, poor and working-class whites, and pregnant women of all races — making these racialized, classed, and gendered subjects targets of state authority.

Virginia's first venereal disease prevention campaign came during the First World War. Federal public health officials and military leaders believed venereal disease threatened national security during the wartime emergency and launched a nationwide campaign to combat it. At the outset of U.S. involvement in the war, Congress established the National Commission on Training Camp Activities to treat and prevent the spread of venereal disease among military personnel. Cities and states across the country responded to federal initiatives, passing antiprostitution laws and trying to police illicit sexual activity.[4]

In 1918, as pressure mounted nationwide to halt the growing incidence of venereal disease at military training stations and industrial sites, the Virginia legislature created a Division of Venereal Diseases within the Department of Health and hired a full-time director to run it. The federal government's Interdepartmental Board of Social Hygiene contributed $22,415.59 to this effort in 1919, and the state contributed another $11,000.[5] The Division of Venereal Diseases worked to suppress activities that spread venereal disease, to treat people who had contracted it, and to educate the public about its transmission. Rules adopted by the State Board of Health mandated the reporting of infection by examining physicians, the instruction of infected persons on how to avoid spreading the disease, the examination of individuals suspected of having it, and the quarantine of those suspected of spreading it.[6]

Federal funding for venereal disease control did not last long after the conflict in Europe ended, since the wartime emergency had provided the primary impetus for the program. Congress ended appropriations for the Interdepartmental Board in 1921. In 1920 federal leaders reduced Virginia's funding to $12,246.65 and made further cuts in following years, until all federal funding stopped in 1926. A small increase in state appropriations failed to save the program. With no director of venereal disease control and little financial support, most of the control work stopped in Virginia. Venereal disease control programs were terminated for similar reasons in other southern states in this period as well.[7]

Prevailing cultural currents in the 1920s contributed to the declining popularity of venereal disease control efforts across the nation. A desire for a return to normalcy in the postwar period, coupled with a growing challenge to Victorian sexual mores, led to a waning of public support for extensive government involvement in controlling and repressing sexual behavior. Young people sought increased sexual freedom, but this was accompanied by a growing disinclination toward open discussion of sexual diseases and threats, bringing an end to most venereal disease control programs in the 1920s and early 1930s.[8] Public opinion indicated that education about sexual behavior should have a strong moral component, and leaders in the American Social Hygiene Association (ASHA) concurred. The ASHA even opposed chemical prophylaxis for venereal disease, a measure introduced during the war, saying such treatments promoted immorality and promiscuity.[9] The vice reforms of the Progressive Era, with their mission to uplift prostitutes from their apparently degraded lifestyles and to clean up American cities, also waned significantly in this decade.[10]

Those who argued against venereal disease control in Virginia spoke from positions of significant power. Walter Plecker was skeptical of many public health efforts, because he feared they took time and money from eugenic measures. "Is it not of greater importance to the welfare of the state," he asked, "to give some thought to the quality and value of its future citizens than to lavish all its energies and money upon prolonging the lives and increasing the number of unfit?" Plecker also suggested that eugenic improvements, not spending on treatment and testing, were central to eradicating venereal disease. Good health and good morals, he believed, were part of the genetic heritage passed down from generation to generation. While venereal disease was not caused by poor genes, Plecker believed that many of the traits — the mental inferiority and moral weakness discussed in the previous chapters — that led people to become infected were. Plecker made it clear that he considered eugenics to be the answer to public health problems; venereal disease control was at best peripheral and at worst a distraction.[11]

Ennion Williams argued more directly against expanding governmental efforts at venereal disease control and took action to block those already in place. In the 1929 annual report of the Department of Health, Williams wrote testily, "It is probably not necessary for me to restate my position on this subject. I have never been able to understand why we should operate clinics for the treatment of venereal diseases and not operate clinics for the cure of all communicable diseases." Williams did not support such an expansive public health program but was rather making the point that, since the state did not operate such general public clinics, it should not have specific clinics for venereal disease. He concluded, "Venereal disease clinics, to the contrary, seem to me to be the least defensible of public health encroachments on the field of the private practitioner."[12]

Williams opposed venereal disease education as well, though the state's commitment to this had always been meager. The Bureau of Social Hygiene employed only one full-time educational worker, Mrs. Fereba B. Croxton. Croxton incorporated venereal disease information into "sex hygiene" presentations to clubs and groups of students in high schools and colleges, reaching for the most part only middle- and upper-class Virginians.[13] Her focus on students reflects the influence of ASHA's model of social hygiene education, which focused efforts on the middle class and on the teaching of morality.[14] The only other state activity in this regard was an agreement that the Virginia Social Hygiene Council would purchase antisyphilitic drugs at wholesale rates and distribute them at cost to physicians.[15]

Part of Williams's opposition to venereal disease education was due to his belief that it was a threatening and possibly dangerous undertaking. In the 1927 annual report of the Department of Health, he wrote, "I have never thought it wise for us to do any work, other than educational, in the direction of venereal disease control. Even in this restricted line there is always danger, for an unwise director could make mistakes that would be almost irreparable."[16] In the 1929 report, he noted his objection to the discussion of "sex matters" in "schools, colleges or in public places to mixed audiences of male and female, young or old."[17]

In 1930 Williams succeeded in ending all publicly funded sex-education programs except the distribution of state-approved informational pamphlets on venereal disease and the sale of antisyphilitic drugs at cost to physicians.[18] But rather than simply ceasing to request state appropriations for sex education, he took a less direct approach. Williams conducted a survey of Virginia educators asking them whether they thought sex education should be carried out by the state, and if so, whether it should fall under the purview of the Department of Health or the Department of Education. The results of the survey were mixed, though a majority expressed reservations about sex education and showed some support for the Department of Education to sponsor programming. Williams used these results as the rationale for further reducing the budget for sex education in his department, and in 1930 he spent only $2,500, earmarked for the printing and distribution of literature.[19] Staff in the Department of Education—possibly resentful that the health director sought to define the agenda of their department—did not, in turn, expand the department's programming, as Williams had suggested they should. Consequently, state sex education and venereal disease prevention efforts continued at a minimum level for several years. Venereal disease disappeared from the health department's annual reports for 1932, 1933, and 1934, except in tabulations of mortality statistics.

The plan to all but eliminate venereal disease control work went largely unchallenged by other state officials until the mid-1930s, indicating complicity with Williams's actions, if not outright agreement. At least one member of the State Board of Health, Assistant State Health Commissioner Roy Flannagan, offered perspectives on venereal disease and sex education contrary to Williams's.[20] However, Flannagan and his allies were not able to marshal enough political clout to change the policy, nor were they willing to take the political risk of undertaking an unpopular campaign.[21]

This decline in state programs for venereal disease control runs counter to the trend historians have observed in other public health initiatives in the South during these years. Indeed, many southern state public health programs expanded in this period, benefiting from the growing commitment by the states to public welfare that was born during the Progressive Era and that deepened with the onset of the Great Depression. As the state health commissioner, Williams had backed other programs that expanded the government's role in public health. In fact, Williams cut venereal disease control programs at the same time he sought to expand rural health and sanitation efforts.

Some in the medical profession expressed concern about the impact of public health on private medical practice. The American Medical Association (AMA) questioned public health programs, particularly large-scale, federally funded efforts that might undermine the work of private physicians.[22] The Medical Society of Virginia (MSV), the state association of white physicians, joined the AMA in denouncing certain public health efforts, including the Sheppard-Towner Maternity and Infancy Act. The MSV faulted the Sheppard-Towner Act, which gave money to states for the promotion of maternal and infant health, for "tending to promote communism." The MSV found similar danger in a plan to extend the services of the Veterans Bureau, labeling the expansion of veterans' hospitals "communistic in character."[23]

Virginia doctors were concerned not only with federal public health programs but also with state efforts that might compete with private medical practices. Some of Virginia's physicians expressed concern that establishing state-run venereal disease testing and treatment centers would deter patients from seeing private physicians and paying for the drugs and treatment themselves. The 1929 annual report of the state health department (authored by health director Williams) suggested, in fact, that venereal disease clinics represented a "public health encroachment on the field of the private practitioner."[24]

Williams's opposition to venereal disease control was based on more than skepticism about government's impact on private medical practices, as evidenced by his opposition to venereal disease education as well. The fact that young middle- and upper-class white students were a primary focus of the state's venereal disease control work suggested these populations were likely to have or to acquire venereal disease and marked this part of the population as unclean and dangerous. Targeting these populations threatened elite rule, which rested on the principle that this part of the population was superior in every way to those they governed. The purity of white southern women might also be undermined by the information venereal disease educators gave them and by the state's suggestion that they needed to learn about such sordid topics.

Williams's position brought him into conflict with a national movement that sought to revive and expand venereal disease control. The inspiration for a new fight against venereal disease came from a small but dedicated group of scientists backed by philanthropists and coordinated by the ASHA and the U.S. Public Health Service's (PHS) Committee for Research in Syphilis. Impressed by the prevalence of the disease and concerned about its impact on individual lives as well as on the nation as a whole (impacts the war experience had demonstrated), this group sought to use the new advances in treating venereal disease to curb what they considered an epidemic.[25] Their work supported research in syphilis treatment and the dissemination of such information in the PHS journal *Venereal Disease Information*.[26]

Encouraged by the national movement and already convinced of the efficacy of public health campaigns such as hookworm eradication, some private physicians in Virginia began to lobby locally for recommitting the state to venereal disease control. In 1928 a group of Virginia doctors organized the Virginia Venereal Disease Society during the annual meeting of the MSV, the year after Williams had spoken out against venereal disease control work in his department's annual report. The new group planned "to promote all medical and popular measures for preventing the venereal diseases." R. W. Garnett (the Danville physician who had earlier encouraged an accelerated pace of eugenic sterilization) served as its first president, T. P. Latane as vice president, and Dudley C. Smith as secretary. Their effort drew motivation and encouragement from national venereal disease control advocates. Walter Clark of the ASHA attended the organizing meeting and showed a film produced by the ASHA titled *The Diagnosis and Treatment of Syphilis*.[27]

The new organization sought the attention of policy makers and physicians, trying to convince them that a venereal disease eradication drive would benefit the state in a number of ways. They sought to convince physicians that public health efforts would not encroach on their business by crafting policies that would protect private medical practices and offer benefits to local medical professionals. In addition, they utilized the language of progress and modernization to gain support from physicians and policy makers. In fact, arguing for venereal disease control's connection to progressive government became an important part of the campaign. The *Virginia Medical Monthly*, the monthly journal of the MSV, helped the effort by publishing at least one, and often several, articles per year on the public health threats of venereal disease and the importance of a comprehensive program for its eradication. Many of these articles were reprints of addresses given before the society's annual meeting or other health-related meetings across the state.[28] In an address before the MSV, Roanoke physician C. B. Ransone made the case this way:

> You are loyal citizens of Virginia, intensely interested in her material and social progress and, as interested intelligent citizens, may I urge that you use your influence in your several communities to create a public sentiment in favor of a more adequate venereal disease control program for Virginia, embracing education for the non-infected, early diagnosis, and adequate therapy for the infected, with quarantine for the depraved and lawless.[29]

The MSV members did not all speak with the same voice, and there was some variation in the arguments they made in support of statewide venereal disease control, but common themes and trends certainly emerged in the advocacy of these programs by the organization, its members, and its various local chapters and committees.

According to Allan Brandt, the nationwide venereal disease control movement of the early 1930s attacked the previous efforts of the ASHA and others for being moralizing and prudish. "Doctors urged that the time had come to reject euphemism, reduce moralism, and address the venereal problem on the level of science and medicine."[30] Some Virginians calling for venereal disease control in the late 1920s took this approach, including Dudley C. Smith, a doctor at the University of Virginia, who spoke before the MSV in 1927. Smith directly challenged the view that syphilis control should be equated with the control of immoral behavior. Rather, he criticized the equation of a medical problem with a moral problem and noted, "In other words, the moralist in attempting to help the sanitarian has often, as ironical as it seems, handicapped him. This infection has been so completely walled in and protected by secrecy, ignorance, prejudice and indifference that it could not be attacked properly by medical measures." Equally noteworthy was Smith's reminder that the transmission of syphilis could occur in both immoral and "innocent" interactions: "one in every three syphilitic infections were acquired innocently." He advocated the use of "personal prophylactics," rejecting the argument made by the ASHA and others that the use of such devices would increase immorality. Finally, he argued for state-subsidized treatment of venereal disease for citizens who could not afford treatment: "No case should be allowed to go untreated or to stop treatment before cured."[31] In a comment following Smith's talk, Assistant Health Commissioner Flannagan echoed Smith's perspective that a broad range of the population was at risk for venereal disease:

> Every physician should suspect syphilis in his patient. Everybody is susceptible to it; it does not mean any particular reflection on anybody to make a Wassermann [a test for syphilis]. It should be done in every case. In fact, I had it done upon myself recently when I was sick, not only blood Wassermann, but spinal fluid. Every doctor that practices for a number of years is laying himself open to infection.[32]

These two men are particularly notable because they rejected the equation of diminished mental capacity with immorality and venereal disease, a formulation held by eugenicists such as Plecker. For Flannagan and Smith, disease did not recognize boundaries of race, class, or morality.

Smith's and Flannagan's more egalitarian view of venereal disease was not to become the dominant perspective in the state. Others in Virginia took a different position, suggesting that certain parts of the population were more likely to spread a venereal infection and targeting them for strict enforcement and punishment. At the 1930 MSV meeting, C. B. Ransone spoke at length on venereal disease, but his approach differed from Smith's. Focusing on the risk of immoral behavior, Ransone suggested targeting particular segments of the population for disciplinary action. He said the majority of transmissions of venereal disease took place in "unlawful and immoral conducts — sex intercourse out of wedlock." Ransone also claimed that people infected with syphilis fell into three "classes." One comprised the feebleminded and otherwise mentally handicapped, who should be institutionalized indefinitely, apparently regardless of whether their venereal infection had been treated and cured or not. People in the second group "understand the seriousness of their condition" and should be left to their own devices, because they readily sought treatment. The third, "composed mainly of prostitutes," knew that they had a dangerous disease but willfully infected others. Ransone proved willing to identify women, specifically prostitutes, as the most dangerous class of diseased individuals. In his mind, these lower-class, sexually promiscuous women were so irresponsible that they refused medical care and thus needed the strictest discipline from the state. This "scum and driftwood of society" should be "placed in absolute quarantine."[33]

Though Ransone's comments differed from those of Smith and Flannagan by connecting venereal disease to immorality and dividing the population into dangerous and trustworthy citizens, he was similarly silent regarding connections between race and infection. His moralistic language positioned him as more of a traditionalist than Smith and Flannagan in one sense, but his silence on race distinguished him from previous generations who had viewed venereal disease as primarily an African American problem. The idea that African Americans had a higher rate of infection than whites had long been held in the South, particularly by those partial to the ideas of eugenics and pseudoscientific studies of racial difference. Claims of black immorality, sexual excess, physical inferiority, and general irresponsibility had led turn-of-the-century observers to label African Americans "a notoriously syphilis-soaked race."[34] By avoiding overtly racist constructions of venereal disease, this group of Virginia doctors distanced themselves from the previous generation of physicians and scientists whose comments on the connection between race and venereal disease had reflected a virulent racism. This marked the new campaign as modern and different from past venereal disease control efforts.

Relative silence on the issue of race also generated a clear difference between the venereal disease control campaign and eugenics. In some ways, these two campaigns followed similar paths. Emphasizing the modern and scientific agenda of venereal disease control echoed the rhetorical strategy that eugenic advocates had used to gain legitimacy and support from the

General Assembly. But while the language of eugenics was clearly one of race, the early venereal disease control effort kept racial issues in the background. This is not to say that leading venereal disease control advocates did not believe in eugenics. Indeed, much evidence suggests that they remained committed to eugenic principles asserting the physical and mental inferiority of African Americans. But their decision to de-emphasize racial issues distinguished the venereal disease effort from the one Plecker was leading.

There are a number of explanations for why they adopted this rhetorical strategy. For one, Virginia's physicians were following a national trend in this regard. The extreme racial rhetoric of earlier years, according to historian James Jones, declined nationwide in the 1920s "as medical discussions became more quantified and physicians concentrated on clinical manifestations."[35] But it is also likely that these doctors sought some distance from Plecker, in particular, because of his stated opposition to venereal disease control work. Since for Plecker everything seemed to revolve around race, these venereal disease control advocates marked their campaign as distinct from his work by avoiding his racist approach. Furthermore, as demonstrated in the previous chapter, Plecker's star, after shining brightly in 1924, had already begun to dim by the end of the decade. For all of these reasons, sidelining racial rhetoric and adopting the attitude of progressive moderates made sense in the late 1920s.

Ransone's focus on the particular dangers women posed was not wholly shared by his fellow venereal disease control advocates. Flannagan, in contrast, emphasized that venereal disease could be spread by men as well as by women. In 1925 he read a poem before the Richmond Academy of Medicine about a venereal disease doctor who falls asleep and dreams of patients in hell. The *Virginia Medical Monthly* published the poem, titled "The Devil's Masque. A Dream — Time, A.D. 1918." The poem describes a play performed in hell by some of hell's residents who died of venereal disease. Four groups of characters take turns telling the stories of their downfall. First, a group of "damned young men" who contracted venereal disease prior to marriage bemoan the fact that they "brought to our homes / this blight from the past." Next, women who had "many, many a mate" tell how they caught and then transmitted the disease. While this group of speakers claims to be the "wise ones" who understood the risks they were taking with multiple sexual encounters, they note that some female victims had "no minds" and "are but babes." They explain that feebleminded women caught venereal disease because they yielded to men's desires at every opportunity. Third, young wives, "wizened, dejected, and lame," speak of how they became "unsexed" by the venereal disease they caught from their husbands. And finally, in the "Song of the Completely Unfit," those "blasted and broken / by prenatal blight" speak of the worthless lives they experienced, having contracted venereal disease at birth.[36]

The poem illuminates two important aspects of Flannagan's understanding of venereal disease and its relationship to gender and class. First, though some women were innocent victims, infected by their husbands, he does not portray any innocent male victims. Flannagan was less willing to call on old stereotypes of female sexual danger in his venereal disease control advocacy. Men were just as dangerous. Second, though he underscores the fact that men and women of all classes could contract venereal disease, he suggested that infections in upper-class men and women have their origins in cross-class contacts. Male immorality brings the disease into the upper classes:

The disease of the slum
To the palace will come
When men from the palace go down
To the red lighted way
With its denizens gay
Secluded but always in town.[37]

Neither Flannagan's poetry nor other elements of this campaign brought any immediate results. They did not dissuade Williams from taking the final steps in dismantling the state's venereal disease education program in 1930. They also failed to marshal support in the legislature for funding greater venereal disease control work. Success would not come until the language of race reentered the calls for venereal disease control, accompanied by hints that lower-class whites and pregnant women of all races brought sexual danger as well.

Beginning in 1928, the work of the Julius Rosenwald Fund brought a different focus to venereal disease control in Virginia, reviving discussions of the prevalence of these diseases among African Americans and contributing to a new focus on venereal disease in pregnant women. Julius Rosenwald had established the fund in his name to support a wide range of philanthropic initiatives with the money he made from Sears, Roebuck and Company. His earliest philanthropic interests lay in the establishment of schools in the South, primarily schools for rural African Americans. But in the 1920s Rosenwald and the Rosenwald Fund also began to focus on supporting public health programs in the South, realizing that poor health posed a significant barrier to education.[38]

In 1928 Health Commissioner Williams wrote the Rosenwald Fund seeking money for rural sanitation improvements. Cognizant of the group's interest in African Americans, Williams sought a grant to pay the salary of a field agent who would travel around a nine-county area in eastern Virginia (a part of the state with a high percentage of African Americans) promoting sanitation efforts. Using the economic arguments that had worked so well to promote earlier health proposals, Williams emphasized that poor sanitation "makes so many of our rural people, both colored and white, unproductive."[39]

Williams did not seek state employment for this field agent but instead asked for the fund to channel the salary through the Negro Organization Society of Virginia, which would be the agent's employer.[40] In any other context, it would be reasonable to assume that Williams framed the proposal this way to keep the size and cost of government small. If the Negro Organization Society was involved, it would be up to that group, not the state, to pay for or eliminate the position when Rosenwald money ran out. However, in this case race was also an important factor. Virginia's leaders had a history of avoiding the hiring of African Americans in high-status posts in the state government. This explains Williams's request that the position not be a state job.

In his response, Rosenwald staff member Edwin Embree praised Williams's interest in sanitation but explained that the fund was more interested in promoting public health nurses in the region, particularly African American nurses. And he expressed reluctance to bypass the state administration in funding the position: "I wonder if it would not be feasible for such work to be carried on through the State Department [of Health]. In general, it seems to me much better to get such services established under public authority, rather than to leave it to private agencies."[41]

Rosenwald Fund officers approached the South with a quietly subversive agenda that is revealed in the records of these communications.[42] They supported health and education programs with the hope that over time such work would improve the general status and condition of African Americans in the region. M. O. Bousfield, the fund agent who worked closely with the initiatives in Virginia, constantly sought opportunities to use his position to undermine the southern racial system.[43] In addition to improving African American health by funding the maternal health nurses, Rosenwald Fund officers hoped to increase the demand for African American nurses, demonstrate their competence, and get more of these individuals (primarily women) on the state payroll and into positions of authority in the state government.

The immediate result of these negotiations was Rosenwald Fund assistance in paying the salary of a "colored itinerant nurse" charged with the herculean task of doing "maternity and infancy work" in eight counties in eastern Virginia. The state paid $300 toward this undertaking, the Rosenwald Fund paid $550, the eight counties served promised $810, and the president of the Virginia Normal and Industrial Institute (a historically black college in the region) promised to raise $600.[44]

Nurse Rosa Taylor began work on 1 September 1929. She visited each of the eight counties, staying about a week at a time. Traveling by car, she focused on training midwives in sanitation and medical techniques. The next year, state and private contributions paid for another nurse to work in the same region, and by August 1932 six African American women worked as public health nurses in Virginia: Daisy Greene, Emilie Fowlkes, Juanita Scott, Betty S. Davis, Dorothy Hooper, and Frederica Beale. Their salaries came from a combination of Rosenwald Fund grants, state, county and municipal funds, contributions from the Negro Organization Society, and donations from private individuals. Funding for these positions was tenuous, and some jobs came and went from year to year. For example, in 1931 Albemarle County employed nurse Daisy Greene, but in 1932 the county discontinued funding her position. So, in 1932 the state paid half her salary, and the Negro Organization Society and the Rosenwald Fund covered the rest.[45]

In subsequent years New Deal programs would bring a significant increase in federal funds for public health work in Virginia and across the nation, replacing the small-scale efforts of private agencies such as the Rosenwald Fund. Federal money began to support all kinds of public health when Title 6 of the 1935 Social Security Act provided $8 million to be divided among the states for public health campaigns, and more money would follow in subsequent years. Congress intended the funds to supplement existing state-based health efforts, and state health departments had to meet certain standards to be eligible for federal money.[46] By 1 February 1934 Virginia had 130 new public health nurses whose salaries were paid by the Federal Emergency Re-Employment Administration. Maternal health work continued to be an important focus for these new public health nurses, though they involved themselves in many other areas as well.[47]

Soon after providing funding for African American public health nurses in the South, the Rosenwald Fund began to promote venereal disease control efforts across the region. Like other fund projects that aimed to spur southern governments into action, Rosenwald agents hoped to demonstrate the effectiveness and utility of offering blood tests and free (or reduced-cost) treatment for syphilis. Central to this particular undertaking was the debate over whether offering venereal disease testing and treatment to African Americans was worth the effort of public health programs. The Rosenwald study would show that, contrary to prevailing opinion, African Americans would take responsibility for their health and well-being and avail themselves of free testing and treatment when those services were available.[48]

In late 1930 the fund approved an application by Virginia to hold one of these demonstrations in Albemarle County. Located in central Virginia and the home of the University of Virginia, this county was at first glance an odd choice for such a study, as African Americans there had a relatively high standard of living, greater access to health care, and better-quality educational facilities compared with the rest of the state. In short, a county with Charlottesville and the university at its center was hardly representative of the rural or small-town South. But in choosing this location, the fund and Virginia's health leaders were, in a sense, stacking the deck. The study was more likely to succeed in Albemarle County because of its better medical resources (the patients could be seen at the university's clinic) and because African Americans here were, on average, more prosperous and better educated.[49]

The success of the southern venereal disease control initiative was mixed. With the help of Rosenwald money, medical professionals surveyed 19,427 African Americans in five southern states. Rosenwald Fund officers were quick to point out that these studies did show "the practicability of administering modern treatment for syphilis en masse in rural districts where facilities were not available."[50] In Albemarle County, some venereal disease treatment was available for blacks living in or near Charlottesville, but doctors also ran clinics in more remote parts of the county for residents of those areas. The health department sent letters to every African American household, inviting family members to be tested. In addition, African American school children received syphilis tests. In the county, 3,812 people were tested for syphilis over an eighteen-month period. Of that number, 339 (8.9 percent) tested positive for syphilis and received treatment. By the end of the study, just over a third of the county's African Americans had been tested for syphilis.[51]

The paternalistic attitude so common among southern public health leaders was reflected in the letters sent to Albemarle County's African American residents. The letters made no mention of syphilis:

Through the generosity of the late Mr. Julius Rosenwald the colored citizens of Albemarle county and the city of Charlottesville have been provided with the opportunity of having a special health examination.

The files of those making this survey show that you have not had your examination. To date, approximately 4,000 of the colored citizens of this area have taken advantage of this opportunity.

We would like to extend this privilege to you and your family. There is given below the time and place where the examination can be obtained.

Yours very truly,

Joint Health Department and Rosenwald study[52]

The study's leaders approached the population as passive recipients of help, not as people who could be truly educated and encouraged to help themselves. Masking the actual intention of the study, they made no mention of venereal disease at all. Whites would provide benevolent guidance for those too ignorant or irresponsible to take care of themselves.

Though the study did examine and treat many people, it had less success in securing increased support for venereal disease control. Two years after the study ended, the PHS, at the request of the Rosenwald Fund, surveyed southern states to see whether they provided free antisyphilitic drugs to doctors for distribution to those who needed them — one of the most basic elements of a venereal disease control program. Of the twelve southern states surveyed, only three used state funds to provide these drugs to indigent patients only. Two others used federal money. Six southern states reported to the PHS that they did not subsidize these drugs. Included among these six states were four of the sites of the Rosenwald demonstration: Virginia, Georgia, Alabama, and Mississippi. The fifth, North Carolina, paid for the drugs with federal relief funds.[53]

Why not use state funds to subsidize antisyphilitic drugs and provide free venereal disease testing, since the Rosenwald study had just demonstrated the success of this approach? One barrier to this kind of large-scale public health effort was that some physicians were concerned it would harm their private practices. Advocates of venereal disease control countered that a sliding scale could be established whereby patients would be charged based on income; those who could indeed afford a private doctor would not save money by going to a public clinic. Nonetheless, the possibility remained that patients would underreport their income and use the free clinic whenever possible, and thus the fear that public health efforts would threaten private physicians prevailed.[54]

Though offering free tests and subsidized drugs to poor patients might do little to benefit private medical practices, the rewards of the Rosenwald study in Albemarle County were clear to local physicians. The study held significant potential to help the University of Virginia Medical School and biomedical research efforts, which further explains the choice of this county for the location of a syphilis control demonstration in Virginia. Albemarle County doctors supported the Rosenwald proposal because of "the marked beneficial effect it is expected this demonstration will have on the future policies of the Virginia State Dept. of Health; the very great educational benefit to be derived by certain classes of students attending the University of Virginia; and the very wholesome effect that a demonstration of this character should have upon the negro element of the population."[55]

The study's impact on the recipients of care was just one of the reasons to perform this work. Patients were a valuable commodity to medical schools and medical researchers, and the syphilis demonstration helped procure those patients. Thus, projects that had a clear and immediate benefit for the university and for local doctors, such as the syphilis demonstration in one county, got support, whereas those with more dubious benefits to those with political clout, such as free drugs and tests across the state, failed.[56]

While the Rosenwald study did not immediately change public policy, it changed the way doctors and health experts discussed the venereal disease problem and how they framed appeals for new health programs. In short, arming themselves with Rosenwald data allowed them to frame the venereal disease problem in racialized terms that would appeal to those who believed in eugenics or held more general racist ideas. But by using the language of science and medicine, they presented themselves as progressive reformers, not racists. Scientific rhetoric masked the racism underlying their approach.

In the years after the Rosenwald Fund demonstrations, public health leaders increasingly referred to the high rate of syphilis infection among African Americans in arguments for venereal disease control. Soon it was common for public health leaders in the state to dwell on the racial aspects of venereal disease. Armed with data and scientific studies, they used the language of race in ways that made them sound more modern and rational—and persuasive—than previous generations of southerners who had merely railed about the dangers of a syphilitic race.

Lecturing before the MSV annual conference in 1936, R. W. Garnett, for example, noted the particularly high rate of venereal disease among blacks and prisoners, forming a discursive connection between these two marginalized populations. Garnett observed that the prevalence of venereal disease among African Americans varied across the South, ranging from a relatively low rate of 10 percent in Albemarle County, Virginia, to a high of 40 percent in Macon County, Alabama.[57] In another lecture at the conference, U.S. Assistant Surgeon General Raymond A. Vonderlehr paid similar attention to race as a factor in venereal disease prevalence, presenting statistics that indicated a nationwide black syphilis rate more than twice that of whites. Though Vonderlehr's numbers showed that whites had a slightly *higher* rate of gonorrhea than blacks, he did not comment on the causes or implications of that statistic.[58]

Even Ennion Williams came around to supporting venereal disease control by the mid-1930s. In a speech before the Virginia Conference on Social Work outlining the "social significance" of syphilis, Williams underscored the extent of syphilis infection in the state's "colored" population. According to Williams, Virginia's African Americans had a rate of infection that was "three to five times" higher than that of whites. While the white death rate from syphilis was declining, the African American rate of death was on the rise. While not directly endorsing expanded public health efforts to combat syphilis, Williams did note that "It is also the social duty of society in general to provide facilities whereby the individual may receive this necessary treatment."[59] Although officials cited different statistics, their message was the same: venereal disease was rampant among African Americans in Virginia.

State leaders, it seemed, were constantly on the lookout for ways to highlight the high rate of venereal disease among African Americans. In 1938 another study in Albemarle County, funded by the state health department, tested over eleven thousand people for venereal disease. The health department's annual report that year noted the success of the study, saying that 10.1 percent of the African Americans examined had tested positive for syphilis. The report made no mention of white Virginians being tested at all, only listing the total number of tests done and the number of African Americans tested. Doing the calculations reveals that the Department of Health failed to disclose that 3.5 percent of the whites in that study had positive syphilis tests. It is true that the rate for whites was lower, but the disease was certainly present in that population as well.[60]

Public health officials relied on long-held racist beliefs to interpret the high rate of black infection and then framed their plan to alleviate this situation in the language of science and progressivism. Taking as a given the inferiority of the African American temperament, and ignoring other factors that made health care less accessible to African Americans than to whites, they explained that African Americans were irresponsible and unconcerned with health matters. Those running the Albemarle County study, for example, spoke of the "apparent indifference of the average Negro to the possible consequences of syphilitic infection."[61] On another occasion, Assistant Surgeon General Taliaferro Clark (who oversaw the famous Tuskegee syphilis study) noted the "disinclination of the average Negro to seek any prolonged treatment for an ailment that for long periods of time occasions slight if any discomfort."[62]

Following this logic led health officials to conclude that venereal disease control work would have a "wholesome effect" on the character African Americans.[63] Such a wholesome effect might take a number of forms. First, receiving medical treatment might convince African Americans of the importance of receiving health care, despite its discomfort and inconvenience. Of course, African Americans were as conscious of medicine's benefits as any other Americans in this era. What elites read as "indifference" about health matters was often lack of access owing to poverty, rural isolation, and the fact of segregated health care. But Virginia's elites were disinclined to admit to the economic factors that kept these individuals from good health — let alone do anything to change their lot — and policy makers suggested instead that an improvement in moral fiber was in order. After receiving treatment, African Americans might learn that putting up with temporary discomfort had long-term benefits, and this lesson could be transferred into other areas of life where their moral character was also thought to be lacking.

In addition, curing venereal disease might alleviate the supposed laziness of African Americans. One way health leaders measured success in the Albemarle County study was with claims that African American workers were able to do more labor when they were free of syphilis. Data suggested that, prior to the syphilis control demonstration, 50 percent of the patients were physically unable to do a full day's work; afterward, only 7 percent said they could not work a full day.[64] Again, the weakness of the African American character, so obvious to white health leaders, exacerbated the danger of sick farm laborers. People too sick to work hard might — in the racist mind — tempt healthy people into laziness or become spoiled by a more leisurely lifestyle.[65] I do not want to overstate this point and suggest that public health experts did not appreciate the physical difficulties people with syphilis faced. For people trying to provide for their families, the ability to work a full day was important to their survival, but concern for the dependents of ill workers was secondary to many public health officials, at least in these discussions.

If all these rewards seem too much to expect of venereal disease control, it is important to remember the significance attached to the realm of the sexual in American culture. Sex formed the dividing line between moral and immoral, illuminated the path between health and sickness, and inspired a range of fears and hopes. As seen in the previous chapters, sex connected physical, moral, and racial degeneration, and this formulation provided the basis of public policy that regulated sexual behavior. Venereal disease was enmeshed in the realms of sexuality and morality, often signaling the difference between immoral and moral sex, and thus advocates of venereal disease control could successfully imbue this enterprise with great significance.

The attention to syphilis among African Americans by the Rosenwald Fund in the early 1930s built on the idea that blacks were sexually dangerous, but it also reinforced this perception. The Rosenwald study gave those supporting venereal disease control the data to confirm what many suspected: African Americans did have a higher rate of venereal disease. Interpreting infection statistics through the framework of time-honored racial beliefs, venereal disease control advocates made their case in ways that legislators would find persuasive. The historical understanding of southern blacks by southern whites as licentious (and thus more likely to get venereal disease) and lazy (so less inclined to seek medical treatment) made the data believable and the argument for government action compelling. Virginia's public health advocates never cited studies that looked at the relationship between poverty and venereal disease, even though poor, rural whites had venereal disease rates comparable to those of blacks. They framed the risk to the state in racial rather than class terms, reflecting Virginia's long tradition of focusing on racial issues to avoid addressing the problems posed by the vast economic disparity in the state. Though the fund's efforts were arguably quite noble, their results assisted those who sought to aim state discipline at the disfranchised masses, specifically African Americans.[66]

The Rosenwald venereal disease control demonstration established a precedent in Virginia for aiming these efforts at African Americans when work in this area expanded later in the decade. The success of coercive approaches (no mention of securing parental consent was made before children were tested) and underhanded tactics (concealing from letter recipients the actual intent of the tests) set the stage for future strategies.

The other important argument that would bring victory to those seeking expanded venereal disease control work involved the economic losses resulting from such disease. Such claims also helped justify the cost of these programs, echoing the rhetoric of the crusade in the previous decade for eugenic measures.[67] Arguments for the economic benefits of venereal disease control took a variety of forms. Ennion Williams observed that controlling venereal disease could save the state money by decreasing the number of late-term syphilitics who needed institutionalization.[68] Offering another perspective, Roanoke physician C. B. Ransone described the economic benefits of a state syphilis control program this way:

> If the primary aim of public health work is the lengthening of the span of useful human life; the elimination of economic loss from illness; the increasing of earning capacity through good health; then this disease, which so reduces efficiency, occasions so much financial loss and produces so many deaths, surely constitutes the greatest challenge to those engaged in preventive medicine.[69]

Curbing venereal disease could make more useful and productive citizens and help the economy. At times the equation of economic loss with the pain of disease and death comes across as somewhere between heartless and ridiculous, as in the claim by state health officials that venereal disease control could reduce the "toll of illness, inefficiency, and death."[70]

Economic arguments were critical to the association of venereal disease control with progressive reform. Such arguments worked on two levels: real and symbolic. By undertaking a statewide venereal disease control effort, Virginia would raise the level of productivity of its workers, while lowering the number of individuals whose inability to work made them a drain on the state's resources. At the same time, the venereal disease control effort would enhance the state's progressive reputation, impressing those considering the state as a business location.

The attention in Virginia to the problems of venereal disease mirrored a rise in concern across the nation about the impact of venereal disease on the economy. When Franklin Roosevelt appointed Thomas Parran to the position of surgeon general in 1936, Parran committed himself to making venereal disease a national issue. He pushed the PHS to earmark over 10 percent of the Title 6 money for venereal disease control, more than was designated for any other communicable disease. Venereal disease, Parran and others suggested, was more dangerous than any other disease in the country.[71]

Years later Parran admitted that federal officials had deployed economic arguments strategically, assuming that appeals to self-interest would bring support from southern white landowners.[72] Clearly following this strategy, a report on the Rosenwald venereal disease study concluded, "Most of the Negros are laborers on various plantations, so it was felt that the plantation owners would have a very good idea as to the effect of the therapy on the efficiency of their laborers. The planters stated that the average cost per employee of medical care has dropped from $18 to $7 in NC and $4 to $1 in Alabama."[73] Such observations reaffirmed the idea that venereal disease control would be directed at African Americans for the benefit of white elites.

As Virginia's white political and medical leaders came to understand that the venereal disease control program would be targeted at those who presented special danger to the state, their support for this work increased, laying the groundwork for their cooperation with federal attempts to promote venereal disease control in the state. In 1936 the MSV agreed to the PHS's request to appoint a committee to review the syphilis problem in Virginia and put forth a proposal to deal with the disease. The following year the committee completed its study and submitted a plan to the PHS, which in turn recommended a program to the state health department that was based on the MSV proposal. The Department of Health approved the plan later that year, and the MSV endorsed it at its October meeting.[74] The plan focused primarily on syphilis control, since syphilis could be rendered non-infectious within twenty-four hours of treatment, while at that time gonorrhea took much longer.[75]

In 1938 the Virginia legislature committed funds to the health department for a new venereal disease control program. The Division of Venereal Disease Control, established in December 1936, received $70,898 for its work in 1938—$11,915 from the state, which qualified Virginia for $58,983 in matching funds from the federal government under the Venereal Disease Control Act of 1938 (also known as LaFollette-Bulwinkle Act).[76] The next year federal money nearly doubled, to $106,397.[77] In addition, in 1938 the PHS assigned one of its physicians, Dr. Otis L. Anderson, to Virginia to assist in the planning process. The PHS paid Anderson's salary but asked the state to reimburse him for travel expenses within the state.[78]

The role of Virginia's white physicians in mediating between federal and state governments and the extent to which this mediating role enhanced the power of physicians in Virginia are noteworthy. Federal campaigns against venereal disease funded by the Social Security Act would be overseen in Virginia by the state's physicians. The federal government enlisted the help of the MSV in drafting a statewide venereal disease control policy and then pushed the legislature to approve this plan. Then federal officials used the promise of matching funds to push the state to provide the project with ongoing funding. The MSV made itself indispensable as a go-between for federal and state projects.

One way that Virginia's white physicians became so powerful was by holding out for more authority in federal programs, suggesting that they would resist top-down directives unless they were involved and their interests safeguarded. The MSV opposed the Sheppard-Towner Maternity and Infancy Act and critiqued some of Roosevelt's health programs for promoting communism. But they had supported programs that might help local doctors, specifically the Rosenwald venereal disease demonstration in Albemarle County. Now the MSV made itself essential to designing and implementing the new venereal disease control program, ensuring in the process that the interests of their members would be protected.

The new plan would benefit the state's physicians in a number of ways. A streamlined method of reporting venereal disease cases would save time, and the free distribution of antisyphilitic drugs to doctors would save them money. The burden of tracing contacts and tracking delinquent patients now fell primarily on the state. Expanding the state's system of public clinics had never been popular among Virginia's white doctors, as some feared an expanded state health system could threaten private practices. But advocates of expanding public funding for venereal disease control carefully responded to these concerns, suggesting that the absence of public clinics had cost many private physicians dearly. "Most individuals prefer treatment by a private physician even though only a small proportion can pay for such services. This tendency on the part of the patient usually places the costly burden of treatment on the private physician, thus relieving the local health authorities of their proper financial responsibility."[79] Enhancing the public health system in the right ways would help private physicians, too.

This participation in the lobbying and legislative process brought the MSV and its members a number of benefits. The group solidified its reputation as an important voice in state politics, a move that enhanced its membership and stature. More generally, by emphasizing the social danger unchecked venereal disease posed, doctors, as they had the previous decade with eugenic sterilization, elevated their importance to the state. All of this brought more research grants, higher salaries, and more prestige for Virginia's doctors. The MSV had learned the importance of political clout in 1926, when chiropractors had sought the creation of a separate licensing board for their profession. The State Board of Medical Examiners, a board controlled by physicians, had long been hostile to chiropractors, and a separate board would enable the profession to develop free of the hostility of doctors. With intensive lobbying, the MSV defeated the proposal, but only by one vote.[80]

The new venereal disease control program in Virginia expanded treatment, prevention, and epidemiological research. In two years the number of venereal disease clinics in the state grew from nineteen (in January 1937) to sixty-five (in January 1939).[81] The state health department distributed free antisyphilitic drugs to hospitals, clinics, and private physicians to treat all cases, regardless of the patient's financial status. A new system of reporting was implemented with the hope that it would improve contact tracing and follow-up for patients "delinquent from treatment."[82] The state and some cities provided more free and reduced-price testing opportunities and treatment facilities for poor and indigent Virginians. In addition, health officials encouraged employers to test workers in certain occupations and required tests for individuals arrested on morals charges. Preventative and epidemiological measures included the tracing of sexual partners of people with syphilis, reporting by physicians of positive syphilis tests, and mandatory treatment for people who had the disease. The initial policy recommendation also suggested a premarital venereal disease testing requirement, which the legislature enacted a few years later.[83]

Both the *Richmond News Leader* and the *Richmond Times-Dispatch* covered the new venereal disease control efforts thoroughly and favorably. Although some of the newspapers in other states questioned the propriety of discussing venereal disease openly in mass-subscription publications, neither of the two Richmond papers held back in their use of potentially controversial terms such as "venereal disease" and "syphilis."[84] The *Times-Dispatch* printed the word "syphilis" for the first time in 1937 but showed no reluctance to use the term after that. In fact, local newspapers became boosters of the new venereal disease control program, emphasizing in particular the economic costs of such infections. The papers were also quick to point out any tangible progress the program brought. For example, just six months after one public clinic expanded its services as part of the statewide campaign, the *Times-Dispatch* proclaimed "syphilis treatments show big gain," when, in fact, the only "gain" that occurred was a 25 percent increase in the number of patients seen at the clinic that year.[85]

As important as the new statewide program was, much of the real work of venereal disease control came from local governments, particularly those in Virginia's urban areas. Richmond, the state's capital and largest city, took the lead in Virginia by implementing a citywide venereal disease eradication effort. Examining this undertaking at the local level offers insight into how these policies touched the lives of the citizens of Virginia and how the racial language used in making the case for venereal disease control shaped the kind of policies subsequently implemented.

The drive for expanding venereal disease control efforts in Richmond received a boost with a 1937 PHS study titled "Prevalence and Incidence of Venereal Diseases in Richmond, Virginia — with Recommendations." The study involved surveying all patients under "observation or treatment" for venereal disease in the city. The report made much of the racial disparities in venereal disease infection, noting that African Americans had five times the incidence of syphilis as whites. Rates of gonorrhea had declined in both races, but this disease was also problematic, because many patients thought it was less serious than syphilis and therefore were less likely to seek treatment for it.[86]

An accompanying study proposed a complete overhaul in Richmond's venereal disease program. Its authors recommended the city hire a full-time venereal disease control officer to run a separate division in the health department. Richmond should also improve epidemiological services (by contact tracing and follow-up for "recalcitrant" cases), expand the free laboratory services offered physicians for blood tests, and furnish free antisyphilitic drugs to physicians for all patients. Finally, the report recommended expanding and reorganizing the various public clinics in the city.[87]

Though the PHS report was written by "outsiders"— federal employees — they came at the request of local leaders, including state and city health officials and members of the Richmond Academy of Medicine. Once the *Virginia Medical Monthly* publicized the results, Richmond health leaders used the study's recommendations to buttress their case. Soon after the report's publication, civic leaders, including church leaders, education professionals, and physicians, met with the mayor to voice their support for the creation of a new venereal disease control division.[88] The only words of caution came from the mayor, who warned that expanding government programs cost money, and this money might have to come from a tax increase. The possibility of higher taxes could not quiet the fervor for venereal disease control, at least among those meeting with the mayor that day. The *Richmond Times-Dispatch* reported that one citizen told the mayor that parents "would gladly pay added taxes if it brought protection from this scourge."[89]

This rise in support for city venereal disease control work confirms other accounts of Richmond politics in this period. State officials had sought to promote Virginia's reputation as modern and well-governed, but Richmond's leaders had the city's own reputation in mind as well. Since the early twentieth century, many Richmond leaders had hoped that the city would become a leader in the region, modeling good governance, efficiency, and growth. Richmond historian Christopher Silver writes that a tendency to-

ward fiscal conservatism in the city was replaced by "proponents of an ac-
tivist and city-promotion-minded government" in the late 1930s. Business
leaders took the lead in pushing for change, though Silver notes that their
concerns were primarily with business growth, not "social reform." The
clamor for venereal disease control in Richmond in 1938, however, suggests
that public health efforts such as this fit easily into the agenda for economic
progress.[90]

Richmond soon implemented a new campaign against venereal disease,
hiring Francis Upshur to serve as venereal disease control officer in April
1938. Some of the funds for the early stage of this project came from the Red
Cross, which gave $2,400 to the cause that year. The Red Cross also paid the
salary of a nurse, Virginia H. Campbell, to do follow-up work with venereal
disease patients. The Medical College of Virginia expanded its out-patient
department, increasing access to free care for those unable to pay for private
physicians. Upshur soon implemented a system for reporting cases and delinquent patients to the state.[91]

The new venereal disease control program brought a significant expansion in the number of individuals tested for venereal disease. The 1937 PHS
study had recommended that this kind of testing be increased, and Upshur
began to implement the proposal in 1938. Thousands of citizens in Richmond received venereal disease tests each year, making this element of the
venereal disease control program the most significant by far in terms of the
number of people affected.

Looking at who was tested for venereal disease in Richmond and under
what circumstances reveals patterns in the experience of state discipline.
Venereal disease testing disproportionately affected particular groups of citizens: the poor and working classes, students, women of all races, and those
in police custody. Many venereal disease tests were performed involuntarily
or were coerced. Each of these groups had tenuous or contested claims to
the full rights of citizenship and were thus obvious targets for paternalism
and coercion.

Venereal disease tests on working-class individuals were often performed
as a condition of employment for both industrial and domestic workers.
Performing such tests on industrial workers had a history in Virginia that
predated the campaign of the late 1930s. In this earlier period, positive tests
results could lead to dismissal. For example, Richmond's Nolde Bakery
tested employees for syphilis and fired any employee found to have it. The
American Tobacco Company also checked its employees annually for syphilis but handled positive results differently. Those who had been working for

the company for more than five years were treated if found to have syphilis, but the company fired newer employees with the disease.[92]

The testing of workers at the DuPont de Nemours rayon plant in Richmond predated Upshur's citywide industrial campaign, but it followed the procedures Upshur would recommend. Dupont required confidentiality and discouraged punishment for positive tests. The company implemented a preemployment examination for all job applicants and annual blood tests for syphilis for all employees—a group that included men and women, black and white. Management required that the company physician administering the test keep the results confidential; in theory at least, management and supervisors did not know who tested positive for the disease. The company doctor required anyone found to have syphilis to undergo treatment as a condition of continued or future employment. The company itself did not offer treatment but instead expected the employee to seek care from a physician and to bring in weekly statements from the doctor certifying that the appropriate drugs had been administered.[93]

Dupont required infected employees to follow a specific course of treatment, consisting of continuous, weekly injections, rather than the standard procedure of allowing periodic rests between the doses. This heavy-handed approach brought the company into conflict with some physicians who disagreed that this was the best way to treat the disease and resented being told how to treat their patients. Ultimately, however, mandatory testing and treatment, coupled with educational programs for employees about venereal disease, did succeed in reducing the incidence of syphilis among the plant's employees. According to company managers, cases of syphilis in employees dropped from 6.4 percent in 1933 to 0.22 percent in 1942, and they claimed that no workers had been fired for having the disease.[94]

There was, of course, no medical validity for testing workers in, for example, rayon or cigarette factories. Transmission of venereal disease through casual contact was very rare, and virtually impossible through shared handling of cigarettes or synthetic fabrics. At the time Upshur began pushing for employee testing, scientific studies had clearly demonstrated that most employees posed no risk at all of transmitting venereal disease through their jobs. However, officials in cities such as Richmond continued to implement policies mandating these examinations.[95]

The city's new program also targeted those who worked in the service sector. City leaders encouraged employers of cooks or domestics to bring their workers in for testing, as well as those who employed individuals in hotels, cafes, and hair salons.[96] African Americans dominated this portion of the workforce, though it did include some lower-class whites as well. Hospital employees were also subjected to testing, though this group fell into a different category both because they came from a wider array of socioeconomic backgrounds and because there was greater medical validity for testing them.

Upshur sought to soften the blow of the expanded testing effort on the lives of workers by seeking guarantees from employers that infected individuals could keep their jobs as long as they participated in a treatment protocol.[97] While it is likely that larger industries followed this recommendation, there is evidence that some employers, particularly those who employed one or two people in their home, did not.[98]

When Norfolk's health officials began expanding that city's venereal disease testing efforts, they followed Richmond's pattern of primarily testing poor, working-class, and/or African American workers. Of the 11,630 people tested for venereal disease in 1940 at the main public clinic, 35 percent worked as food handlers, 40 percent were unemployed, and 8 percent worked as oyster shuckers, maids, barbers, and beauty shop operators. Twenty percent of these individuals were found to have syphilis or gonorrhea.[99]

Industrial workers in other parts of the state received venereal disease education and underwent testing as well. State industrial hygiene officials worked with factory owners at knitting and woolen mills in Orange County and Albemarle County in 1941 to educate employees on venereal disease and encourage testing. Employees watched venereal disease education films, listened to lectures on venereal disease, and received printed pamphlets. Though the state underscored the fact that employee testing was "voluntary," the factories chose to make venereal disease tests a requirement for new employees.[100]

Some workers apparently resisted the mandatory tests, though there is little documentation of this. One source suggested that some industry heads were wary of initiating testing programs for "fear of labor difficulties as a result of compulsory Wassermanns among employees." Labor difficulties did not arise, Virginia's industrial workers failed to mount a significant challenge to the mandatory testing, and the program continued.[101]

There is also no evidence that African Americans collectively opposed venereal disease testing or other disease control measures. In fact, African American groups supported efforts to combat venereal disease in their community by including venereal disease control in National Negro Health Week events and spreading information about the dangers of these diseases.[102] But African American community leaders had their own reasons to support venereal disease control, and their endorsement of it was not merely passive acceptance of the agenda of the white public health establishment. Health issues had long been a significant area of concern for African Americans, and the barriers to accessing adequate health care had formed rallying points for the community as well as avenues for political engagement, such as advocating equal access for African American doctors to hospitals and professional organizations.[103]

The specific notion that African American domestic workers, particularly women, might introduce contamination to their employers has a long history, particularly in the South. For generations, African Americans working in the homes of white people interacted in intimate ways with the white families that employed them. The physical intimacy of such employment produced sites in which all kinds of contamination might be imagined and/or occur. Close contact with slave women had, one interpretation went, provoked moral weakness in white men. The product of this moral contamination, mixed-race offspring, might also be considered a form of racial contamination. Experience proved that some kinds of infection could come from simple proximity. Employers had long worried about the risk of tuberculosis and other infections from their employees, particularly those doing domestic labor.[104] The most famous example of such contamination is "Typhoid Mary," a New York cook who infected dozens of people with typhoid fever in New York City in the first decade of the 1900s.[105]

Some whites articulated specific fears about venereal disease contamination from African American domestic employees. A medical textbook from the 1930s claimed that childhood gonorrhea "is most commonly received from toilet seats soiled by infected members of the household, such as colored maids."[106] Some black leaders, including Booker T. Washington, sought to use white fears of contracting contagious diseases from African American workers to increase white concern about the health of African Americans. Historian Susan L. Smith has argued that Washington's descriptions of black workers infecting white households served to remind whites how important African Americans were to southern society, a message that would have simultaneously empowered African American audiences.[107]

Thus, the act of taking a domestic employee—or being taken by an employer—to the health department to be tested for venereal disease was an act with multiple layers of meaning. At the center of this act was a reiteration of the power the (almost always white) employer had over the (usually African American, usually poor) employee. The employee's body was the property of the employer, a site of danger that had to be examined and monitored. If not lessening the possibility of sexual contact between male employer and female employee, venereal disease testing would decrease the danger of white upper-class venereal infection if such cross-racial sexual contact occurred. The sexual dangers female domestic employees posed could be managed by the process of forcing them to be tested.

Placing white upper-class women in charge of ensuring their domestic workers underwent testing for venereal disease connected the domestic order with the public order.[108] Women were, of course, traditionally responsible for ensuring the cleanliness of the home, a fact local leaders recognized in charging them with venereal disease control. But the state's goal in promoting such testing was the defense of white upper- and upper-middle-class homes — the homes of those wealthy enough to employ domestics. The state protected these families, but these families also then protected the state by undertaking this public health function. The state and the white elite family both participated in the regulation of the lower classes and African Americans. The state acted in the interests of the white upper classes, the constituency that elected and served in the government. These women acted as agents of the state, monitoring the private sphere, while upper- and upper-middle-class white men (physicians, factory managers, and health officials) oversaw health in the public sphere. But in each case, African Americans and lower-class whites were those being checked and tested. Those outside the white upper-class family, African American domestic workers, were also those outside citizenship, since they were denied the right to vote.

On a more prosaic level, the stated rationale for employee testing was that the more people who could be tested, the better. This is how the ASHA, a group with access to up-to-date knowledge of disease transmission, explained their support for employee testing, despite the absence of medical justification for it. Since working-class and African American individuals were considered more likely to be diseased and less inclined to seek treatment, any excuse to test these individuals was considered a bonus.[109]

City leaders also sought tests for those receiving public assistance from the Social Service Bureau.[110] For these individuals — primarily lower-class blacks and whites — the state made venereal disease tests a condition of public assistance. Individuals were thus required to trade a degree of personal autonomy in exchange for financial help, just as workers were required to trade such autonomy in exchange for employment. And just as workers had to submit to the authority of their bosses and allow their bodies to be inspected, so did welfare recipients have to submit to the authority of the state. For those required to submit to such surveillance, venereal disease testing became a gateway to public assistance. The city would protect itself from these individuals by cleansing them of venereal disease, an act that social service clients were presumed to be too irresponsible to perform voluntarily.

Richmond's leaders also targeted high school and college students for venereal disease testing. The revival of such efforts in Richmond, just eight years after the state had ceased educational efforts for this part of the population, further illuminates the extent of the changes that had occurred over the intervening years. Educating upper- and middle-class white students about venereal disease was again an acceptable undertaking, and policy makers did not have the qualms about it that Ennion Williams had less than a decade earlier. Not content with simply educating youths, officials also sought to test them for venereal disease.[111] Testing young people—even upper- and middle-class white youths—fit in with the paternalistic approach to venereal disease control in general. Young people, like the other groups targeted for venereal disease education, had long been considered appropriate targets of benevolent adult authority. Furthermore, now that public health leaders had now unambiguously marked venereal disease as a disease of the lower classes and African Americans, familiarizing the white upper and middle classes with the process of venereal disease testing could help perpetuate this system. Instilling these upper- and middle-class youths with an understanding of the importance of venereal disease testing prepared them for a future in which they managed industrial sites and employed domestics. Richmond physician Thomas Leonard illustrated this perspective when he wrote, "High school pupils, teachers, and parent teacher organizations form a very intelligent group, through which knowledge upon the subject is disseminated to less fortunately situated people."[112] These young white boys and girls would grow up to require venereal disease testing of those at the lower end of society, and this helps explain the city's motivation to teach them about the benefits of it at a relatively young age. Educating young upper- and middle-class women about venereal disease no longer risked sullying their purity but now prepared them to be responsible housewives.

Finally, health officials singled out pregnant women from across the spectrum of race and class for testing, another population with a long history of paternalistic surveillance and intervention. Various private, local, and national initiatives—including work sponsored by the Rosenwald Fund—had promoted attention to maternal health among poor women for several decades. But now women of diverse class and racial backgrounds underwent scrutiny for venereal disease when they were pregnant. In Richmond, Upshur encouraged local obstetricians to test all pregnant women who visited their offices and to examine all newborns for signs of syphilis as well. In 1938 he visited sixteen obstetricians in Richmond, including all who had overseen five or more births the previous year. All promised to administer a syphilis test on every pregnant woman who visited them, treat all infected women, and check all newborn babies for syphilis.[113] Venereal disease control campaigners encouraged those training physicians for maternal health work to include instruction in doing blood tests for syphilis.[114]

Clearly proud of the city's success in examining this part of the population, the Venereal Disease Control Division listed its record of prenatal examinations and treatments performed at the city's public clinics first in the five-page list of tables in the division's annual report in 1938.[115] Pregnant women had little choice but to allow doctors to test them for venereal disease if they wanted to receive prenatal care. Furthermore, given the urgency with which health officials viewed the treatment of syphilis in pregnant women, it is likely that if a woman chose to discontinue her treatments before giving birth, she would be high on Nurse Campbell's list of delinquent patients needing follow-up. Again, then, the state required part of the population traditionally denied full independence and autonomy, in this case pregnant women, to submit to surveillance as a precondition of health care. The long-standing focus of paternalistic intervention in the lives of pregnant women made white elite policy makers consider them particularly appropriate targets for state authority. In promoting venereal disease control in pregnant women, health officials promoted the examination of female bodies from all classes and races in the interest of public health.

Upper- and middle-class pregnant women could be tested and, if necessary, treated by their private physicians, but poor and working-class women had to be tested and treated at public clinics. A 1937 report on Richmond's venereal disease control program offers some insight into how working-class pregnant women experienced the public health system. Surveys found women at the City Home, a facility that would be described today as a homeless shelter for pregnant women, had a high rate of venereal disease and needed treatment before giving birth. However, social workers found some procedures at the clinic to be inadequate: "It is recommended that separate clinic session be held for pregnant syphilitic women. This is advisable not only because of possible embarrassment to the expectant mothers of being in a large public waiting room containing both colors and sexes but also because more time and care must be given in the diagnosis and treatment of such women."[116] This quote is notable because it indicates that some of the waiting rooms at public clinics were integrated, or at least imperfectly segregated. Many public clinics saw African American and white patients at different times and on different days, and it is hard to believe that integrated public clinics were the rule in Richmond. There is a history in the South of being more concerned with separating whites of the higher class than those of the lower class from blacks, so perhaps this perspective combined with space constraints to occasionally integrate clinic waiting rooms.[117] Whatever the explanation, it is clear that city health officials considered testing working-class pregnant women for venereal disease to be an important priority for the health department, but also a delicate task.

Social workers, perhaps more intimately connected with and sympathetic to the dignity of their charges, made some gestures toward protecting the privacy of poor pregnant women with these recommendations. But despite this attempt at protecting the dignity of these individuals, the reality remained that the health issues of economically disadvantaged pregnant women, and indeed the economically disadvantaged in general, were often in the public eye. The attention of public health workers made working-class bodies, collectively and as individuals, more exposed to public scrutiny. Public health staff believed the health issues of the lower classes and welfare recipients were matters of public concern. And the means of delivering health care to this population tended to be more public — as housewives escorted domestics to the doctor, factory managers oversaw the testing and treatment of their workers, and other lower-class individuals waited their turn in public clinics.

One must be careful not to make too much of the parallel between requiring venereal disease testing of domestic and industrial workers as a condition of employment and including venereal disease tests among the many exams performed on pregnant women by their doctors. The medical utility of testing pregnant women is undeniable — in sharp contrast to the medical necessity of testing housekeepers or rayon plant employees. And educating doctors about developments in disease prevention and other elements of medical practice is a valuable function of the public health system. At the same time though, by telling doctors to pay special attention to venereal disease in pregnant women, city health leaders defined these women as more appropriate targets of scrutiny than other citizens. And it connected escalation of this scrutiny — the success in persuading doctors to perform these exams — to the success of the larger venereal disease testing campaign. The increased number of pregnant women tested offered further evidence that the larger authoritarian and paternalistic health plan, aimed at those on the margins of political and economic power, had succeeded.

The final group targeted for testing in Richmond had little or no choice in submitting to these procedures: individuals arrested in the city. Data on these tests are incomplete but indicate that some involuntary tests were performed on this part of the population. We do not know which individuals police singled out for testing, but the number of individuals tested, according to these reports, represented a small fraction of the total arrests. It is likely that city authorities subjected those arrested for sex-related crimes to venereal disease testing.

These figures offer some additional insight into the racial and gendered aspects of involuntary or coerced venereal disease testing. Most significant, the number of African American men tested exceed the number of white men tested. Between 1938 and 1940, 850 African American men underwent venereal disease tests at the city jail or at the request of local courts. In contrast, only 509 white men were tested. Since more whites than African Americans were arrested, this means the city tested a higher percentage of African Americans following arrest than whites. Though more men were tested than women (367 white women and 225 African American women), one must remember that arrests of men of both races outnumbered arrests of women by about ten to one in this period. So, a higher percentage of arrested women underwent venereal disease testing than men.[118]

In 1930s Virginia, the design and implementation of venereal disease control was connected to the distribution of political, social, and economic power and rooted in constructions of race, class, and gender. In a time and place where white elite males held a near monopoly on political power, those advocating new policies that expanded the authority of the state over the lives of citizens structured their arguments to appeal to the beliefs held by this governing class. Building on the consensus that African Americans, lower-class whites, and pregnant women were sexually dangerous helped legitimize and naturalize the new venereal disease control plan.

So, too, did the claim that venereal disease control was a symbol of progress and a key step toward building a modern state. Doctors who encouraged policy makers to support a comprehensive venereal disease control effort believed that it would enhance the reputation of the state as a leader in the region. The authority of science and medicine made sexual regulation part of a progressive vision that appealed to those in power.

Political and health leaders targeted African Americans and lower-class whites for venereal disease control measures because of their tenuous claims to citizenship. Their exclusion from citizenship placed them in a terrain that was within the accepted realm of state authority. White elites used the control they had established over politics to direct the authority of the state at those with the least power. African Americans and lower-class whites became subjects of disciplinary authority because social constructions of sexual danger were reinforced by the structure of political and economic power. These individuals faced suspicion of sexual danger because of the South's racial and class system, but their potential sexual danger was reinscribed because of their inability to vote and the conditions of their employment.

The echoes of the 1920s are unmistakable. In the previous decade, physicians and health officials used the language of eugenics to make sexual regulation seem to be markers of modern, progressive government. In the 1930s physicians framed venereal disease control the same way, as a form of sexual regulation of the dangerous classes that would bring progress to Virginia and improve its reputation. In both decades medical men were central to shaping Virginia's destiny, and the cultural authority of science gave weight to observations and social prescriptions. Furthermore, the association of science and medicine with rationality and progress made sexual regulation part of a progressive vision.

Finally, venereal disease control laws underscore the importance of sexual discipline in naturalizing and sustaining white elite rule. From this perspective, working-class and poor whites and African Americans were ignorant and irresponsible in ways that threatened the state and had proved themselves incapable of full citizenship. Putting venereal disease control in this context underscored the importance and benevolence of elite governance. Elites were wise enough to protect their workers and the larger society from the terrible danger of venereal disease — a danger that health officials constantly emphasized. Sex was thus critical to defining and defending the division between those who governed and those who were governed.

Conflict, Dissent, and Venereal Disease Control

The history of Virginia's venereal disease control program in the 1930s demonstrates how a group of physicians, motivated by a vision of economic and social progress in which they played a starring role, convinced policy makers to, in effect, change course by reviving and expanding state efforts to control venereal disease. Though this story has a certain elegant simplicity, it is wrong to assume that proclamations of the dangers of venereal disease resulted in guaranteed support for and passage of all measures aimed at controlling it. White elites did not have a monopoly on venereal disease control work, nor did venereal disease control efforts only serve to perpetuate the existing distribution of political power in the state.

This chapter further explores the connections between race, class, gender, sexuality, and political power in 1930s Virginia by examining contested elements of venereal disease control policies. Some aspects of venereal disease control generated debate, and these conflicts can shed light on the particular kinds of sexual regulation and state discipline Virginians constructed. Though white elites seized any opportunity to reinforce their dominance, they disagreed at times over how venereal disease control efforts would fit into this agenda. In addition, new sexual regulations could make space for challenges to the established power structure, sometimes planting seeds of unrest or aiding those seeking political change.

Virginia politics was not without dissent in this era, despite the white upper-class dominance of electoral politics. African American protest, disagreements between lower-class whites and African Americans, and class tensions within the white community accelerated in the 1920s and 1930s, shaking the foundation of white elite rule.[1] Venereal disease control proved to be a site for such kinds of disputes as well. This chapter examines three episodes in the history of venereal disease control and asks how in each case racial and class conflicts shaped the ways in which the state disciplined sexual behavior.

The first example of conflict generated by venereal disease control policy stemmed from a Public Health Service (PHS) offer of funds for a venereal disease clinic for African Americans in Norfolk. This move by federal health experts generated tension between the PHS and Virginia officials. The disagreement was never publicized but is reflected in the surviving correspondence among these individuals.

Prior to 1938, when the state legislature began supporting venereal disease testing and treatment work, efforts in the city of Norfolk to control venereal disease were minimal and treatment for low-income individuals there was limited. The all-white Norfolk Medical Society opened the first clinic in the city devoted exclusively to treating venereal disease in 1936, drawing on a number of resources to staff the facility. The City of Norfolk and the federal Works Progress Administration (WPA) furnished three and four staff members each (clerks and nurses), and physicians from the Medical Society of Virginia (MSV) staffed the clinic on a volunteer basis. The clinic operated three hours per week for treatment and five hours per week for tests, with separate times designated for African American and white patients. Aside from contributing a few hours of city employees' time, Norfolk's city government spent no funds on the clinic, and the demand for services far outstripped the clinic's ability to provide.[2]

The only other significant facility in Norfolk for testing and treating venereal disease on a free or reduced-cost basis in this period was the "Public Clinic (Colored)" at 449 East Bute Street, run by David W. Byrd and E. D. Burke. Byrd, a 1900 graduate of Meharry Medical College in Nashville, Tennessee, had served as president of the National Medical Association (NMA, the professional organization of African American physicians) from 1917 to 1918 and chaired the executive committee of the Old Dominion Medical Society (the African American equivalent of the segregated MSV) for several years.[3] Patients who could afford it—about half of them—paid twenty-five cents per treatment; the clinic treated the rest for free.[4]

Like many health and social service programs for African Americans in the South during this period, most of the clinic's financing came from private contributions.[5] Byrd, Burke, and two other African American physicians volunteered their professional services, and seven African American women worked, also without pay, as clerks, nurses, and technicians. The only public support for their work came in the form of a city nurse who worked there one

day per week and a full-time WPA worker who made house calls and did follow-up work.[6] Their combined efforts kept the clinic open from 1:30 to 4:00
P.M. on Thursdays and from 2:00 to 3:30 P.M. on Sundays. Between 1932
and 1936 the staff administered 24,000 syphilis tests and 50,000 treatments
for the disease.[7]

Byrd's work in the 1930s demonstrates that he came to see venereal disease control as more than a public health campaign. In particular, he believed the concern about venereal disease among African Americans and the
increasing involvement of the federal government in these health matters
might offer ways to improve the health of the African American community
while also furthering the quest for racial equality. Where white health leaders saw African American pathology, Byrd saw opportunity. While the state
government used venereal disease control to reinforce white supremacy,
Byrd's venereal disease control work sought to undermine it.

Though Byrd was not alone among African American leaders in believing
that venereal disease control work could further a broader political agenda,
he played an important leadership role in promoting this work on both a
national and local level. In 1936 Byrd pushed the NMA to become the first
nationwide medical group to endorse the PHS's new syphilis control program. The same year, he helped establish the NMA's Commission on the
Eradication of Syphilis and became the commission's first chairman. His
colleague at the Norfolk Public Clinic, E. D. Burke, served as secretary and
vice chairman.[8]

The endorsement of venereal disease control by the NMA attracted the
attention of Surgeon General Thomas Parran, and Byrd and Burke led a del-
egation from the group to meet with PHS officials in Washington, D.C., in
the fall of 1936. Byrd and Burke brought with them letters of introduction
from W. R. L. Taylor, the mayor of Norfolk, and F. C. Smith, the medical officer in charge at the U.S. Marine Hospital in Norfolk. Mayor Taylor described
Byrd as "an outstanding man of his Race" and "highly cultured." The NMA
committee members discussed with Parran the ways that their group could
assist with the fight against syphilis.[9]

The two physicians apparently impressed Surgeon General Parran and
Assistant Surgeon General Raymond Vonderlehr, because following this
meeting the two federal officials worked to bring PHS funding to assist Byrd
and Burke's work in Norfolk. Vonderlehr went so far as to send blank grant
application forms and a sample of a completed application to the PHS representative in Richmond, asking him to encourage Byrd to apply for PHS

support and assist him in completing the application. The effort paid off, and in 1938 the PHS approved a research grant of $2,000 to the Norfolk Public Clinic. Byrd and his staff would "study the efficiency with which a syphilis clinic can be conducted which is staffed entirely with Negro personnel." The PHS renewed the appropriation the following year. Fifteen hundred dollars of the money paid the salary of Dr. Byrd, and the PHS designated the remaining $500 for supplies.[10]

The grant allowed the clinic to see more patients, expand its work to locate "delinquent" patients (those who failed to return to the clinic for follow-up treatments), trace "contacts" (individuals who had sexual contact with infected patients), and pay staff members. In 1937, 27,000 visits were made to the clinic by individuals seeking treatment, examination, or advice. Clinic staff took 11,471 blood samples, finding 1,488 women and 745 men infected with syphilis. Caseworkers made 2,077 visits to contacts and 6,437 visits to delinquent patients. They also instructed women with syphilis about birth control matters, educated student nurses about the importance of having blood tests and following the full course of treatment, examined school children, and more.[11]

The reaction of Virginia's white public health and medical establishment to the PHS's support for Dr. Byrd and the Public Clinic was far from positive. Although Vonderlehr and Parran articulated on numerous occasions their desire for Byrd's grant to be coordinated with the city and state health programs, city and state officials refused to assist the project. Parran suggested that the State Department of Health "act as the distributing agency" for the federal funds, but this did not happen, and the PHS ended up channeling the money through the U.S. Marine Hospital in Norfolk, at least through 1939, when surviving correspondence regarding the grant ceases.[12]

By giving money to Byrd's clinic, the PHS ruffled some feathers in the state and local public health bureaucracies. Some of these objections were due to PHS money for venereal disease *research* being directed to Byrd, and it is true that, by saying Byrd and Burke's clinic was conducting research in how effectively African Americans could run a venereal disease clinic, the PHS employed a rather generous definition of "research." However, the fact that the PHS circumvented the state health bureaucracy to fund an African American clinic especially nettled the white medical establishment.

Further evidence of antagonism roused by the PHS grant can be found in a 1938 letter marked "personal" from Surgeon General Parran to his assistant, Otis Anderson. Parran wrote:

Your letter of June 13th has been received and I note the proposed action of the Norfolk Medical Society [the white organization] in the event assistance is extended to Doctor Byrd for a research project in his clinic. The answer as I see it is that the Public Health Service is free to act in supporting research in accordance with the law, and if the Norfolk County Medical Society has a research study which can be demonstrated to be of great scientific value the Public Health Service would be glad to consider such a project.[13]

Parran also noted to Anderson that he had enclosed some forms for Byrd to fill out that would "strengthen our hand," further suggesting a controversy was brewing. Parran's letter indicates that representatives of the white medical society had expressed resentment that the PHS had given money to Byrd's clinic and threatened some kind of retaliatory response to Byrd's grant, though no such action was reported in the newspapers or the state medical society's monthly journal. Later that year Virginia's health commissioner, Irl Cephas Riggin, told PHS staffer Robert Olesen that the state would be unable to support Byrd's work because of technicalities in "methods of disbursement." Olesen responded that the PHS would welcome any assistance the state could provide Byrd's clinic. He closed his reply to Riggin by noting that Norfolk had a high venereal disease rate, a fact that he hoped Riggin would take into consideration when planning future public health projects.[14] Tension between federal and state representatives, though not directly stated, rumbled below the surface.

By supporting Byrd's work, PHS officials had, intentionally or not, chosen a side in a conflict that had begun years earlier.[15] Byrd and other African American doctors had long been working to undermine the control that white doctors held over health and medicine in Virginia. African American doctors, in alliance with African American nurses and other medical professionals, sought equal respect and access in medical employment as well as equal membership in professional organizations. They considered this effort to be part of a bigger battle against white supremacy and the exclusion of African Americans from economic, social, and political equality. The ability, for example, to vote equally with white doctors in the American Medical Association (a privilege that could only be achieved by joining the MSV, which barred African Americans from membership) would have great symbolic value in a region where African Americans were denied the franchise in public elections.

African American and white doctors had clashed before over the employment of African American physicians in Norfolk. In 1924 the city's Colored Physicians Club had announced that African American doctors would no longer volunteer their time at the "colored health clinic" operated on a periodic basis at the Community Center on Princess Anne Avenue. Behind the city's (white) director of public welfare's accusations of selfishness lay the fact that African American physicians withdrew their support because of the city's failure to hire them for any city jobs. African American leaders pointed out that the city had been happy to utilize their services when they were free, but requests for paid employment, even of one person on a part-time basis, had been rejected.[16] White city leaders believed that employing African American doctors in the city government would confer a degree of respect for the abilities of black professionals that might threaten the preeminence of white professionals. It is also possible that white health leaders did not want to appear to concede to the demands of black doctors. If protests like the withdrawal of support for the community clinic succeeded in this case, it might encourage similar actions in the future.

In this context, the subversive nature of the PHS grant to Byrd becomes clear. Dr. Byrd had circumvented the authority of white public health leaders and the white medical society by negotiating with federal health officials on his own. The federal government chose to support Byrd's Public Clinic rather than the white MSV clinic, suggesting to some a preference for Byrd. Virginia officials refused to administer the grant, so the PHS turned to the (federal) Marine Hospital instead. Norfolk's African American doctors, a group with a record of causing trouble, had found a new ally in federal health officials.[17]

To make matters worse, in the eyes of Virginia's white leaders, Byrd became more politically active in the years to come, building on his relationships with PHS leaders to further his racial agenda. In 1938, as the controversy brewed over his grant from the PHS, Byrd testified before a federal congressional committee on behalf of the Venereal Disease Control Act, along with the NMA's president-elect, George Bowles. Byrd's testimony and work continued to impress Parran, who sent him a personal note after he returned to Norfolk:

> My dear Dr. Byrd:
> The work that you are doing among your own people and the spirit with which you do it has always been a real inspiration to me. May I just say a word to tell you how much I appreciated your testimony before the hearings on the La Follette bill? If it passes and is made law, I hope it may

be within my power to advance greatly the cause in which we are mutually interested.

Very Sincerely yours,

Thomas Parran

Surgeon General[18]

Always strategizing, Byrd wrote to the Rosenwald Fund's M. O. Bousfield later that year advising him to work to ensure that some of this new federal venereal disease control money went to African American doctors and nurses. Otherwise the money would be distributed to state governments, and in southern states this meant it would go only to white medical professionals. The following year Byrd and other NMA members successfully campaigned to convince the editor of a medical textbook to change its assertion that white children caught gonorrhea from sharing the toilet with colored maids.[19]

In 1940 Byrd took on the issue of segregation in the MSV directly, angering whites and dividing African American leaders over the wisdom of his approach. The controversy began when some liberal white physicians allied themselves with African American doctors seeking to negotiate the right to practice on a limited basis in white-run hospitals. Byrd rejected this plan and convinced his African American colleagues in the Old Dominion Medical Society to demand full and equal access instead. Byrd's uncompromising position took many people aback, including many he considered his allies. M. O. Bousfield, the Rosenwald agent whose dedication to racial advancement equaled that of any of his contemporaries, wrote to NMA president A. W. Dumas that Byrd's "whole hog or none" attitude was impractical.[20] In the long-standing debate over the merits of gradualist approaches to equality, Byrd had taken a stand that conflicted with many in the African American establishment by insisting on full equality. Byrd, correctly as it turned out, realized that the changed political context gave African American doctors in Norfolk more leverage than they had had in the previous decades. The growing involvement of the federal government in matters traditionally left to states — in this case, public health work — offered opportunities for African Americans to challenge the local distribution of political power.[21]

The story of Byrd's venereal disease work in Norfolk also shows how the high rate of venereal disease among African Americans, used as a means to justify and preserve white dominance, also offered an opportunity for politically engaged African American leaders to fight for racial progress. For white health leaders, the high rate of venereal disease among African Americans had led them to step up surveillance and control over the black population. For Byrd, the crisis of African American venereal disease justified the expansion of health clinics run by and for the black community.

Just as Byrd looked for ways the campaign against venereal disease could help advance his racial agenda in the 1930s, so too did a group of white barbers hope to advance their own racial and professional interests by joining the fight against venereal disease. In 1930 a group of white barbers asked the legislature to create a state board of barber examiners to be charged with regulating the health, hygiene, and moral standing of barbers. The board's power would center on its ability to grant licenses to barbers, without which they would be barred from practicing their profession. This plan, presented as the "barber bill," was rejected by the General Assembly in 1930. Delegate Daniel Coleman of Norfolk, one of the measure's most vocal proponents, revived it in subsequent Assembly sessions, and it provoked debate for several years.[22]

Those supporting the barber bill argued that some of the barbers in the state were unhygienic and risked spreading disease to their customers. According to these claims, the close contact between barbers and clients made the spread of tuberculosis, syphilis, and other diseases a possibility. Thus, a state board should be established that would investigate the health of barbers by testing them for diseases as part of the licensing process. In addition, this board would ensure that only people of "good moral character and temperate habits" could work as barbers, and it would make sure that barbers knew their trade and were properly trained and skilled. The bill's supporters suggested that, if Virginia failed to establish this regulatory board, diseased barbers who had been barred from practice in other states would move to the Old Dominion, placing the state's whole population at risk. Without this law, the state might become a "dumping ground" for unfit barbers from other states.[23]

Delegate Coleman and other advocates of the plan followed the lead of those who pushed for eugenic sterilization, racial integrity, and venereal disease control, echoing their rhetoric and strategies. Building on arguments about public health with which legislators were already familiar, advocates of the barber bill highlighted the danger posed by diseased barbers and suggested that the only solution was expanded government oversight. The state had to keep up with its neighbors in regulating barbers, because lagging behind could have dangerous consequences when diseased barbers from out of state caught wind of Virginia's relative laxity.

A succession of public health advocates spoke against the bill before the legislature, including State Health Commissioner Ennion Williams, his successor, Warren F. Draper, and Draper's successor, I. C. Riggin. Both white Richmond newspapers published editorials against the measure as well. Within the General Assembly, one of the barber board's most vocal opponents was Senator J. Belmont Woodson, a physician and superintendent of the Piedmont Sanatorium. Woodson told the Senate in 1930 that labeling the plan a "health measure" was "absurd" and "an insult to the intelligence of the Legislature of Virginia." African American barbers opposed the measure unequivocally.[24]

Woodson and others argued that the barber bill was motivated by more than threats to public health and was, in fact, an attempt to drive African American barbers out of business, particularly those barbers who served white customers. According to an editorial by Virginius Dabney, the editor of the *Richmond Times-Dispatch*, advocates of the barber bill admitted to him that this was the bill's real purpose. African American barbers charged lower prices, so closing them out of this trade would increase profits for white barbers. Even though one amendment to the bill exempted currently practicing barbers from its licensing requirements, a supporter admitted privately to Dabney that the plan might all but eliminate African American barbers "in ten to fifteen years."[25] A similar attempt to cut into the white client base of black barbers in Atlanta, Georgia, had succeeded when the city council there passed an ordinance prohibiting African American barbers from cutting the hair of white customers. Health leaders there had backed the move, saying the plan would promote sanitation.[26]

How would this seemingly benign licensing scheme curtail the population of African American barbers? First, the plan rested on the assumption that African Americans were more likely to have venereal disease and tuberculosis. It also assumed that white barbers would control the licensing board and would thus be able to skew the process sufficiently to protect their own, while driving out African American barbers. Since literacy tests and other measures aimed at restricting the electorate had done such an efficient job of suppressing African American voting, it is not surprising that white barbers assumed they could harness the mechanisms of public policy to their advantage in this area as well. Though avoiding a direct reference to voter registration boards, Dabney's editorial suggested that barber boards might follow a similar approach, asking unreasonably difficult questions of African American barbers and simple questions of white applicants. He also pointed out that "the requirement that applicants be 'of good moral character and temperate habits' offers unlimited possibilities for discrimination."[27]

Though many of Virginia's leaders supported the campaign against venereal disease and were willing to entertain the possibility that barbers should have their health regulated, they felt that the particular regulatory mechanism proposed in this bill—a state board that, according to one editorial, would be almost as powerful as the "supreme court of appeals and general assembly combined"—made the abuse of power quite likely. The *Richmond Times-Dispatch* pointed out that ensuring hygienic barbers could be done on a local level, and in fact several Virginia cities had employed barber inspectors. African American barbers backed a plan whereby they would pay an annual fee to the state health department, and the health department would use this money to hire inspectors and enforce sanitary laws. State health officials concurred, saying that if the Department of Health had enough money to hire inspectors, current laws would offer sufficient health protection. All of these alternative proposals rejected the idea of a barber board, agreeing that such a powerful and unchecked body would be subject to widespread abuse.[28]

This account of the barber bill shows how those on the margins of political power saw venereal disease control work as a means to gain access to the state and to the authority the state possessed. White barbers understood that in other contexts fears of sexual danger had enabled elites to use the apparatus of state government to gain more authority over lower-class whites and African Americans. White barbers, members of the middle and lower-middle classes, hoped to use similar techniques to make African American barbers the targets of state discipline. African American barbers would suffer at the hands of the barber board, while white barbers would gain access to the political machine and receive higher incomes. With more economic and political power, white barbers would be elevated to a new status in the state, moving into the upper-middle class and strengthening their relationship with the governing upper class.

It is telling that this plan for the advancement of barbers combined racial and sexual fears. Barbers behind the bill sought to gain legitimacy by appealing to racist interpretations of black sexual morality and risk for venereal disease. They hoped that historical constructions of sexuality and race would lead legislators to readily agree that the state should monitor the health and morality of African American barbers. But at the same time, the plan relied on the racially skewed distribution of political power. Since African Americans were excluded from electoral participation, their voice mattered little in the legislature, and African American barbers had no chance of persuading legislators to vote against the plan. Furthermore, once the barber board had been created, African Americans would lack the political power to influence its membership or its policies. Hoping to gain power through sexual and racial ideologies and traditional distributions of political power, white barbers planned to advance themselves at the expense of African Americans.

The planned barber board failed because its opponents were more politically powerful than its supporters. The state's public health establishment viewed the proposal as a threat to their power over health matters and refused to endorse it. The MSV joined the debate on the side of state health leaders, and the group's Committee on Legislation and Public Health passed a resolution recommending the plan's defeat.[29] Public health leaders refused to cede authority over any aspect of health to another part of the government, let alone a board with suspect credentials. That is why men like Health Commissioner Riggin opposed the creation of a barber board but supported the idea of increasing funds (perhaps through the licensing fee plan) for the health department to enforce barbering laws.

White elites opposed the barber bill because it was an attempt from below to undermine their management of race and class relations. The bill threatened one of the most significant African American professions, and African Americans would surely react with outrage to such an assault. Furthermore, some southern elite leaders saw the African American middle class — of whom barbers were a key element — as bringing stability to the African American population and helping to quell more dangerous working-class elements. Thus, when Dabney, writing in defense of African American barbers, said, "The Negro barbers are among the most valuable elements of Negro citizenship," he meant that he believed African American barbers were part of a class that played an important role in preserving Virginia as it was, run by white elites.[30]

A different approach to controlling venereal disease attracted more support from the public health establishment in the late 1930s: premarital venereal disease testing. Those backing the proposal hoped that transmission of venereal disease from one spouse to another would be prevented by checking the health of men and women prior to marriage (assuming neither acquired an infection from another partner after marriage). A law passed in 1918 had prohibited the marriage of individuals with venereal disease in the state, but it made no provision for testing. Instead, it simply allowed clerks of the court who issued marriage licenses to request an affidavit from the man certifying that neither he nor his prospective wife had venereal disease.[31] The new proposal would require men and women to undergo blood tests before obtaining a marriage license.

The General Assembly first debated a premarital testing bill in 1938 that would have required individuals to be tested for syphilis before marriage and would have prohibited them from being married if they had the disease. Its supporters made a number of arguments in its favor. In addition to stopping the transmission of venereal disease within (monogamous) marriages, they hoped the law would also help prevent the birth of children with syphilis, who often were blind or had other physical abnormalities.[32] Other supporters expected that the plan would reduce the "increasing number of hasty marriages" that were blamed on Virginia's "lax legislation on the subject." Rash, impulsive marriages, they believed, were more likely to end in divorce.[33]

Though supporters of premarital testing did not overtly embrace the eugenic agenda, many of the assumptions of eugenics underlay the justifications for the measure. And many in the Virginia legislature were familiar with this agenda and found its ideas persuasive. Beyond the obvious benefits for the individuals involved, preventing birth defects had social value for those who sought progress and modernization. Healthy babies would grow up to be productive workers whose labor would enrich the state. Marrying hastily also signaled the possibility of mental unsoundness or degeneracy. The poor and unfit were thought to be more likely to give in to their impulses and passions, whereas the well-off would make rational decisions and plan marriages well ahead of time. Anything that might deter the marriage and reproduction of the unfit would win support from those who favored eugenics.

Despite the appeal of such arguments, the plan for premarital venereal disease testing initially met with serious opposition. In fact, when a Senate committee first considered the measure in 1938, committee members tabled it with a six-to-four vote. A number of individuals and groups spoke against the bill before the panel. One doctor at the Medical College of Virginia pointed out that the blood test was not accurate, because the disease had an incubation period of up to 135 days. An Episcopal priest argued that since medical tests could be wrong on occasion, a false-positive diagnosis could be made, resulting in embarrassment and "stigma." Others asserted that the bill would increase illegitimacy, because people who had syphilis would be prevented from marriage but would engage in sexual relationships anyway. People who could not afford the test might simply avoid getting married. A legislator cited rumors that some county clerks across the state opposed the bill because they feared a loss of revenues when people went to other states that did not require testing to be married. Finally, a group of Christian Scientists opposed the bill since it required medical treatment, which they rejected in favor of divine healing, as a prerequisite for marriage. The Senate committee delayed further debate on the proposal until the next biennial session in 1940.[34]

Opponents of premarital testing were ultimately unable to derail the plan, and in 1940 the General Assembly approved mandatory syphilis tests for couples contemplating marriage. But the bill was revised from the original version proposed in 1938, revisions that diluted some of the plan's possibly deleterious effects as well as its strengths. First, the new law did not prohibit marriage by infected individuals but instead required that they begin treatment that would render them noninfectious prior to marriage.[35] Second, on the occasion of a positive test result, the test would be repeated, in case the positive reading was the result of a laboratory error. Finally, poor people would not be dissuaded from legal marriage by the cost, as state health officers and venereal disease clinics would offer the test for free to people unable to afford it. Legislators did not address the concerns of Christian Scientists in the new version of the law, though one legislator tartly suggested that Christian Scientists would not be required to undergo treatment prior to marriage if, in fact, they could heal themselves through prayer and thus produce a negative blood test.[36]

Virginia and North Carolina both enacted laws in 1940 requiring premarital blood tests for syphilis, making them the first two states of the former Confederacy to do so.[37] Virginia's law differed from those passed previously by many other states, however, because it did not prohibit marriage of syphilitics but only mandated their treatment.[38] Legislators wrote the law this way so that it would not discourage marriage. Whether the Virginia premarital testing law was consequently more or less coercive than its mostly northern predecessors is debatable. On the one hand, it did not deny individuals the right to marry, but on the other hand, it forced them to undergo medical treatment and even provided for monitoring of this treatment by the state.

The new premarital testing law did not require that blood tests be performed at a public health department. Private physicians could also perform the test, but if patients could not afford a private doctor, the state had to provide the test for free. If an indigent patient did not live near a public health office, the state would pay a private doctor to perform the test. But even if individuals went to a private physician for testing, public health officials would become involved in any positive test results. Physicians had to certify to state health officials that if one party to the marriage tested positive, the other party had also been informed of this result. Individuals who tested positive would have to continue the treatment after marriage, and patients who did not continue treatment would be reported to the state health commissioner. Failure to take treatment was a misdemeanor, punishable by a maximum of twelve months in jail. And in counties where local health departments had the capacity to do so, health professionals would meet with individuals with syphilis to obtain the names of their sexual contacts, in an effort to locate the source of the infection and prevent any further transmissions.[39] In the first eleven months after the law took effect, 1,718 Virginians with plans to marry tested positive for venereal disease, all of whom then had to be monitored by the state.[40]

Legislators allowed for the participation of private physicians in these tests as a concession to the powerful medical lobby in Virginia, specifically the MSV. A leading Richmond physician described the situation in terms of the "rights" of these doctors. He argued that "the question of infringing upon the rights of private physicians is to be considered" when trying to expand venereal disease testing.[41] The rhetoric here is striking. In a state where many rights were denied to the disfranchised masses, physicians had established themselves as an element of the citizenry whose rights were very important. In this case, doctors in the MSV were asserting their right to maintain their privileged status and to shape government policy. They did not want government clinics and government employees performing the test, and the state conceded. As the MSV had hoped, health care remained a primarily private, not governmental, undertaking.

The opposition to the premarital testing legislation represented the first serious discussion in Virginia about the implications of the new venereal disease control efforts for civil liberties. Leading citizens scrutinized the bill and made their feelings known to the legislature. They had been silent when state and city governments had required venereal disease testing of employees, certain prisoners, students, and pregnant women. No one warned the legislature about the stigma of false positives when these politically marginal individuals underwent mandatory testing. But the premarital testing bill attracted the attention of doctors, ministers, and community leaders, and these individuals demanded that politicians take their concerns seriously.

The debate over premarital testing and the bill's subsequent revision indicate uneasiness with increasing governmental regulation of sexuality when the elite, enfranchised class would feel the impact of this power. Premarital testing was a broad-ranging proposal that was likely to touch the lives of most citizens. Wary Virginians studied the proposal and demanded that the legislature rewrite the bill so that its effect on the presumably well-behaved upper classes would be minimal. Those citizens who questioned premarital testing comprised only a small percentage of the state's population, but they wielded a disproportionate amount of political power. Their lobbying paid off. The legislature bowed to their demands and made a number of amendments to the bill. Positive tests would be repeated in case the first result was incorrect. The state would not use the occasion of a syphilis infection to prevent individuals from marrying, only to require they undergo treatment. Well-off patients would be able to go to their private doctors for tests rather than join the masses at a common public clinic — though government did intrude on upper-class lives nonetheless by requiring they be tested.

This wariness of government involvement in the sex lives of the wealthier classes was not merely a reaction against the potential inconvenience of submitting to the state's authority. Rather, these individuals felt threatened by the potentially leveling power of the state. Premarital venereal disease testing scrutinized rich and poor, black and white, in equal detail. Previous venereal disease control efforts had, as we have seen, primarily targeted those on the outside of political power. But everyone had to undergo venereal disease testing prior to marriage. And anyone who tested positive for syphilis had to give the names of those with whom they had had sex and undergo treatment (or risk time in jail). Thus, the new law risked undermining some of the privileges of white elites in Virginia, making the state an agent of equality rather than of racial and class privilege.

Though southern elites opposed any encouragement of social leveling, the kind of equality suggested by mass venereal disease testing had particular symbolic weight, given the context of racial, sexual, and gender politics in the South. White men had long avoided scrutiny of their sexual behavior. But the new law required that all men with syphilis inform their fiancées of their infection prior to marriage. And the system of contact tracing raised the possibility that men would be asked to name their previous sexual partners. Contact tracing would even require women, white or black, to give the names of their partners as well, further opening white male sexuality to scrutiny. The premarital testing plan monitored and revealed male sexuality to an unprecedented extent.

Involving the state in monitoring the sexual behavior of white women as well shifted the relationship between female sexuality and the state. White women, according to southern tradition, were supposed to be morally pure and sexually innocent prior to marriage. The 1918 venereal disease law that had required men to promise that their brides did not have venereal disease was rooted in these notions of female purity and male authority. It assumed unmarried women to be pure and placed their sexuality under the watch of their future husband. After 1940, however, the law would expose "impure" women if they had contracted and failed to cure venereal disease prior to marriage. Giving the state the power to reveal the promiscuity of white women meant that the state, in addition to the spouse and family, monitored female sexuality.

Premarital testing not only regulated individuals seeking marriage, it also helped shape the social meaning of marriage. Such testing helped construct marriage as a pure institution, marking married individuals as clean and disease-free. Marriage would cleanse and discipline individuals, and the disease-free married couple would be a model for a disease-free society. In this sense, premarital testing echoed the drive to test domestic workers in Richmond for venereal disease a few years earlier. In both cases, the home was a site of purity, and cleanliness in this private sphere would improve the health of the entire society.

The debate over the merits and logistics of premarital testing demonstrates how elites fought trends toward social equality, but the drive for self-preservation by this class is also reflected in the debates over federal funding for the "Public Clinic (Colored)" and the barber bill. On the surface, the response of white state leaders to these two events seems contradictory, because in the first example they worked to hold back the progress of African American physicians, but in the second they defended African American barbers against collusion by whites. Why would the state's white elites protect African American barbers but deny the aspirations of African American doctors?

In both cases the white ruling class acted in defense of their favored social position. They reasoned that federal recognition of the talents of African American physicians might elevate black doctors to equality with white doctors. Giving in to the demands of African American physicians for government pay could only bring about more demands for equality. Instead, African American doctors should be put in their place and denied opportunities to challenge the racial order.

But African American barbers were different, because their social position was far less threatening to Virginia's white elites. Barbers had little potential for upward mobility beyond the middle class. And barbers with white clients engaged in a fairly servile relationship with them, attending their needs but not seeming to aspire to equality with them. In addition, while denying privilege to African American doctors was bound to anger the African American community because it blocked progress, stripping barbers of their livelihood would have infuriated African Americans because it would have been a regressive measure. Taking away rights was bound to cause more dissent than preventing the expansion of them.

The barber bill also provoked a negative response from white elites because they viewed it as a populist measure that was proposed by those hoping to gain political influence. The position of Virginia's leadership class on the bill paralleled their response to lynching in the 1920s. White elites saw lynching as a populist uprising, a rejection of the wisdom of the judicial system, and thus a rejection of their governance of the state. Though they defended African Americans against lynching, white elites were more interested in defending the state against marauding lower-class whites.[42] The response to the barber bill was similar. Virginia's white leaders stepped up to defend African American barbers against a group of self-righteous and aggressive white barbers who were trying to seize the public health system for their own ends at the expense of racial calm.

In 1940 Virginia and the rest of the nation stood on the brink of a war that would bring unprecedented social, economic, and political changes. Among the transformations the South would undergo were changes in sexual behavior and in the racial, class, and gender orders. But in the decade before the war began, stirrings of a challenge to the existing order can be detected in the three stories chronicled here. Each represents a small victory for African Americans in their fight for racial equality, and each also involves questions of sexuality. In the first instance, Dr. Byrd succeeded in using his venereal disease control work to interrupt the monopoly held by the white public health establishment and gain national endorsement. This episode presaged a future in Virginia and other southern states in which federal authorities would side with African American protesters to redistribute political power between the two races. From this perspective, Riggin and other Virginia leaders were correct in their anger at the PHS's action on Byrd's behalf; similar federal actions would bring more trouble for white elites in the future. African Americans also won a modest victory when whites who had hoped to undermine the black middle class failed in their effort to drive African American barbers out of business. Allying themselves with white elites, African Americans preserved the livelihood of a significant element of the black middle class. Later in the century, African American business owners, including barbers, would provide valuable support for the civil rights movement.

The advent of premarital venereal disease testing is the clearest of these examples in showing the potential for sexual regulation to produce small cracks in the bedrock of white elite rule. By testing the blood of all individuals seeking marriage licenses, the state acknowledged that all citizens posed some degree of sexual danger, regardless of their race, gender, or social position. Opposition to mandatory premarital venereal disease testing echoed the rejection more than a decade earlier of mandatory racial registration under the initial draft of the Racial Integrity Act. In 1924 the legislature chose not to require that all Virginians register their race with the state, but after 1940 members of even the nicest Virginia families would have to submit to blood tests prior to marriage. The demands of public health necessitated that white elites could no longer avoid state scrutiny of their sexuality. Southern prejudices were beginning to lose ground to the authority of national advocates of science and public health. Though the tenets of science and medicine were not free of race and gender bias, they did present more egalitarian views of disease and health than did the traditions of the South.

5

Birth Control and Social Progress

While policy makers in Virginia proved willing to expand state efforts to control venereal disease in the 1930s, they proved less interested in involving state government in the provision of birth control. Activists who worked to promote birth control in Virginia, like those in other states, sought state financing for birth control services so that poor and working-class women could obtain contraceptives free of charge. They succeeded in expanding access to birth control through private efforts, but involving the state in the provision of birth control for the lower classes remained elusive until after 1945.

Rather than trace the history of debates over birth control and the varied efforts to provide it in Virginia—a project beyond the scope of this book—this chapter explores the connections between birth control and other sex-related issues that captured the attention of state policy makers between 1920 and 1945. A central question here is the extent to which birth control advocates drew motivation from the same impulses that led Virginians to advocate racial integrity, eugenic sterilization, movie censorship, and venereal disease control. Birth control leaders framed the issue in similar ways and attracted a common pool of supporters. Nonetheless, the birth control movement in Virginia attracted a new set of allies as well, including individuals and groups involved in women's advocacy and social welfare. And while these other campaigns to involve the state in sexual regulation succeeded, birth control supporters failed in this period to secure committed state support for distributing contraception.

Debates over birth control began during the 1920s in the General Assembly when supporters and opponents of birth control mobilized. Although the Assembly's passage of the eugenic sterilization law and Racial Integrity Act made headlines in 1924, a third eugenics-inspired bill aimed at restricting access to birth control drew less attention at the time and failed to gather support. Delegate Thomas William Ozlin of Lunenburg County proposed that Virginia make it illegal "to sell, give away, or possess any appliance or instrument for the prevention of conception." This prohibition would have applied to members of the medical profession as well as laymen and would have thus outlawed all contraception in Virginia.[1] The House of Delegates referred the bill to its Moral and Social Welfare Committee, where it caught the attention of birth control advocates across the country. The American Birth Control League publicly criticized the proposal in the *Birth Control Review* and called on birth control supporters in Virginia to make their opposition heard in the Assembly. Birth control groups from other states sent statements to the committee as well. Ultimately, Ozlin withdrew the measure.[2]

It is not completely clear who supported the bill, as people are quick to claim credit for measures that pass but are more reticent to associate themselves with failed projects, but it is unlikely Ozlin acted alone. Ozlin was not just a minor cog in Virginia's political machine, he was a key part of it, and just two years later Governor Harry Byrd would back his election to Speaker of the House of Delegates. Given Ozlin's connections in Richmond, it is likely he introduced the measure with the support of Walter Plecker, the Bureau of Vital Statistics director who had called on allies in the Assembly to introduce and enact his extensive legislative agenda that year.

The failure of Ozlin's bill or another like it in subsequent years meant that Virginia remained one of the states where contraception was legal, though the Comstock Act (which included information about birth control in the definition of obscene material that could not cross state lines) made access difficult.[3] Those who could afford private physicians had little trouble obtaining birth control and could request it from their doctors, but a significant percentage of the population was too poor to do this. These individuals had to do without or take their chances with "black market" birth control, products often ineffective and occasionally dangerous.[4]

Public birth control clinics were the other alternative for individuals who could not afford a private doctor's visit. A count by the Maternal Health Association in 1932 found that only eighteen states in the United States had clinics where doctors made contraceptives available to those with limited financial means. According to this census, Virginia was home to one of the eighty-six public birth control clinics in the nation in 1932, located at the University of Virginia hospital in Charlottesville. At the time, this was the only public birth control clinic in the state. Two other southern states had such clinics in these years, Florida and Arkansas.[5]

The Charlottesville hospital's involvement in venereal disease control and maternal health made the placement of a birth control clinic there a logical choice. Public health experts hoped that promoting prophylactics among those with venereal disease would curb its spread, and many venereal disease clinics across the country made condoms available to their patients. Prophylactics, of course, would also be useful in preventing conception and in limiting the number of newborn children exposed to syphilis. Maternal health work and venereal disease control efforts often went hand in hand in Virginia, as doctors sought to test pregnant women for venereal disease to protect the child at birth. With birth control, venereal disease control, and maternal health clinics all in the same location at the university hospital, it is easy to see how patients might have overlapped and how services would have complemented each other.

But the university's birth control clinic could only serve a limited number of individuals from a small region of the state. Those who believed birth control offered individual as well as social benefits sought to expand the number of public clinics so that poor and working-class citizens could have access to contraceptives. They clashed with Plecker and his allies over whether or not birth control would bring eugenic improvement to Virginia.

Local disagreements over the social utility of birth control echoed the debate between opponents and proponents of contraceptives across the country. Individuals on both sides appealed to the logic of eugenics to defend their perspective. At the heart of the matter were differing emphases on positive eugenics (increasing the reproduction of the upper classes) and negative eugenics (decreasing birth rates among the lower classes). Some opponents of birth control reasoned that the upper classes would have the easiest access to birth control and that this would bring about racial degradation as the birth rate of the "best" citizens declined. Rejecting condoms and other contraceptive devices, birth control opponents preferred more permanent measures to stop the lower classes from reproducing, such as sterilization and the prohibition of dysgenic marriages. On the other side were those who believed that the promotion of birth control among the lower classes would have significant eugenic benefits. Over the course of the 1920s and 1930s, proponents of birth control gradually outnumbered and out-shouted those who opposed it. Physicians who hoped to curb the reproduction of "undesirables" joined forces with birth control advocates to make birth control more accessible to poor and working-class women.[6]

The arguments over birth control in Virginia mirrored national debates over whether increased access to contraception would bring eugenic improvement or dysgenic degradation, but Virginians articulated their positions in particular ways that reflected the local context. Leading the local opposition to birth control was Walter Plecker, Virginia's most powerful and vocal eugenicist, who warned that birth control would bring disastrous consequences. Plecker made his most vehement public statement on the topic of birth control at a lecture on "Racial Improvement" that he gave before the Medical Society of Virginia (MSV) in 1925. In all likelihood, the timing of his remarks was well planned and his fervor strategic. Success in rallying physicians against birth control could produce the momentum needed to revive Ozlin's birth control ban in the legislative session that would begin four months later.[7]

Plecker began the talk by tracing the history of racial amalgamation in the state but soon turned his attention to birth control or "race suicide." Birth control was an "evil" that was "selective in its diabolical work" because it exacerbated a tendency among the better classes to have fewer children. While the elites failed to reproduce their number, lower-class whites and blacks, according to Plecker, had an increasing birth rate. In particular, he noted, the "lowest strata," the feebleminded, criminals, and "other undesirables," had the highest birth rate of all. These low-grade citizens threatened the future of the white race: "Racial pride will disappear, and then our complete amalgamation of the whites with our present twelve millions of negros will rapidly follow." In other words, once "undesirables" had succeeded in undermining the high quality of the white race, there would be no reason to avoid interracial mixing. The state would become a chaotic mix of degenerates.[8]

Plecker did not hesitate to include young members of the middle and upper classes in his criticism. Virginia's better citizens who failed to reproduce at sufficient levels had given in to "selfish and indolent desires." To save the race, this generation had to change its ways. Young men and women needed to follow the lead of their parents and grandparents "and show their patriotism and love for their State and race by producing six, eight, ten or twelve children as was the custom in the recent past."[9]

Further amplifying the danger of birth control, Plecker likened its advocates to outsiders bent on destroying the South, as Sherman's army had done in 1865. Connecting birth control and Yankee invaders was the assertion that both slowed the reproduction of elites while accelerating that of the masses. According to Plecker, the war had decimated Virginians of its leading men, while lower classes survived unscathed. "While our best were laying down their lives freely for their ideals, the lower fourth . . . naturally untrustworthy and unfit for duty at the front, either skulked at home and es-caped, or, if drafted, were assigned duty as teamsters, or as manual laborers, always in the rear and away from danger." After the war, many upper-class women were forced to either remain unmarried or marry inferior men be-cause of a shortage of upper-class young men. Plecker lamented, "Women have been known to apologize for their husbands, saying that they took the best that were left." In a similar way, birth control would affect the wealthy while sparing the poor. Plecker would sound a similar theme in 1935, saying that birth control had a more dysgenic effect on the state's population than all the wars Virginians had fought since 1607.[10]

While Plecker hoped his reference to the Lost Cause would underscore the urgency of the situation, Virginia's medical establishment remained un-convinced. Shortly after his speech aimed at rallying doctors to "do their part in saving their race and country," the *Virginia Medical Monthly* published a noncommittal reply as its lead editorial. The editors proved less certain than Plecker that birth control would bring irreparable harm and argued instead that the subject be studied more thoroughly. More remarkable, the editorial expressed uncertainty about the whole premise of eugenics:

> Should we not take into consideration that the very parents who have given the world defectives have also given the world some of its most use-ful citizens? Shall we stop the propagation of both? Queen Elizabeth's father was a syphilitic and a murderer and her mother a prostitute but we are proud of the Elizabethan age of culture and we feel that if it had not been for Elizabeth the English speaking colony in America would prob-ably have not succeeded.[11]

Over the course of the next decade, the MSV and its official organ, the *Vir-ginia Medical Monthly*, continued to remain officially uncommitted on the issue of birth control. Though avoiding public disagreement with Plecker, the organization sought ways to quietly voice support for expanding access to contraception. In 1934 Wright Clarkson, chairman of the MSV's legisla-tive committee, wrote to Virginia's Senator Carter Glass asking him to sup-port the "doctors only" bill pending in the U.S. Congress. This proposal would have changed the postal code to allow birth control information to be mailed between doctors, patients, and pharmacists. Activists hoped the doctors-only bill would make it easier for doctors to prescribe contracep-tives and thus be a step toward bringing birth control clinics to areas that lacked them. Endorsing the doctors-only bill meant supporting the larger project of making birth control more readily available to poor and working-class women, a goal that appealed to Virginians who sought racial improvement through reducing the reproduction of the lower class.[12]

Clarkson told Glass that although the MSV took no official position on birth control legislation, "in talking to outstanding men in the profession throughout our State about this matter I find that most of them are in favor of this bill, in fact all of them who really know anything about the problem."[13] A year later, the MSV polled its members on the subject, finding that 86.5 percent of those who returned the ballots were favorable toward contraceptives. The group published the results of the poll prominently in the *Virginia Medical Monthly*.[14]

The MSV refused to take on Plecker directly, but one Richmond doctor was willing to disagree openly with the state's most famous eugenic advocate. Though praising Plecker's commitment to racial improvement, Richmond physician Mary B. Baughman minced no words in criticizing his opposition to birth control. Baughman publicly remarked on the matter in a direct response to Plecker's pronouncement in June 1935 that birth control was pushing the nation toward race suicide. Speaking to the press four days after Plecker had made headlines, Baughman explained her opinion that birth control was the first step toward "scientific regulation in production of the members of the race," and not, as Plecker had suggested, a dysgenic mistake. Doctors, she said, faced a "heavy load" in caring for "unsocial" individuals. "It should be permissible for physicians to see that the population does not increase by the birth of people of that type." Furthermore, Baughman said, controlling the reproduction of defective individuals would bring about an increase in the population of fit citizens. "When we have prevented the reproduction of more mentally and physically deficient children, the state can fulfill its legitimate function of providing environment into which eugenical parents will not hesitate to bring their offspring."[15]

Public criticism of Plecker was rare, but Baughman was a rare individual. As a young woman, she competed as a gymnast and later opened the first gymnasium for women in Richmond. In 1918, at the age of forty-three, Baughman entered the Medical College of Virginia (MCV) as a member of the school's first class that included women. After finishing her medical education, she served as a clinical instructor at MCV and opened her own medical practice, specializing in gynecology.[16]

Baughman played an important leadership role in Virginia's birth control movement, speaking out publicly and working with other activists. Her belief in eugenics, possibly acquired when she spent a summer at Cold Spring Harbor Laboratory in 1901, played a significant part in her advocacy for birth control.[17] But Baughman cited other reasons beyond eugenics to explain why increasing the availability of birth control would benefit the state and its citizens. She hoped that making contraceptives more widely available would encourage young people to marry. Some, she said, deferred marriage because they did not have the financial resources to raise children. Birth control would thus promote marriage by allowing individuals to marry but remain childless for a time. This would also decrease the state's high rate of illegitimate births.[18]

Baughman also pushed for expanded availability of birth control because she hoped it would reduce the number of abortions. She spoke publicly about abortion a few weeks after an honorary luncheon she attended with Margaret Sanger, an internationally known birth control advocate and founder of the American Birth Control League. Abortion, Baughman said, was murder, but birth control was not. "It isn't murder to prevent conception, for before conception there is no life." Public birth control clinics would help stamp out a procedure that she believed to be both dangerous and immoral.[19]

Baughman's position on abortion was typical of birth control advocates of this era, who publicly condemned abortion while supporting the expansion of birth control. Birth control supporters underscored the immorality of abortion to build a case for the morality of contraception. They faced a challenge, however, in the fact that many women who sought "birth control" were actually seeking abortions. Differentiating between birth control and abortion became an important project for the birth control movement during this period, and Baughman's remarks on the subject demonstrate her connection to the national movement.[20]

Baughman's claim that birth control would help decrease the number of abortions brought her into another public conflict with Plecker in 1937. Plecker rejected the notion that birth control was needed to prevent abortion, insisting that the procedure was rare in Virginia and that reports of deaths from it were exaggerated. When Plecker wrote the annual report of the Bureau of Vital Statistics for 1936, he announced that only two women in the state had died from abortions that year, the same number as had died from the procedure in several preceding years. A *Richmond Times-Dispatch* reporter contacted Plecker to ask why Virginia's figures were so much lower than estimates in other states. Plecker defended his data, saying that while some deaths from abortion may have gone unreported, his experience in Virginia led him to believe that the problem was greatly exaggerated. The reporter could not find any male physicians willing to comment to the press on the story.[21]

While male doctors were reluctant to question Plecker, Baughman, according to the *Times-Dispatch*, "scoffed" at Plecker's statistics. Baughman claimed that her work as a gynecologist gave her a different perspective on the matter. Many patients had requested that she perform the illegal procedure, though she refused to do so. But, Baughman observed, less scrupulous doctors as well as "professional abortionists" without medical training did perform abortions, and many women were hurt or died as a result. Baughman told the *Times-Dispatch* reporter that she received several requests for abortions every year, and in the past, when she had a street-front practice, such pleas were even more common. Careful to situate herself in the mainstream of her male-dominated profession, Baughman said that she believed most of her male colleagues received a similar number of appeals for help terminating pregnancies.[22]

Because the historical record contains limited information on the exact nature of Baughman's views, any attempt to compare her positions on these issues with those of Plecker (whose words have been better preserved through the decades) must be partly speculative. Baughman's public pronouncements suggest some areas of agreement with Plecker, particularly with regard to the value of eugenics and the goal of racial improvement. Baughman also expressed support for sterilization, specifically of anyone with more than one illegitimate child. The two shared general beliefs about the risks of uncontrolled sexual behavior and the role government should play in protecting the state from its dangerous effects. Baughman positioned herself as morally traditional, avoiding any hint of sexual liberalism and emphasizing instead the importance of marriage, the immorality of abortion, and the utility of sterilization.

But underneath this traditional and conservative façade was a woman who recognized the inequities of gender and sought expanded independence for women, a position that put her at odds with Plecker. Her intellectual roots and political inspiration came not only from eugenics but also from the Progressive Era women's movement. This not only led her to endorse positions contrary to Plecker's but also to find wisdom in challenging him publicly. Her contacts with individuals like Margaret Sanger, who confronted established ideas and systems of power, and her mission to change the lives of women set her apart from many male physicians in the state who often ceded to Plecker's authority.

Baughman sought to rectify gender inequality by giving women more power. Though she disagreed with abortion, she sympathized with the desire that her patients had for greater control over their reproductive lives.

She saw expanding access to birth control as a step toward helping women control their sexuality and reproduction. And she looked for ways the state could play a role in this, even to the extent that she sought state assistance in locating "fugitive" men who rejected the responsibility of paternity. At the heart of her opposition to abortion as well was her concern for women's health and safety. The *Richmond Times-Dispatch* reported, "But Baughman is not so much concerned with the moral aspect of [abortion] as with its injury to women. Even when it is successful and when no complications develop, harm is done, she explained, for the operation upsets the ovarian cycle."[23]

Though we do not know exactly how Baughman's position on eugenics compared with that of Walter Plecker, we do have more information about the ideology of a key birth control advocate on the national level, Margaret Sanger. Historians who have studied the birth control movement in the United States have looked closely at the role of eugenics in shaping Sanger's beliefs. Carole McCann has pointed out that Sanger's agreement with eugenicists about the goal of racial betterment and the role of contraception in that effort did not mean that Sanger agreed that reproduction by the lower classes inevitably threatened the genetic stock. Rather, McCann has concluded that Sanger saw environmental causes, not genetics, as primarily responsible for physical and mental defects. Avoiding biological determinism, Sanger believed that women needed to be able to control their fertility so that family size did not exceed the capacity of the mother to care for the children and the ability of the father to provide for them financially.[24] These ideas set Sanger apart from Plecker, who had repeatedly underscored his conviction in the central importance of heredity in shaping mental and physical health.

It is possible that Baughman shared Sanger's position on eugenics, as the two women had met and both had attended national birth control conferences. Whatever Baughman's particular stance on eugenics, her more general interest in helping women control their reproductive lives suggests that eugenics was a secondary motivation for her support for birth control. Baughman's dedication to these issues led her to team up with others in Virginia to build support for birth control clinics. This effort gathered steam in the 1930s as a growing number of individuals and organizations voiced their support for expanding access to contraception in the state. Arguments about the eugenic benefits of birth control played a significant role in mobilizing assistance for this effort.

A visit by Margaret Sanger to Virginia helped stimulate local activism in 1933. Shortly before Sanger's arrival, national birth control organizers from the American Birth Control League came to Virginia to help form a state chapter of the group. Gathering at Richmond's elite Jefferson Hotel, a small group of women and men formed the Virginia Birth Control League (VBCL). First on the new group's three-part agenda was "the promotion of the understanding of contraceptive methods to the underprivileged classes." The VBCL also hoped to publish information about birth control—limited because of the Comstock Act—and to establish birth control clinics.[25]

Catholic opponents of birth control implored Governor John G. Pollard to stop Sanger's Richmond talk. Since she would be speaking at a state university, they asserted, the governor had the power to do so. Though they joined Plecker in opposing contraceptives, Catholics did not share his eugenic agenda. Rather, Catholics opposed both birth control and eugenics on moral grounds. In a letter to Pollard, the Catholic Layman's League of Virginia compared birth control to infanticide and called it "injurious to humanity." Pollard refused to stop Sanger's talk, citing his beliefs in freedom of speech and academic freedom.[26]

Sanger planned her visit to Virginia to gain support for the "doctors only" bill in the U.S. Congress. Many Virginians welcomed Sanger and were moved by her message. A number of organizations endorsed her visit, including the local chapters of the American Association of Social Workers, the American Association of University Women, the Junior League, and the Graduate Nurses Association.[27] Business and Professional Women's clubs in Arlington, Charlottesville, Farmington, and Waynesboro voiced their support for the expansion of birth control clinics, as did the Richmond YWCA and the Richmond Council of Jewish Women.[28] She spoke before the Virginia Federation of Labor's annual meeting in Clifton Forge. The group responded positively and formally endorsed the doctors-only bill.[29]

The next day she drew a crowd of fifteen hundred people at the MCV in Richmond. Her speech focused on the need for birth control among the lower classes. She emphasized that it could save taxpayers money by preventing the birth of "unfortunate and often malformed children," born as a result of lack of information about birth control. Sanger also praised the state's eugenic laws for their success in improving the population's health. "Virginia, which is one of the most progressive states in the union, and her wonderful eugenics laws, which have accomplished a remarkable achievement in increasing her birth rate while decreasing her death rate, will undoubtedly, I believe, shortly establish birth control clinics in her borders."[30]

Support continued to build in Virginia for efforts to make birth control more widely available to low-income individuals in the state. The movement aspired for Virginia to become known as one of those forward-thinking states that dealt with the difficult problem of birth control in well-planned ways. It would be a place where scientific birth control triumphed over the "contraband, half-bootleg distribution of information and materials."[31] In 1935 Mrs. Thomas Hepburn (actress Katherine Hepburn's mother) visited the state at the invitation of Baughman. Hepburn had served as legislative "chairman" of the American Birth Control League. Addressing the annual convention of the Virginia Federation of Women's Clubs, Hepburn called for birth control clinics in every community in the country. Immediately after her talk, the group unanimously endorsed a proposal supporting the idea. Explaining their support for these efforts, club women cited the "burden" poor citizens imposed on the state and their expense to taxpayers.[32]

Enthusiasm for expanding access to birth control continued with the establishment of the Virginia League for Planned Parenthood (VLPP) in 1940. At the organization's founding meeting, leaders stressed the importance of helping poor women in the state, especially poor mothers, and linked birth control to improvements in the lives of their families.[33] A pamphlet published by the group noted, "We cannot fail to emphasize the social consequences of the fact that one-half of the annual baby crop is now born to that one-third of our population least able to care for them."[34] An article written for the *Virginia Club Woman* by VLPP president Mrs. Carter H. Harrison explained, "While the Virginia League for Planned Parenthood is interested in the promotion of responsible parenthood for all classes, yet it is deeply concerned that in Virginia today from fifty to sixty percent of babies are being born into families where there is poverty, illness, inherited disease; ... where there is crime [and] delinquency."[35]

Nearly every public statement made in favor of birth control in Virginia during this period mentioned the importance of increasing the availability of birth control to the lower classes, reflecting the continuing influence of eugenic ideology. Examples from diverse sources abound. A *Richmond News Leader* editorial endorsing birth control noted that the only citizens who failed to practice birth control were "those whose ignorance or poverty least fits them to rear large broods of children."[36] Thomas G. Burch, a Democratic representative to the U.S. Congress, emphasized his concern that tenant farmers and "negroes" have access to birth control, since they needed it the most.[37] The state Federation of Women's Clubs emphasized the "constant tax burden of the poor" when it endorsed birth control at its annual meeting.[38]

Birth control supporters in Virginia did contend that contraception would bring a range of benefits beyond reducing the number of poor citizens who burdened the state. That is, eugenic improvement was not the only reason to make birth control available. Social danger aside, the Great Depression made reducing the number of children born to families on relief seem to be economically beneficial.[39] Indeed, Representative Burch's comments spoke as much to concern for the needs of the poor as to a eugenic agenda. Although birth control advocates suggested that making birth control more widely available would help the larger society, they underscored the benefits to individual well-being as well. Maternal health was a benefit in its own right, and birth control supporters hoped that contraceptives would help women who were too sick to safely bear children avoid pregnancy. Birth control would help poor families avoid having more children than they could afford and would protect the health of women whose medical problems made pregnancy risky or even life-threatening. A VLPP pamphlet titled "Public Health and Planned Parenthood" observed that child spacing would reduce maternal and infant deaths. The pamphlet went on to stress that maternal and infant deaths caused both "human misery" and "a loss of human and material resources which seems stupendous."[40]

The VLPP directed particular energy toward making contraception available to patients at the two public tuberculosis sanatoriums in the state. In 1941 Dean Cole, who had been president of the Virginia Tuberculosis Association, joined the VLPP's board, and the organization published a pamphlet about birth control for individuals recovering from tuberculosis. It told patients that birth control could help them plan their pregnancies, enabling them to avoid getting pregnant while still weak from illness and to space their pregnancies to allow for their strength to recover fully after giving birth.

Birth control supporters also used appeals to states' rights in making their case to Virginia legislators. This approach contributed to the support for the "doctors only" bill expressed by Senators Harry Byrd and Carter Glass. In April 1934 birth control advocates met with Byrd and suggested that present federal laws denied states the right to decide this issue on their own. A month later Senator Byrd responded to a letter from R. W. Garnett, a Danville physician stating his support for the bill, Byrd's first public endorsement of birth control. Reports from birth control lobbyists indicate that Senator Glass's support for birth control was primarily due to this states' rights argument. In 1936 he responded to a constituent's letter that "I do not care to express an opinion about it beyond saying that I am utterly opposed to delegating power to the federal government which properly belongs to the states."[41]

Physicians played significant leadership roles in the VBCL and the VLPP. Both groups sought to enhance their legitimacy and respectability by allying themselves with the medical profession. The VLPP's newsletter highlighted this relationship by proclaiming in the masthead, "All our activities are first approved by our Medical Advisory Committee." Doctors in turn welcomed the opportunity to enhance their personal and collective visibility while doing what they felt was good work. Numbered among the prominent physicians and public health officials who served on the VLPP's Medical Advisory Committee were C. J. Andrews of Norfolk, Flavius Ogburn Plunkett of Lynchburg, and H. Hudnall Ware of Norfolk. Leaders in nonmedical fields on the VLPP Advisory Council included newspapermen Douglas Southall Freeman, William Shands Meacham, and Louis Jaffe. Several Richmond clergymen were involved, including Rabbi Edward Calisch and the Reverend Carter H. Harrison. Others on the board of directors included Richmond architect Coleman Baskerville, Hampton Roads businessman and wartime chairman of the Hampton Roads Defense Council Raymond Bottom, and MCV president William T. Sanger.[42]

Male physicians had a hand in many of these efforts to expand state regulation of sexual behavior, but unique to the birth control movement was the significant involvement of women. Many of the women advocating for birth control were socially and politically active in a variety of causes. Mrs. M. M. Caldwell, who was on the state board of the VBCL, had been a leader of the Roanoke Women's Civic Betterment Club.[43] VLPP Advisory Council member Cynthia Addington Boatwright of Coeburn was the first woman in Wise County to run for public office, serving as a member of the Coeburn Town Council from 1934 to 1938. She was also president of the Virginia Federation of Women's Clubs from 1941 to 1944 and served as a delegate to the 1952 Democratic National Convention.[44] Other VLPP board members in the 1940s included Cornellia Adair, a well-known Richmond educator who had been president of the Elementary Teachers Association.[45] Eudora Ramsey Richardson served as the acting state director of the Federal Writers Project for Virginia.[46] And Jesse Wetzel Faris served from 1932 to 1950 as the executive director of the Virginia Nurses Association.[47] Women held key positions of authority and outnumbered men in the state's two birth control organizations. The board of directors of the VLPP in 1941, for example, comprised twenty-eight women and sixteen men. A woman presided over the group, and two of the three vice presidents were women, though men also had a significant degree of authority and visibility, as they held all the seats on the Medical Advisory Committee.[48]

Birth control supporters did succeed in expanding access to contraceptives in Virginia by establishing a number of privately financed public clinics. In 1936 the Old Dominion had six birth control clinics, more than any other southern state except Florida, which also had six.[49] Activists worked with local hospitals, health departments, and community groups to establish and staff these facilities. In Newport News, for example, the local chapter of the VLPP helped raise money to support a birth control clinic in the city health department. In Richmond the state league paid the salary of a full-time nurse who worked at a clinic in the MCV. Community groups gave space for other clinics, such as in Salem, where the Community Nursing Association donated part of its facility for use as a birth control clinic.[50] Funding for this work was uncertain, and several clinics closed and then reopened over the years.

But the state government failed to support the effort to build a statewide program of "planned parenthood," despite continued pleas from birth control groups.[51] The public clinics pieced together funding from various sources, but the state health department refused to provide financial backing. Though some city health departments did offer space for the clinics to operate, most notably in Newport News, most of the public clinics operated out of hospitals or charitable health clinics.[52]

Despite the significant effort private groups put into making birth control more available to poor and working-class Virginians in the 1930s and early 1940s, without the commitment of the state health department Virginia lost its position as a regional leader in providing birth control. Several of Virginia's southern neighbors made a greater effort at promoting birth control by bringing state health departments into this work. In particular, North Carolina soon made Virginia's birth control efforts seem all but trivial. Beginning in 1937, Virginia's southern neighbor began to establish birth control programs at all of the state's public health clinics with the assistance of Dr. Clarence J. Gamble, a Boston philanthropist. By March 1938 the state operated thirty-six birth control clinics, and in the following year it would open twenty-six more. According to historian Johanna Schoen, this effort continued to expand into the late 1940s, until financial support began to drop off.[53]

Birth control supporters in Virginia tried to point out that North Carolina was pulling ahead and doing a better job of expanding access to contraceptives and seizing the progressive mantle from Virginia in this particular area.

In a pamphlet distributed by the VLPP in the 1940s, the group's president, Mrs. Carter H. Harrison, wrote, "What North Carolina, South Carolina, and Alabama are beginning to do effectively, Virginia can do." Medical Advisory Committee member Bathurst B. Bagby concurred, saying the state would soon find that "some of our sister states have forged ahead of us by their more realistic approach to this question."[54] But these warnings failed to spur the development of a comprehensive, statewide program in Virginia.

Birth control clinics remained grassroots efforts and did not become institutionalized in the state bureaucracy. Top health officials refused to take strong, public stands in support of expanding birth control. For example, state health director I. C. Riggin expressed private support for birth control but would not take a lead in supporting the issue. And advocates were unable to persuade the state to make birth control available at county health departments.[55]

Formal support from the MSV for birth control finally came in 1942, when the group voted at its annual convention to endorse a proposal put forward by its Maternal Health Committee. The four-part resolution encouraged private physicians and state health departments to give birth control information to patients who had medical reasons to avoid pregnancy. It also recommended birth control advice be given to patients at the state tuberculosis sanatorium. Finally, it urged "interested lay persons" to supply contraceptives to individuals whose doctors recommended them. The resolution focused on access to contraception as a health issue, using the argument that birth control was a medical necessity for some individuals.[56]

Four years later the MSV's Maternal Health Committee endorsed a plan whereby representatives of the VLPP would work with maternal health clinics in county health departments to provide contraception. Soon health department physicians began referring patients to VLPP fieldworkers, who provided birth control information and assistance. Financial support for the VLPP's work came from local organizations, particularly women's clubs and business and professional women's clubs. This program was an important breakthrough for Virginia's birth control movement and meant that, although the state was not actually providing contraceptives, local health departments were essentially facilitating their distribution.[57]

Comparison with the venereal disease control campaign in Virginia underscores the paucity of the birth control movement's progress and the implications of its failure to obtain state support. By 1941 Virginia had 108 public venereal disease clinics but only 21 birth control clinics.[58] By that time the MSV had campaigned for venereal disease control for more than a decade, but the group did not officially endorse birth control until 1942. Virginia's health departments did not begin to offer access to contraceptives for poor and working-class citizens until 1946. In short, venereal disease control, like other sex-related efforts discussed in this work, soon attracted government support and became part of public health policy in Virginia, but birth control lagged behind throughout this period.

The drive to bring public birth control clinics to Virginia was connected in many ways to other efforts aimed at controlling sex in the name of public health but departed from them in important respects as well. A basic connection was that many supporters of birth control also had been involved in these other projects. Several members of the board of directors of the VLPP had close ties to the movements for eugenic sterilization, venereal disease control, and prostitution control. Board member and physician R. W. Garnett had helped form the Virginia Venereal Disease Society in 1928 and had been an advocate for eugenic sterilization in the 1930s. Mrs. Aubrey Strode also served on the VLPP board; her husband had represented the state in *Buck v. Bell*. Bathurst B. Bagby was a particularly active member of the VLPP's Medical Advisory Committee, while at the same time chairing the Committee on Venereal Disease Control of the Richmond Community Council. Another Advisory Council member, Rabbi Calisch, had spoken out on the issue of movie censorship a decade earlier.[59]

Providing poor women with contraceptives both inspired the birth control campaign in Virginia and became its central goal. This emphasis reflects the local movement's focus on the particular danger that uncontrolled reproduction by the lower classes posed. Though the deployment of eugenic rhetoric was not particular to Virginia, the fact that these citizens found such arguments convincing and believed them to be useful ways to persuade other state leaders to support expanded access to contraception further demonstrates the connection between the birth control movement in Virginia and the other drives for sexual regulation. By the mid-1930s, the combined efforts of supporters of eugenics and of venereal disease control had convinced many leading citizens in Virginia that sexual behavior by the lower classes threatened the state. And they had set a precedent for action by the state government and the expansion of public health work in these areas. As a result, Virginia's civic leaders and politically active elites understood and responded to the calls for expanded access to birth control and recommendations for increased government involvement in providing it in the context of similar issues with which they were already familiar.

Despite Plecker's opposition to birth control, he and his allies shaped the movement in Virginia and laid the groundwork for the plausibility of its appeals. Making birth control available at public clinics was a way to respond to the arguments of Plecker and his allies that birth control would only affect the upper classes. Increasing the availability of contraceptives to poor and working-class families became another facet of the larger project of improving the state by regulating the sexual behavior of the lower classes. At times the rhetoric of birth control supporters in Virginia sounded remarkably similar to that of Plecker himself. When the VLPP wrote in 1941, "More healthy, normal women can and should be encouraged to do their part, and relieve the ill and unfortunate among us from the unjust and socially dangerous proportion of race reproduction they now bear," it seemed to echo Plecker's call for middle-class youth to have "six, eight, ten or twelve" children to demonstrate their "patriotism and love for their State."[60]

Public policy regarding birth control also reflected the political consensus about sexual regulation that had been formed in the context of these other issues of sexual regulation. In other instances, Virginia's elites had been comfortable directing the regulatory power of the state at the lower classes but reluctant and often unwilling to allow the state to restrict the activities of the wealthier classes. This context helps to explain why the legislature rejected Ozlin's effort to outlaw the provision of birth control by private doctors. Ozlin's plan aimed state power at the upper classes and would have restricted access to birth control for those who could afford private physicians. It also would have, of course, restricted the behavior of physicians by stopping them from practicing medicine as they saw fit. From this perspective, Ozlin's bill bears important similarities to Plecker's unpopular attempts to tighten the enforcement of interracial marriage laws. Like Plecker (and likely in alliance with him), Ozlin sought to use the power of the state to regulate white elites as well. And like a number of Plecker's efforts to reign in white elites and physicians, the effort failed.

Several factors help explain the lack of enthusiasm in Virginia for birth control among political leaders and elements of the public health establishment. First, some leaders continued to believe that public health work threatened the livelihood of private physicians and thus were slow to support any expansion in government efforts. Second, Plecker's vehement opposition to birth control did dampen support for expanding it. Many doctors, even some who disagreed with Plecker, would have been reluctant to challenge such an important health leader.

But a final element in the birth control movement's relative lack of success in this period was the fact that birth control differed in significant ways from venereal disease control, eugenic sterilization, racial integrity, and movie censorship. Each of those other policies aimed primarily to discipline, control, and scrutinize sexual behavior. While birth control encompassed a kind of regulation — which was evoked by those who cited its eugenic benefits — it also gave women more sexual autonomy and more control over their lives. Poor women got more freedom, not less, from contraceptives. African Americans across the nation made calls for birth control part of their political agenda in the 1930s, because they believed that access to these products would improve their economic status and social position. And lower-class women of all races took risks and made sacrifices to obtain access to birth control.[61]

Supporters of birth control also differed in significant ways from those who had advocated for these other sex-related regulations. Other efforts were almost entirely undertaken by men, but women played a key role in pushing for expanded birth control in the state. These women had broader agendas than birth control, and many sought to help women and poor families in other ways beyond limiting their reproduction. The contrast between Mary Baughman and Walter Plecker highlights these conflicting ideologies of gender, with Baughman seeking to give more power and autonomy to women, while Plecker had devoted his career to reigning in the sexual behavior of women and men. Similarly, the rhetoric of organizations like the VLPP indicates roots in both eugenic ideology but also in the social welfare movement.

Those seeking birth control tried to harness the rhetoric of eugenics and progress through sexual regulation that had been so successful in persuading the legislature to expand the reach of the state. But offering birth control to poor citizens bore more resemblance to social service programs than to disciplinary measures such as eugenic sterilization. Birth control reformers embraced a vision of government that focused more on the provision of welfare than the enforcement of discipline. Policy makers in Virginia had supported efforts to control the sexual behavior of poor and working-class whites and African Americans but were less enthusiastic about committing state funds to measures that offered women in these groups sexual freedom, economic advancement, and social improvement. Thus, the birth control movement in Virginia during the 1930s faced a much more difficult struggle than the campaigns for venereal disease control, eugenic sterilization, racial integrity, and movie censorship.

6

The Second World War in Richmond

Protecting Social Hygiene

The sexual regulations that seemed so progressive to Virginia policy makers in the 1920s and 1930s were outdated and obsolete in the changed social and political climate of the 1940s. Eugenics could no longer pass for cutting-edge science, even in Virginia. Warnings by the surgeon general that venereal diseases threatened military strength demanded large-scale programs aimed at rapid eradication. Federal health officials called on city leaders across the nation to increase their venereal disease control work by eliminating prostitution and monitoring young women who sought sexual relationships with soldiers. The federal mandate for preventing dangerous behavior increased demand for sexual regulation in Richmond, but the city's history in this period demonstrates how these federal directives intersected with local distributions of political power, constructions of sexual danger, and conceptions of the state to produce public policy on the local level.

Though the war brought social and economic changes to Richmond, other cities experienced much greater upheaval in this period. The city's industrial sector did not expand significantly with wartime production, although many local factories converted to defense-related work. Military personnel came to the city to train as pilots at the University of Richmond or to work at the newly designated Richmond Army Air Base, but these were small deployments. Richmond avoided the rapid influx of new residents common to other cities in this period. The city's population remained fairly stable, rising from 193,042 in 1940 to an estimated 227,000 in 1945. Much of that population increase can be attributed to the annexation of Henrico County in 1942, which added 20,280 people. The most significant way the war taxed municipal services was in the large number of soldiers who visited the city when on leave; these visitors numbered some 35,000 per week during the war.[1]

Reforms aimed at preventing prostitution had begun in Virginia and other southern states several decades earlier. The earliest organized efforts took the form of social purity crusades launched in the late nineteenth century by women's groups such as the Woman's Christian Temperance Union (WCTU). WCTU members and others who engaged in these campaigns believed women to be essentially innocent or pure in morals, and they worked to rescue those who had been led astray into a life of vice. Raising the age of consent became a key focus of this movement, as reformers sought to protect those they considered most vulnerable to the lures and deceptions of men.[2]

Organized approaches to moral reform changed after the turn of the century as antivice campaigners sought more governmental involvement in their efforts. Though a variety of factors prompted this new strategy, a key motivation was the increasing evidence that many women who worked as prostitutes resisted efforts at reform. By rejecting efforts at uplift, they failed to fit the model of the helpless sexual victim. Reformers changed their focus to emphasize the enforcement of existing laws against prostitution and the passage of more stringent ones.[3] In the South, suffragists helped to elevate the issue of prostitution to a prominent position on the reform agenda while using it to advance their arguments for the vote.[4] They gained fuel for their arguments from the nationwide social hygiene movement, which began to emphasize the threat venereal diseases spread by prostitutes posed to "innocent" and "virtuous" victims.[5] Suffragists asserted that male voters and politicians had ignored threats such as these that women faced. To get protection from the government, women needed access to the ballot.[6]

In many U.S. cities, including Richmond, the antiprostitution campaign of the 1910s took the form of agitation against organized prostitution districts. In 1912 Richmond vice reformers rallied local clergy to preach against the existence of the city's regulated prostitution district. In these designated areas, also called "segregated districts," authorities permitted prostitutes to practice their trade without fear of prosecution, as long as they complied with certain regulations.[7] Citizens pressured for an end to this system, and city leaders responded by establishing a vice commission charged with investigating the situation and recommending changes. The vice commission found that the regulated district failed to confine the trade to one area and described 120 houses of vice scattered across the city outside the vice district. Blaming the police for failing to enforce the law and deeming the system of segregated districts a failure, the commission called for the closure of the districts, reform of the police department, and rehabilitation for women who worked as prostitutes.[8]

The city's commitment to eliminating prostitution turned out to be more rhetoric than substance, and the council failed to appropriate any money for the vice commission's operation. Consequently, the group's members borrowed money personally, signing their own names to a loan to pay initial costs.[9] Realizing they had to work with very limited financial resources, commission members did not propose measures that would have been costly to implement, with the exception of a general recommendation that the city work to rehabilitate prostitutes. The city council ignored the call for rehabilitation and did nothing to help the newly unemployed prostitutes. Instead, Dr. Joseph T. Mastin, the secretary of the State Board of Charities and Corrections, who lived in Richmond at the time and had spent much of his career working to help delinquent women and girls, took on the task himself, contributing some of his own money and enlisting financial help from an executive at the local Florence Crittenton Home for unwed mothers. These meager resources did little for the more than one hundred women who sought Mastin's help, and for the most part he just gave them a few dollars with which to leave the city.[10]

On the statewide level, the renewed interest in campaigning against prostitution produced several new laws in 1916. The General Assembly raised the age of consent from fourteen to fifteen years and passed a law forbidding any private employment agency to send a woman into a house of ill fame. A "nuisance abatement bill" aimed at segregated prostitution districts operating in urban areas gave local law enforcement the power to use injunctions to close them down. Other states passed similar statutes in this era. In addition, the legislature allowed the appointment of policewomen in cities of more than fifteen thousand residents. No money was allocated for the actual hiring of policewomen, since police were funded by local governments, and none of these new laws required the establishment of any new state governmental agencies.[11]

The nuisance-abatement plan did provoke some controversy in Virginia. The General Assembly defeated the bill when it was first proposed in 1914, with some arguing that segregated districts were preferable to having unchecked houses of prostitution scattered all over the city.[12] Two years later, in light of the Richmond vice commission's assessment that the segregated system was failing, the legislature passed the proposal. State Senator Harry F. Byrd cast the only "nay" vote. In 1925, when Byrd ran for governor, supporters of his opponent, G. Walter Mapp, circulated a letter suggesting that Byrd's vote on this issue indicated a weak moral character. Byrd responded by saying that he was, of course, opposed to prostitution but felt that the existing statues would have been sufficient, if properly enforced. Further-more, he had feared that the law would unfairly penalize property owners because "upon complaint of any private citizen, any house can be closed for a year, no matter how innocent the owner of the house may be, if some tenant was guilty of lewdness." The *Richmond News Leader* defended Byrd's willingness to take a stand against popular but poorly written legislation. The paper noted that in those years proponents of moral legislation virtu-ally controlled the legislature, and criticism of any "moral reform" efforts was rare.[13]

Shortly after the United States' entrance into the First World War, Presi-dent Woodrow Wilson established the Commission on Training Camp Ac-tivities (CTCA) to address concerns about prostitution and venereal disease and their connection to national security. Members of the commission worked with local and state authorities to close down red-light districts, en-listed the help of charities such as the YMCA to provide "wholesome" recre-ation for soldiers, and tried to restrict the "promiscuous" behavior of young women. The CTCA also encouraged local governments to arrest women sus-pected of being venereally infected and/or promiscuous.[14]

Twenty years later, with war in Europe again threatening to turn global, federal administrators believed it necessary to revive and intensify the ve-nereal disease control effort of the First World War. Emphasizing the im-portance of social hygiene to national defense, a coalition of groups advo-cated for an expanded venereal disease control effort with antiprostitution work at its center, soon after President Roosevelt declared a limited national emergency in 1939. The American Social Hygiene Association (ASHA), in-strumental in the earlier venereal disease control campaign, worked to push this agenda in Richmond and countless other cities across the nation.[15] Be-fore long, the military, the U.S. Public Health Service (PHS), and the Office of Community War Services joined together to expand social hygiene work in the name of national security.[16]

Congress moved to strengthen federal power when municipalities failed to reduce the problem in their area. Early in 1941, Representative Andrew J. May of Kentucky introduced legislation that would make prostitution within a "reasonable distance" of military and naval establishments a federal crime and thus permit federal agents to enforce antiprostitution laws in these dis-tricts. Congress passed this measure, known as the May Act, in July.[17]

Later that year Surgeon General Thomas Parran and Assistant Surgeon General Raymond Vonderlehr attacked existing federal efforts against vene-real disease in their book *Plain Words about Venereal Disease*. They recalled the lessons of the previous war, when the military lost more hours of service to venereal disease than to any other ailment. Parran and Vonderlehr asserted that military officials were dealing inadequately with venereal disease, largely owing to their weak attempts at controlling commercialized prostitution. Although the May Act gave the military strong tools to curtail prostitution around military bases and thus (at least in theory) to cut venereal disease transmission to enlisted men, federal officials rendered the act useless by refusing to designate particular defense areas to be under May Act control, except in the rarest of circumstances. The prostitution industry continued to boom across the country, acting, according to PHS leaders, as a "torrential source of the rising level of syphilis and gonorrhea in our new army."[18]

The other document guiding federal planning for venereal disease control was the "Eight Point Agreement." In 1939 military and public health leaders had divvied up responsibilities for venereal disease control in defense areas. According to this plan, the military would educate soldiers about venereal disease and treat their infections, report contacts and vice problems to health authorities, and "lend all assistance possible" to reduce prostitution. Local and state governments would diagnose and treat venereal disease in the civilian population, "forcibly isolate" "recalcitrant infected persons" pending treatment, repress prostitution, and educate the civilian population about venereal disease. The PHS would provide information and assistance to aid local and state efforts, unless local officials failed to deal with venereal disease problems, in which case the PHS would "intensify efforts" toward developing necessary programs. The Social Protection Division (SPD) of the Office of Defense Health and Welfare Services and the ASHA would fill roles similar to the PHS, gathering information and encouraging specific programs and measures as needed.[19]

The initial response of Richmond leaders to these federal directives was to increase local efforts at eliminating prostitution. In February 1941 the city's Committee on Venereal Disease Control held a public meeting on "social hygiene and national defense" to drum up local support for an expanded venereal disease control effort.[20] A few weeks later the committee's chair, Bathurst B. Bagby, who also worked as the city health officer, called for a stepped-up venereal disease control drive that focused on treating and possibly quarantining "streetwalkers."[21] Echoing national health leaders, Bagby cited the blows the national defense had suffered from venereal disease during the earlier world war. Since venereal disease was "one of the most destructive forces in the military and civilian population," it had to be defeated if the United States wanted to prevail over its foreign enemies in the conflict that seemed to loom on the horizon.[22]

When local officials adopted federal recommendations and undertook an antiprostitution effort, they were not simply responding to inspiring federal rhetoric. Richmond leaders raised specific local concerns about the impact of venereal disease and looked for ways an expanded campaign against venereal disease would benefit the city. In March 1941, following the introduction of the May Act legislation (but before Congress passed the bill), Bagby expressed the fear that, if venereal disease spiraled out of control in Richmond, the army might prevent soldiers from coming to the city. He undoubtedly knew that Congress was considering the May Act legislation and realized it could have a negative impact on the city's economic revival if it limited access by soldiers to Richmond businesses. Soldiers on leave brought money into the city, helping local companies and enhancing the city's economy. Local officials were anxious to promote Richmond's economic success by maintaining an orderly and hygienic image.[23]

Of course, highlighting the economic advantages of sexual discipline was not new to the 1940s, and in fact Virginia's political leaders had been making such arguments for two decades. Because of this historical context, assertions that venereal disease control and the regulation of prostitution would help the city fell on sympathetic ears. Policy makers were well disposed toward claims that venereal disease control might have economic as well as public health benefits.

Despite federal calls for sweeping changes in local venereal disease control efforts, such work in Richmond during the early years of the war mobilization differed little from the efforts of the previous decade. Officials still focused primarily on African Americans, further reinforcing white notions of black danger, irresponsibility, and ignorance. Local leaders continued to promote testing for domestic servants and encouraged employers to oversee testing and treatment of their workers.[24] When the military began to draft men in September 1940, induction officials tested new recruits for venereal disease as part of their medical exam. When the first 2,384 men were registered and examined in Virginia, 140 of them were found to have syphilis. Of those 140, 124 were African Americans.[25] The newly enacted premarital testing law generated more statistics to reinforce the idea that venereal disease was primarily an African American problem. Newspapers seized opportunities to assert the relative absence of the disease in whites. A *Richmond News Leader* headline, appropriately printed on April Fools' Day, declared "No Syphilis Found in Whites Here" after city health officials claimed that for the past six months no premarital syphilis tests of whites had detected the disease.[26]

By 1942 Richmond's leaders began to make changes in the city's venereal disease control program, broadening the population suspected of sexual delinquency and targeted for state discipline. A central factor in this shift was a statutory change made that year that gave the state more power over those suspected of participating in the sex trade. A 1918 law had mandated venereal disease testing for individuals *convicted* of prostitution or of keeping "houses of ill-fame or assignation." A new law, passed at a special session of the General Assembly in October 1942, broadened the population targeted for mandatory venereal disease testing to include all individuals *arrested* for these offenses. The Assembly also expanded the categories of arrestees to be tested to include "inmates of a house of ill-fame or persons soliciting for immoral purposes."[27]

Though Virginia's lawmakers backed the expansion of venereal disease testing to all who were arrested for prostitution, there is evidence that concern existed among some General Assembly members about vastly increasing the power of the state over these individuals. Under the Senate version, individuals did not have to be tried or granted bail until they were tested for venereal disease. Thus, theoretically, they could be held indefinitely. The House of Delegates amended the Senate bill to require that within three days of arrest the individual be tested and held for treatment, granted bail, tried, or released. Pending venereal disease tests could not be used as an excuse to keep these individuals in jail.[28]

Though these new provisions had widespread local support, federal pressure also played a role in stimulating this legal change. The SPD had pushed cities and states across the nation to revise existing prostitution statutes to allow authorities much broader control over women whose sexual behavior stepped outside traditional boundaries. Though these laws might also target the male customers for testing, in practice they primarily targeted women.[29] With federal encouragement, some U.S. cities also expanded disorderly conduct and vagrancy laws.[30] In Virginia the navy backed the new legislation, and Manley H. Simons, the commandant of the naval base in Norfolk, lobbied Governor Colgate Darden in support of the change. Since women could be tested and treated following arrest, the evidence did not have to be sufficient to convict them; in fact, these women could be arrested, tested, treated, and then released without ever going to court, as long as police performed the venereal disease test within three days.[31]

Arrest statistics for Richmond between 1941 and 1945 demonstrate the impact of the revised vice law and the city's expanded commitment to regulating commercial sex. In 1941 Richmond police arrested 467 people for "prostitution and commercialized vice" and for "sex offenses." In 1942, with the expansion of venereal disease testing having passed toward the end of the year, arrests rose to 760; they climbed again in 1943, to 1,185, before dropping to 979 in 1944. Arrests peaked in 1945, with 1,424 individuals arrested for these two crimes. Arrests for disorderly conduct followed the same pattern.[32]

The crackdown on women's sexual behavior as a means to protect male soldiers from venereal disease reflected the growing wartime focus on female sexual danger that led to increasing arrests of women across the country.[33] Immoral, diseased women, policy makers held, brought contagion to healthy soldiers. The actions of these women, then, were to blame, while male soldiers were considered to be following "normal" urges.[34] In Virginia the relative impact of this campaign on white women and white men was particularly clear. The number of white women arrested for all crimes increased in this period, from 1,408 in 1941 to 2,311 in 1945.[35] Police not only arrested white women more frequently but also held them in jail for longer periods of time while they underwent treatment. The course of injections for venereal disease treatment could last several weeks. In contrast, police in Richmond arrested declining numbers of white men from 1941 to 1943, though totals began to rise again in 1944. A total of 16,550 white men were arrested in 1941 but only 10,858 in 1943.[36]

Evidence of the novelty of the increased wartime incarceration of white women can be found in the fact that the city jail was ill-equipped to handle them. The rising number of white women arrested, combined with their lengthened jail stays, caused logistical problems, because the city jail had limited space for white female inmates. In this period of racial segregation, all such facilities had to have separate spaces for white women, African American women, white men, and African American men. White women had traditionally been arrested in smaller numbers and had been the least likely group to spend time in jail. With no historical precedent for incarcerating larger numbers of white women for extended periods of time, Richmond was unprepared.

Low levels of incarceration for white women had also been true historically on the state level. The Virginia prison system had maintained dangerous and inadequate facilities for women and men throughout much of its history, and only the most delinquent white female felons were sentenced to time in the state penitentiary. In the mid-1800s officials at the state penitentiary had overseen the construction of a two-story, wooden building for female prisoners. Located near the main men's building, this unsafe and overcrowded facility both housed women and provided space for them to do all the washing for the entire penitentiary. White women rarely were incarcerated there. In 1881 the legislature appropriated $20,000, supplemented by profits from prison contracts, to build a new brick building for the women prisoners. Judges still perceived, probably correctly, this building to be dangerous and unsanitary and continued to avoid sentencing white women to serve time there. The fact that the facility had no space for segregating the races made judges even more reluctant. In the 1890s, for example, an average of eighty-two black women were incarcerated at the state penitentiary annually, while only four white women, on average, served time there per year.[37]

Threats to sexual morality and the need to control sexual behavior, used in so many other contexts in Virginia to compel government action, helped provide the impetus for the construction of better prison facilities for women in the early 1920s. Since Governor E. Lee Trinkle had declared himself an advocate of woman suffrage and women's rights, penitentiary superintendent Rice Youell saw Trinkle's governorship as an opportunity to lobby for a new women's prison.[38] In the 1923 annual report of the state penitentiary, Youell wrote:

> I recommend a separate prison for women. Present conditions are a menace to the discipline and welfare of the inmates of the institution. I do not believe that men and women should be placed in visual contact in prison. It causes moral perversion, sexual diversion, and degeneracy. As a first principle of moral education, there should be a separation of the sexes and improved quarters for women are needed.[39]

Finally acknowledging the requests of Youell and others, in 1930 the General Assembly authorized the construction of a new corrections facility for women in Goochland County. Soon, this State Industrial Farm for Women held white women sentenced to the state prison system as well as those sentenced to time in city jails.[40] This facility adequately fulfilled the needs of local governments and the state during the 1930s and early 1940s. But after the passage of the 1942 law requiring women with venereal disease to spend a week or more in jail while they received treatment, the Goochland County facility proved completely insufficient. It could not possibly hold all the women arrested in cities across the state for the period of time needed. As a result, cities themselves had to deal with the problem.[41]

Unable to send white misdemeanant women to Goochland, Richmond's leaders had to face the challenge of incarcerating white women without state assistance. City leaders soon obtained help from the federal government in the form of an $80,250 Federal Works grant under the Lanham Act to build a "rapid treatment center" for people with venereal disease. City officials located and purchased a building, a former convalescent home in north Richmond, with state and city money, the Federal Works grant paid for its renovation, and staff admitted the first patients to the new Richmond Municipal Hospital on 17 August 1943—less than six months after the mayor had applied for federal money and only ten months after the General Assembly passed the law creating the overcrowding problem. The PHS furnished the doctors and nurses for the facility.[42]

The new rapid treatment hospital allowed the city to treat infected women whom police had arrested for prostitution and other sex-related crimes. Though the facility was officially designated a hospital and not a detention center—in fact, the U.S. Congress specified that Lanham Act funds were for hospitals, not jails—hospital officials invoked communicable disease laws and quarantined people who refused treatment. Staff at the eighty-bed hospital sought to not only treat venereal disease but to move women out of lives of prostitution and vice. Rehabilitation services—counseling and vocational training—would help women avoid going back to delinquency. Most of the patients were women, but some men received treatment at the new hospital as well. The facility served black and white patients in segregated areas. City residents had first priority in the hospital, but when extra space came available, the hospital also admitted people from other parts of the state.[43] The facility enabled city officials to deal with the problem of limited jail capacity for white women, whereas cities without such facilities had a much more difficult time treating this group of infected women.

Leaders of the new venereal disease control campaign ambitiously planned for a large increase in the incarceration of white women, but the number of white women held by the city for prostitution and venereal disease treatment failed to meet expectations. The rapid treatment hospital was underutilized within a year of its completion. On a visit to the Richmond facility in July 1944, the chief of the PHS's venereal disease division, J. R. Heller, noted that the facility only held thirty-five patients. City leaders admitted difficulty in finding patients to treat in the new hospital and discussed closing it later that year. There were a number of possible explanations for this. Venereal disease rates may have been lower than expected. Women arrested and subjected to venereal disease tests would have been released if they were free of infection. A more likely explanation was that enforcement of prostitution laws declined after an initial rally. Fewer arrests would have meant fewer individuals tested for venereal disease and thus fewer positive test results requiring treatment. The arrest statistics cited above bear this out and show that total arrests for prostitution, sex offenses, and disorderly conduct did decline in 1944.[44]

Arrest and incarceration rates of African American women in wartime Richmond remained higher than those of white women, but the wartime venereal disease control campaign had a limited effect on the number of black women who encountered the criminal justice system. The total number of African American women arrested for all crimes increased by only 14.5 percent during the war, from 2,289 in 1941 to a peak of 2,622 in 1945.[45] Statewide, African American women continued to be convicted of felonies at a rate much higher than that of white women, but delinquency was a misdemeanor, as were most other prostitution-related offenses. The misdemeanants at the State Industrial Farm for Women—the women sent to Goochland when city jails filled up—were almost exclusively white, as the facility had little space for black women and used the space it had to hold felons. The small number of black misdemeanants at the state farm increased little between 1939 and 1945.[46] African American women were held in city jails and at facilities like Richmond's rapid treatment center, but space in these locations was limited. Though I have not found statistics describing the racial makeup of inmates at the Richmond rapid treatment center, a similar hospital opened in Norfolk the following year that had space for forty-five white women and thirty black women.[47] There is no reason to believe that the relative size of black and white populations at the Richmond facility would have been much different.

Nationwide, the wartime concern with venereal disease spurred a broader campaign that went beyond controlling the behavior of women who traded sex for money. Federal, state, and local leaders widened their attention from an exclusive focus on professional prostitutes toward a more general concern with female sexual promiscuity, embodied in the supposedly new phenomenon of "pickup girls." According to public health leaders, pickup girls were young women, usually in their teens, who liked to meet and have sex with soldiers.[48] They were not prostitutes, because they did not exchange money for sex and did not make a living at this activity. But health officials nationwide said that pickup girls spread venereal disease to military men at a rapidly increasing rate and thus presented a significant threat to the nation's defense. The national media focused a great deal of attention on these women, also referring to them as "victory girls." The SPD spearheaded the campaign to stop pickup girls from spreading venereal disease.[49]

In Virginia, concern about pickup girls grew with pressure from military officials. In October 1942 the chief of the navy's venereal disease control staff, Lieutenant G. W. Mast, attended the annual convention of the Virginia Police Executives Association. Mast warned the assembled police chiefs that venereal disease was a particularly urgent problem in Virginia and that the commonwealth posed the greatest threat of any state of infecting servicemen with venereal disease. While prostitutes contributed to the venereal disease problem, Mast said, "a growing army of Virginia pickup girls" presented a rising menace.[50] Surveys by the army and navy added to the evidence that pickup girls, or "amateurs," were a key source of venereal disease.[51]

Richmond leaders were quick to agree that pickup girls posed a threat. Judge J. Hoge Ricks, head of the Juvenile and Domestic Relations Court, noted a "marked increase" in the number of young girls brought before him on morals charges — an increase he must have believed came from changes in the behavior of young girls rather than of police officers. The city director of public health, Millard C. Hanson, noted that the percentage of venereal disease cases attributed to pickup girls in Richmond was even higher than the state average. The head of the city crime prevention bureau, Herbert C. Ganzert, conceded that pickup girls were on the increase but argued that many of these problem girls were not from Richmond.[52]

Whether or not premarital sexual behavior among girls and young women was on the rise in this period is a matter of speculation. Karen Anderson's study of three wartime cities questions whether juvenile delinquency actually increased in the war years. She suggests that growing concern about juveniles and attention to the issue may have resulted in more arrests of youths, which does not necessarily prove that youthful misbehavior had increased. This may have been especially true in the case of young women, as increased attention to venereal disease across the country inscribed their behavior with a new level of danger, thus bringing their conduct more frequently to the attention of authorities.[53] It is as likely that this was the case in Virginia as in other cities.

Pickup girls could be found in a wide variety of places, and health officials paid particularly close attention to locating where exactly soldiers met them. The city health department sought to document where soldiers met pickup girls from whom they contracted venereal disease. In the final six months of 1942, for example, investigators determined that servicemen got venereal disease from 107 women picked up in a "confectionery, lunchroom, or beer joint"; 41 on the street; 18 in bus terminals; 13 in dance halls; 8 in hotels; 28 in unknown locations; and 163 in "miscellaneous" places.[54]

The search for pickup girls expanded the terrain where sexual delinquency and venereal disease contagion might occur. Venereal disease could come from women in brothels, but more likely, according to the statistics, men might meet women with venereal disease in diverse locations. Accompanying this expanded terrain came a local shift in the construction of the category of sexually dangerous individuals—a class in Virginia historically comprised of poor and working-class whites and African Americans—into a broader segment of the white female population. Sexual delinquency was no longer presumed to reside exclusively in the lower classes. Pickup girls might well come from the middle class and from "decent" families.

The wartime effort to control the spread of venereal disease by pickup girls brought the sexual behavior of young white women from diverse class backgrounds under the gaze of local authorities across the nation. The story of Richmond in this period is notable, because the focus of state discipline on the sexual behavior of white women ran counter to traditional southern understandings of white femininity and the function of government authority. Though eugenic advocates had underscored the sexual danger posed by some white women in the 1920s, as did the venereal disease campaign of the 1930s, the focus of those efforts was primarily on the poorest segment of the female population. While eugenic advocates had carefully focused their accusations of female sexual delinquency and their efforts at discipline on working-class and poor white women, the pickup-girl scare made the sexuality of women of higher classes suspect as well. The 1940s then brought a new development—the suggestion that a broad section of white women engaged in threatening and uncontrollable sexual behavior. Middle- and upper-class women might engage in the sexual practices that had previously been associated with the working class and poor.[55]

Because of these growing fears, class membership might offer little protection for young women who stepped outside the boundaries of acceptable behavior. The SPD promoted the expansion of morals laws to allow the arrest of any woman engaged in "suspect" behavior. In other words, a whole spectrum of public behaviors by women, well beyond anything that fit into a traditional legal definition of prostitution, could result in morals charges. Women who rode buses, worked as waitresses, or drank in bars might be having illicit sex and spreading venereal disease. And thus, under these new mandates, women from diverse class backgrounds might be arrested.[56]

Though the SPD sought to collapse the distinction between professional prostitutes and promiscuous women, Richmond's law enforcement officials and political leaders continued to search for distinctions between pickup girls and professional prostitutes. Prostitutes comprised a well-known category of women: immoral lawbreakers, primarily lower class, and likely mentally deficient. Pickup girls, however, were harder to categorize, because health leaders believed almost any young woman could fall into this pattern. Their motivations were a mystery that required the attention of experts, who tried to explain why ostensibly nice young women would engage in casual sex.

The search to understand pickup girls produced a number of theories. One of the most often cited explanations for their behavior was misguided youthful patriotism. According to the city health director, 78.8 percent of these women were between the ages of seventeen and twenty-five.[57] Policy makers believed these girls felt sympathy and compassion for servicemen who were risking their lives for their country, reckoning—wrongly, in the eyes of officials—that having sex with servicemen showed an appreciation for their patriotic sacrifices. Similarly, officials cited the "lure of the uniform" in attracting young women. Men in uniform were exiting and brave, and girls supposedly found this enticing, leading a *Richmond Times-Dispatch* headline to proclaim, "Young Girls Here Drop Moral Standards When They See Uniform, Records Reveal."[58]

Many blamed parents, particularly mothers who held paying jobs, for the susceptibility of these young girls to delinquency. Editorializing on the impact of the war on the city's young people, the *Richmond Times-Dispatch* noted parents of "incorrigible" children were often "too busy with war work to direct properly the child's activities." Left alone, these youngsters got into all kinds of trouble, including sexual delinquency. The *Times-Dispatch* editorial underscored the association of pickup girls with the middle class, diverting from the tradition of associating sexual delinquency with poverty. In the 1920s and 1930s, those who did not work hard enough and were therefore impoverished were considered the root of sexual danger. But in the war years, public leaders began blaming those who worked *too hard* for raising delinquent girls.[59]

Public health leaders also saw war in general as having a negative psychological impact on the population, which sometimes manifested itself in female sexual delinquency. During the war, Elmwood Street, the director of the Richmond Community Council and the Richmond War and Community Fund, gave a number of radio addresses on social service programs in the city. In several of the radio segments, he discussed why social services had to be expanded during the war. According to Street, one reason that the number of unmarried mothers had increased was the "emotional unsettlement of so many young women." Women who worried about attacks on the United States, threats to their loved ones in the service, and wartime shortages were so emotionally overwhelmed that they could drift into all kinds of irresponsible behavior. This population, too, could encompass women from different class backgrounds.[60]

It is important to note that as authorities increasingly focused their concern on the sexual danger of white middle-class girls, they averted their gaze from young African American women. Sometimes officials admitted outright that they had overlooked this population. In a February 1943 article on female delinquency, the *Richmond Times-Dispatch* noted, "Negro girls are not detained by juvenile authorities as frequently as white girls, Judge Ricks [of the Richmond Juvenile and Domestic Relations Court] declared, because 'police don't take much notice of the Negro girls.'"[61] The State Department of Public Welfare's annual report for fiscal year 1943 concurred, noting that of the sixty women committed to the department for moral delinquency, "in few instances were colored girls committed."[62] A *Richmond Times-Dispatch* editorial in 1942 titled "War's Mark on Youth" left African American girls out of its discussion entirely: "Since the United States entered the war, delinquency among Negro boys in Richmond has increased more rapidly than delinquency among white boys, and delinquency among white girls has gained more rapidly than among white boys." The article never even mentioned African American girls.[63]

Though city leaders chose to focus more on the sexual delinquency of young white women than of young African American women, this does not mean that they considered African Americans any less sexually dangerous and irresponsible now than they had in the past. The combination of epidemiological claims and racial prejudices explored in the last chapter led officials during the war to consider aiming the more draconian venereal disease control measures, such as quarantining, at African Americans. When the first draftees (mentioned above) underwent venereal disease tests prior to induction into the military, of the 140 men found to have syphilis, the first and—as far as I can tell—only one of them jailed for "refusing treatment" was black.[64] Evidence also suggests that state leaders saw quarantine laws as particularly appropriate for use with the state's black citizens. In a letter to the state attorney general, Abram P. Staples, a state health department officer wrote that a recent interpretation of the venereal disease law allowing delinquent individuals to be brought before a court for avoiding treatment "has been of great assistance to the health officers, especially in handling colored persons who have become delinquent. As you know we have a high prevalence of syphilis and gonorrhea, especially in the colored race in Virginia and we are bending every effort in an attempt to control this menace to our public health."[65]

White leaders in Richmond continued to view African Americans as pathological and particularly susceptible to the emotional unsettlement of wartime. A *Richmond Times-Dispatch* editorial pointed out that delinquency by African American boys had increased more rapidly than among any other group of youths in recent months. The editorial attributed this to the fact that black parents "as yet have been unable to adjust to the sudden and drastic jump in income, which has often risen two to three times what it had been."[66] Thus, while the editorial's author explained that "increased earnings for Negro parents are highly desirable," they were also problematic. This was a classic position for southern racial liberals to take — social and racial changes should never happen too fast. In addition, it reflected the racial stereotype of African Americans as irresponsible, even childlike, and thus likely to become reckless with bigger paychecks. Community Council leader Elmwood Street made a similar observation about economic improvement in one of his radio shows, noting that "Negro girls [were] distracted and made jittery by the war," like whites, but were uniquely affected "by the new problems of human relations and of economic opportunity which it creates." Like the writer of the *Times-Dispatch* editorial, Street felt that the increased economic opportunities for African Americans could bring them physical and emotional problems.[67]

White civic leaders in Richmond did not overlook the sexual danger posed by African American women because they did not believe it existed but rather out of racist notions of African American sexuality coupled with a shortage of resources. Sexual delinquency among middle-class white women might have surprised public officials and struck them as a recent trend that should be reversed, whereas they had long been accustomed to considering African American women morally corrupt and sexually deviant. African American women had been more likely than white women to be arrested in Richmond before the war, and this pattern persisted throughout the period. African Americans were presumed to already have a high rate of disease, but statistics that suggested white soldiers and civilian women had venereal disease and transmitted it at high rates would have also struck health officials (rightly or wrongly) as a new development that had to be stopped. Added to all this was the fact that whites had always received better government services than blacks in Virginia, and thus the limited resources for projects such as the medical treatment and rehabilitation of wayward women and girls were primarily focused on whites.[68]

Reluctance to aim disciplinary and reform efforts at African Americans was not always matched by enthusiasm for targeting them at whites. Though state concern with the sexual behavior of young white women from diverse class backgrounds was increasing, regulating this group could be controversial. It is difficult to know how many of the women arrested in Richmond for disorderly conduct or "morals" charges attracted police attention because they seemed to be "pickup girls" and how many were arrested for specific criminal acts. Such specifics of policing were not widely discussed by local officials, or at least not in public forums. But one attempt to control this population did attract open debate, a proposed juvenile curfew. In 1942 Councilman Cecil Harris proposed that unescorted children be kept off the streets at night in order to curb juvenile delinquency. The plan met with opposition from a variety of sources. Visiting soldiers worried that crackdowns on late-night activities by juveniles could also curtail their own nighttime amusements. Since many Richmond businesses made money from these soldiers, it was in their interest to keep them happy, coming to Richmond for fun and relaxation, and spending money there. City leaders were caught between political pressures to eliminate vice in the city and the economic reality that soldiers were more likely to come to a city with a busy nightlife and ample opportunities for heterosocial entertainment. In addition, the *Richmond Times-Dispatch* came out strongly against the curfew idea, arguing that a better solution for juvenile delinquency would be an increase in organized recreation, church groups, and community centers. These nongovernmental groups would be a more appropriate way to deal with juvenile misbehavior than a further expansion of city government efforts.[69]

The common council passed the proposal in 1942, but it failed to pass when the city aldermen rejected it.[70] However, in the next few months health officials and the press expressed growing concern about the involvement of pickup girls in spreading venereal disease. A year after the bill was rejected, another member of the council, Emmet Perkinson, made a similar proposal. This time it passed.[71]

The opposition to the juvenile curfew should be understood in the context of the historical reluctance of Virginia officials to pass laws that regulated the sexual behavior of a broad section of middle- and upper-class whites. As they had in the debate over the premarital testing law and movie censorship in earlier years, Virginians challenged policies aimed at the whole population, upper- and middle-class citizens included. All juveniles in the city who went out at night would feel the impact of this law, not just those potentially getting into trouble. As a result, the plan met with suspicion and opposition, even though it eventually passed.[72]

More palatable were educational and welfare efforts that sought to check delinquency and sexual promiscuity without invoking the disciplinary power of police and courts — the sorts of efforts that the *Richmond Times-Dispatch* had proposed as alternatives to the juvenile curfew. One popular approach to curbing wartime social problems involved public mental health programs. Columns in the *Virginia Medical Monthly* in 1942 emphasized to doctors across the commonwealth the importance of psychological health and education and advocated expanded involvement by the medical profession in this area.[73] The Virginia Conference on Social Work, held in April 1942, featured a number of presentations on war and mental health, including one on the "effects of war on delinquency and crime."[74] Richmond's Planned Parenthood branch met to discuss "parenthood in wartime," hoping to teach working mothers how to prevent their employment from having a "disastrous" impact on their children. One such disastrous impact, of course, was sexual delinquency, as those seeking to reign in pickup girls were quick to point out.[75] State Health Commissioner I. C. Riggin added to the effort by launching an "anti-worrying campaign" in 1942.[76]

Another angle on the problems of pickup girls and venereal disease involved efforts to shape the behavior of male soldiers. Like many other cities in this era, Richmond worked to provide soldiers with housing and recreation facilities when they visited the city on leave. Little distinguished these activities in Richmond from those in other communities across the country. Local programs for soldiers began in 1941, when the Community Recreation Association established the Richmond Defense Services Unit. The first recreation planned for the soldiers was a series of dances held at the Mosque — a former temple purchased by the city in 1940 for community events — beginning in April 1941. Later dances were arranged at Camp Lee, and organizers transported local women the twenty-five miles to the base in Petersburg. Other local civic groups, private social agencies, and the Richmond USO sponsored dances and offered recreation facilities. All such recreation was racially segregated, utilizing separate facilities for blacks and whites.[77]

The goal of curbing sexual delinquency permeated these efforts, as organizers hoped their programs would guide soldiers away from recreation in bars and dance halls that could bring them into contact with delinquent women.[78] Young women were recruited from the local population for these dances, and chaperones monitored their behavior. For dances held at Camp Lee, the Richmond Defense Services Unit provided buses to transport the "junior hostesses" to the base. As was typical of such events across the country, every attempt was made to locate "nice girls" for these dances. Organizers invited friends and daughters of local club women, and dances held at the Mosque allowed entry only to young women who had been registered with organizers and thus deemed acceptable.[79]

Dances and discussions of mental health problems served another important function for Richmond — they made city leaders seem focused and engaged with the problem of curbing sexual delinquency. This may have been the most significant aspect of Richmond's wartime effort to control venereal disease. Though venereal disease testing did impact the growing number of citizens arrested on morals charges, coercive measures that disciplined the population remained relatively modest in comparison with the rhetoric of the time. The first clue to local restraint came in 1942, when the General Assembly checked the authority of local police to hold those arrested for sex-related crimes indefinitely without performing venereal disease tests. Later, the more than half-empty rapid treatment hospital indicated that federal calls to step up venereal disease treatment met with cautious compliance that failed to satisfy expectations. Arrests for sex-related crimes rose but then fell again in 1944 as enthusiasm for enforcement waned. A proposed juvenile curfew met with opposition from one of the city's leading newspapers, and the city council delayed passage for a full year.

This reluctance was masked by the establishment of "wholesome" dances for soldiers, radio shows on mental health issues, even an "anti-worrying campaign," programs that created the image that Richmond's leaders had sprung into action. Though reluctant to vastly expand state disciplinary measures that targeted a broad segment of the white population, city leaders maintained the image of order and control that was so important to Richmond's image as a well-governed leader of the South. However limited or powerful the city's wartime social protection campaign actually was, Richmond's health and safety leaders had a variety of motivations for encouraging the perception that they had cleaned up venereal disease and vice in the city. City leaders sought to impress federal officials (specifically the military and the SPD, who monitored local situations closely) that they were doing a good job of keeping the city "clean."

At times, however, the inflated rhetoric of city leaders conflicted with the reality of their efforts. In March 1943 the *Richmond Times-Dispatch* reported that, in an application to the Federal Works Agency asking for more money to fight venereal disease, public health director Millard Hanson had characterized the city's efforts as "wholly inadequate."[80] But four months later, Hanson explained in his six-month report for the health department that local increases in venereal disease were due to higher rates of reporting, not higher rates of infection. Figures were "not actually as alarming as they appear[ed] on the surface," and the health department was fighting venereal disease well with vastly increased efforts that year.[81] The bottom line is that politics in wartime America was full of bluster and propaganda, and Richmond officials employed these techniques like everyone else. The city could alternately be helplessly overrun with diseased women or be a bright shining example of social hygiene, as the public relations need arose.

The concern with venereal disease and the sexual behavior of young women that swept the nation in the war years intersected in Richmond with local constructions of gender, race, and class. Federal directives demanded that city leaders impose disciplinary measures that broke with local tradition by expanding the reach of state authority into the sexuality of upper- and middle-class whites and challenging local conceptions of the purity of white womanhood. Richmond's leaders responded by building a consensus about sexual danger and government efforts to prevent it. They recognized that an expanded notion of sexual danger demanded expanded state authority but insisted on their own standard of moderation in disciplining the general white population. This restraint helped city leaders avoid alienating the white middle and upper classes who elected them. Richmond's venereal disease control efforts were not imposed from above, at the demand of federal authorities, but were instead constructed by local leaders with local rewards in mind. The result, in contrast to Norfolk, Richmond's neighbor to the east, was a venereal disease control effort widely considered a success.

7 The Second World War in Norfolk

Struggling for Control

From the earliest days of America's involvement in the Second World War, federal leaders in the Public Health Service (PHS) and the American Social Hygiene Association (ASHA) had a clear conception of how cities should address the venereal disease and prostitution problems. Local governments needed to educate the public about these diseases, repress prostitution in their areas, and provide treatment for infected citizens. The federal government would help by providing planning and financial assistance. To illustrate how all this would work, the ASHA printed a "pictograph"—a cartoon chart—showing the responsibilities of the army and navy, the Federal Security Agency (which included the PHS and the Social Protection Division, or SPD), the local community, and the Department of Justice. This pictograph of faceless cartoon figures shows uniformed, official-looking men giving lectures and arresting people; patients being examined and treated; and women being sentenced in courts and led off to jail. Everything in this diagram is very orderly. All the authorities appear authoritative, and all the criminals look suitably repressed.[1]

In Norfolk, Virginia, during this time, none of the actual people the cartoon characters supposedly represented filled their roles so obediently or well. Chaos and crisis, not order and control, described public health and vice control in Norfolk in the war years. The national press labeled the city America's "worst war town," printing articles with such titles as "Norfolk, VA: Confusion, Chicanery, Ineptitude."[2] As a result, Norfolk became nationally known in the early years of the war as a city of rampant vice with few redeeming features. Although the press's focus on Norfolk was more about selling magazines than about documenting and explaining the shortcomings of public policy, this attention presaged Norfolk's fate throughout the war years. A parade of experts would expose and diagnose the city's problems during the war, while almost simultaneously other authorities worked to deny or minimize them. Was Norfolk suffering from chaos or from an image problem? Either way, the city appeared unmanageable. The clashing agendas of local, state, federal, and military leaders made for a confusing mix of policy that is a fruitful site for studying the regulation of sexual behavior and the connections between sexuality and the state.

The city of Norfolk is on the southern side of Hampton Roads harbor, one of the nation's best natural ports. Norfolk, Portsmouth, Hampton, and Newport News have developed on different sides of the harbor, and in the twentieth century all of these cities have been home to naval and maritime industries. When military planners decided to significantly expand the U.S. Navy at the outbreak of the First World War, they chose the port of Hampton Roads as the site for the nation's biggest naval base. As a result, the city of Norfolk and the rest of the region changed rapidly in the second decade of the twentieth century. Between 1910 and 1917 the number of residents of Norfolk increased from 67,000 to 130,000, leading to a shortage of housing and social disorder. The vice industry thrived in this environment, and the city became known for what one local preacher called "immoral indulgences."[3] In an effort to reestablish good local government, city residents voted by referendum in 1917 to establish a "commission-manager" system and appointed a city manager to oversee Norfolk's daily governmental operations.[4]

Municipalities across the country hired city managers and formed city commissions in the first two decades of the century, following the leads of Galveston, Texas, and Stanton, Virginia, the first cities to adopt such innovations. Commission-manager governments exemplified the spirit of the Progressive Era, as urban reformers sought to replace corrupt and inefficient political machines with professionally trained experts.[5] Norfolk's first city manager, Charles E. Ashburner, had been the first to hold this position in Stanton and had also worked for the Richmond government. As Norfolk's new city manager, he vowed to run the city in a more effective and efficient way, and city officials orchestrated a crackdown on prostitution, arresting hundreds of women in conjunction with a national campaign to curb venereal disease during the war.[6]

As interest in vice reform declined after the First World War, city officials decided that, since they could never eliminate prostitution, they should try to control it through the establishment of segregated vice districts. In the city's biggest segregated district, East Main Street, an estimated four hundred women worked as prostitutes under the stipulation that they have their health checked every week, carry a card certifying a clean bill of health, and not work outside that area at night.[7] When health inspectors found that one of these women had a venereal disease, they quarantined her while she received treatment in a building that was jointly leased by area brothel owners.[8]

Though there is no record of exactly when city officials decided on the policy of segregated districts, the system was in place by the mid-1930s. Norfolk's third city manager, Major I. Walke Truxtun, took office in 1925 and devoted much of his attention to public safety and public health issues.[9] He likely conceived of the segregated district plan as a way to contain problems posed by the vice industry. Leaders of many turn-of-the-century American cities had implemented similar systems of regulated prostitution districts as a solution to some of the changes brought by urbanization.[10] Richmond established a vice district in 1905 but closed the district in 1914 at the recommendation of the city's vice commission.[11]

There is little evidence as to the racial makeup of the customers or the prostitutes in the East Main Street district. Some documents from the period indicate that some of the prostitutes were white and that the area was a white neighborhood. It is a fair assumption that the customers in the district were almost exclusively white. The South's long history of segregation and its prohibition on sex between white women and black men made it quite unlikely that black men could have purchased the services of white women in such a strictly regulated area.[12] However, some brothels may have had black women working there. One source describing Norfolk on the eve of the Second World War mentions that in the "dark alleys of Main Street . . . Negro girls tried to pick up a pitiful quarter by enticing sailors back into the shadows," suggesting a hierarchy among prostitutes based partly on race, with higher status, primarily white, women working in the more controlled, safer brothels.[13] Given the strict racial segregation throughout the city, brothels that supported exclusively African American prostitutes and African American customers more likely existed elsewhere in the city, in the black neighborhoods.

Though the existence of the segregated district in the city was a tacit expression of defeat in the war to suppress prostitution, public criticism never threatened the policy. However, a brief uproar occurred in 1936 after revelations of narcotics sales in the East Main Street district. After a federal grand jury hearing on drug-related arrests, those present reported they were "appalled" by the existence of "white slavery" and the sale of narcotics and liquor in the city and recommended a cleanup of the area.[14] Though local newspapers publicized the report extensively, city officials never responded to it.

The federal judge who heard the case said he was very busy and could not comment, and the city manager said he was waiting for the federal authorities to make a statement on the subject before he took any action. After a few days of trying to make a story out of the absence of a story and printing headlines reading, for example, "Authorities Still Silent on Vice Report," newspapers dropped the issue and the segregated district continued to operate.[15]

When the nation began to mobilize in the late 1930s to assist European countries at war with Nazi Germany, the navy called upon Norfolk to aid the war effort. The navy allocated $12 million in 1938 for new construction at the naval base and the naval air field, and soon even more federal contracts poured in. By 1940 the naval yard was adding one thousand new workers per month, and other local military facilities expanded just as rapidly. Once again, Norfolk became a city with too many people and too few resources. Housing was scarce, schools and roads were overcrowded, and city services were taxed beyond capacity.[16]

While Norfolk officials tried to deal with the needs of the city's growing population, national public health officials had begun their campaign to stamp out venereal disease, as discussed in the previous chapter. A sudden increase in venereal disease among navy men stationed at Hampton Roads prompted a visit to the city by an ASHA physician, who reported the existence of the segregated district to Surgeon General Thomas Parran.[17] Norfolk officials found themselves caught in the middle of a national debate between public health leaders such as Parran, who believed prostitution should be completely eliminated, and some members of the medical profession, who endorsed the segregation/regulation approach. Despite criticism from some doctors, Parran ordered the closure of districts in Norfolk and other areas across the country.[18]

City officials protested, saying the closing of the district would just scatter the prostitutes to different neighborhoods, but City Manager Charles Borland vowed to comply with the federal recommendation: "As segregation has met with much opposition, we shall have to abolish it and change our methods."[19] The *Norfolk Virginian-Pilot* expressed support for closing the district, along with skepticism that the closure would actually end commercialized vice in the city.[20] Borland ordered the East Main Street brothel owners to shut down their establishments by 1 January 1941. Two weeks later police officers raided businesses that remained open, arresting two female operators of brothels, three female prostitutes, and four male patrons.[21]

The officials who had protested the change were proven right; the prostitution industry suffered little from the new policy, and by all accounts it flourished in the following years. The segregated East Main Street district closed, but prostitution would continue to be a problem throughout the war. Furthermore, as predicted, prostitution spread throughout the Norfolk and Hampton Roads area, making it more difficult to control. From January 1941 until the end of the war, the story of prostitution and venereal disease control in Norfolk was one of city officials struggling with little success to curb illicit sexual behavior. This is not to make a counterfactual argument — that if the segregated district had remained, the city would have been able to contain the industry and curb venereal disease — but rather to say that abolishing the district certainly did not end commercialized sex in Norfolk.

Norfolk was not alone in its struggle over the closure of organized prostitution districts. One city in a similar situation was Seattle, Washington. Seattle had a semilegal prostitution district, and those who ran it proved far more reluctant than Norfolk's leaders to follow Parran's directive. Federal officials first turned their attention to the situation in Seattle in July 1941, requesting that local police close the houses of prostitution there. Two full years passed before the first serious effort began to shut the businesses down. Seattle differed from Norfolk because police there were simply unwilling to enforce the orders to close the brothels. Federal leaders believed this local recalcitrance was due to bribes paid to police by the well-organized prostitution interests in that city.[22]

Norfolk weathered its first storm of criticism in 1942, when the national press turned its attention to the city. Oddly, the first element of the city's reputation that needed to be defended was its architecture, after an exposé in *Architectural Forum*. The magazine not only criticized the buildings of Norfolk, saying much of the city was marked by a "general drabness," but also remarked on local corruption and mismanagement. "Norfolk is not much of a town," the article's author concluded. Other national publications picked up the story, and soon people across the country were able to read about the prevalence of illegal alcohol sales and prostitution in Norfolk, as well as the housing shortage and other problems.[23] For the most part, Norfolk officials and the local press did not deny the allegations. In fact, they poked fun at the moral outrage these publications demonstrated: "Norfolk a Sinful Place? What of It?," asked one headline in the *Norfolk Virginian-Pilot*. Norfolk hosted a large number of sailors daily, and sailors liked "sin" — "at least in its milder and more understandable forms," said a "well-known public official." After all, "What's a sailor going to do when he comes into town? Go to Church?"[24] No, another article answered, he's going to go to East Main Street, "where love is not exactly free, but generally reasonable."[25]

Though the city's spokesmen were blasé in their public reactions to allegations of vice activity, they were put off by the scrutiny of the national press. "Enemy Hasn't Raided Us but Out of Town Writers Have," proclaimed a *Virginian-Pilot* headline. "Big city papers" had come to town to feed "sensation-hungry subscribers," ignoring the positive side of the city and the many sacrifices residents had made for the war effort.[26] City leaders repeated this strategy of blaming outsiders — in this case, out-of-town journalists — for the city's problems on several occasions during the war years. In fact, Norfolk's leaders even responded to critiques of its architecture this way. Local builders, according to the head of the city's Builder's and Contractor's Exchange, were not responsible for many of the "drab" new units that the *Architectural Forum* critiqued. Instead, they were the work of "foreign" contractors with "outside money," who "swept" into the city when the war boom started.[27]

Although Norfolk's citizens tried to laugh off many of the negative stories as the work of overexcited journalists, they could not ignore the demands of national public health leaders that prostitution, because it spread venereal disease, must be curbed in the interest of national security. Echoing federal leaders in emphasizing the threat that prostitution and venereal disease posed, City Manager Borland observed in 1942, "All of us must present a solid front against this evil, just as the FBI is presenting a solid front against spies and saboteurs."[28] Forming this "solid front" meant treating venereal disease and eliminating the vice industry.

In Norfolk the military soon took on most of the activities assigned to it in the Eight Point Agreement, testing military personnel regularly and treating them for venereal disease when necessary. Service members could avail themselves of the "prophylaxis stations" when they feared they had recently been exposed to venereal disease. These facilities, discreetly labeled "Navy First Aid Station," operated at strategic locations around the Hampton Roads area. In 1944 one such station in downtown Norfolk began to operate twenty-four hours a day.[29]

According to the Eight Point Agreement, the city was supposed to take on its share of the venereal disease control job. Military and civilian planners saw this element as crucial. "The fact that the conditions are *local* and must in large measure be dealt with *locally* is constantly emphasized. . . . The Federal Government can assist with plans, advice, and money: but nothing really effective happens unless it happens *locally*," an official from the federal government's SPD wrote.[30] For city leaders to follow the Eight Point Agreement, they had to take responsibility for testing and treating the disease in the civilian population and for preventing activities likely to spread the disease.

City leaders sought to enforce antiprostitution laws by arresting those involved in the trade. A significant number of those arrested were white women, but their arrests posed a problem for local officials because the city had limited facilities in which women could be incarcerated. The problem of jail space in Norfolk for white women produced one of the key faults in the city's plan of controlling vice by removing sex workers from society. Before 1940 the situation in Norfolk paralleled the one in Richmond; neither city had built many spaces to jail white women because, traditionally, white women rarely went to jail. Norfolk could incarcerate only forty-five white women at any one time, unless they filled the cells well beyond the intended capacity. Overcrowded jails, though, also attracted attention and criticism in the press.[31]

The challenge of stopping the sex trade without sufficient resources to incarcerate those who broke the law put city leaders in a frustrating situation. In 1942 City Manager Borland, described the problem this way: "If we don't have more places in which to house these women, then we will be confronted with the situation like that of running a mad dog from my back yard into your back yard."[32] Borland's statement reflects his immersion in ideologies of gender and sexuality that were both misogynistic and preoccupied with sexual continence. But issues of governance and politics informed Borland's reaction as well. Norfolk was the navy's "back yard," and federal officials charged the city with keeping it free of the sex trade by controlling female sexual behavior. In this way, the Eight Point Agreement put women at the center of local venereal disease control efforts. Military men, whom the agreement specified that the military would monitor, treat, and punish, were effectively removed from the local equation.

The first response of local officials to the lack of jail space was to order arrested women to leave town as an alternative to incarceration. City officials requested that judges impose suspended sentences on the condition that these women immediately vacate Norfolk.[33] Such an approach did not sit well with federal authorities who believed it neither stopped prostitution nor curbed the spread of venereal disease.[34] Forced evacuation did not solve Norfolk's prostitution problem, because the women often did not leave town. Instead, they frequently ignored the judges' orders and stayed, hoping that police would not catch them again, or that if they were caught, they would receive a similarly nominal punishment.[35] If they did leave town, the women would often just go to other nearby locations; this was particularly problematic in the Hampton Roads area, as women could easily move between the various municipalities and counties in the region.

Furthermore, simply arresting and releasing the women did nothing to curb venereal disease, a problem that public health officials claimed could weaken America to the point of ensuring a Nazi victory.[36] However, city leaders found that their limited resources made it quite difficult to successfully treat venereal disease in prostitutes. When jail officials released prostitutes who had venereal disease before they had completed their approximately two-week course of treatment, some of the women refused to return to the health department to receive the rest of their shots. When health officials released the women from the crowded jails and sent them to the hospital, that caused another problem since, as Borland put it, "the girls will not stay there."[37] Even if the women did stay at the hospital, H. G. Parker, the city's director of public welfare, explained, "We have tired [*sic*] this repeatedly and found it a completely hopeless proposition. On several occasions only two or three of them at a time have nearly wrecked the institution. The Municipal Hospital is the last place they should go, and they should be provided with an entirely separate unit."[38]

To deal with recalcitrant women with venereal disease, the city needed a new facility. From the earliest months of the war mobilization, city officials had called for the construction of a new, larger prison in which they could both incarcerate women arrested for prostitution and treat those who had venereal disease. When the city authorities had arrested and incarcerated prostitutes during the First World War, they had put them in facilities at the Norfolk city farm and the Newport News city farm.[39] Those solutions were temporary, as were similar approaches used in other cities across the country in that period.[40]

Borland had initially hoped to use the Norfolk city farm again in the 1940s to incarcerate these women, but this plan ran into problems.[41] First, the city council refused to allocate enough money for the project. The small amount of money designated for construction at the site could only build a very small facility that was adequate to hold the city's population of jailed African American women—a group smaller than that of incarcerated white women.[42] Furthermore, Parker expressed to Borland a reluctance to put white women at the farm, asserting that the presence of the women made the men more unruly.[43] In addition to inciting the jailed men, white women caused trouble of their own. According to Parker, "Our experience at the Farm over many years has been that ten or twelve women of this class constitute far more of a problem than two hundred male prisoners."[44]

Desperate for jail space for white women, city officials emptied the building at the city farm of African American women and started sending white women under eighteen years old there.[45] Though there was still some space for incarcerating African American women at the city jail, their exclusion from the city farm so that white women could be held there instead echoes Richmond's prioritization of venereal disease control in white women over black women, as was documented in the previous chapter. The limited resources for venereal disease control would be directed at the white race, emphasizing their health at the expense of African Americans and focusing the city's efforts on the sexual containment of white women.

The space at the city farm consisted of one room into which the women were crowded all day long. The showers had no curtains, and the toilets had no booths. Venereally infected women were instructed to use one toilet, and those who were not infected the other. The young women incarcerated there rebelled against their conditions, attacking guards with chairs until authorities removed the chairs. Next, they set the bedclothes on fire and threw them out the window, producing a fire in the grass outside. The last straw came when the women rioted and broke everything within reach. After that, the experiment at the city farm ended.[46]

In March 1941 Borland met with Charles P. Taft, a representative of the Federal Service Administration. Borland explained to Taft the problems the city had controlling vice and asked for federal help in building a prison in which to hold and treat venereally infected prostitutes, underscoring his conviction that prostitution in Norfolk was not solely the city's responsibility. Defense work had attracted large numbers of military personnel and war industry workers into the city. Others followed who hoped to benefit from the booming population, including women hoping to sell their sexual services. City leaders repeatedly emphasized that most of the women involved in the trade were not Norfolk natives and that, in fact, Norfolk had become "a camping ground for women of ill fame from every State in the Union."[47]

Evidence that local citizens were not to blame for the venereal disease problem came from data indicating that infection rates among local citizens had dropped. Those with venereal disease in Norfolk were recent arrivals, women selling sex and sailors buying it.[48] More proof came from the military's rate of documented local infections. When a serviceman contracted venereal disease, military officials tried to ascertain where he contracted it, and many claimed they had been infected in other cities besides Norfolk and other states besides Virginia. Navy officials printed a map with arrows pointed at Norfolk from all over the nation that illustrated the origins of the women arrested for prostitution in the city.[49]

Norfolk leaders balked at the suggestion that the city was responsible for funding venereal disease treatment for all these new people. In 1942 Borland wrote to Governor Colgate Darden about the overcrowding of white women in the city jail: "It is needless for me to say that this is strictly a State matter. All laws concerning contagious diseases, et cetera, must be State or Federal. These women are now committed in and sentenced under State laws not City ordinances."[50] If venereal disease control was part of the war effort, then money from the federal defense budget should pay for dealing with and treating diseased women.

Taft promised federal money to build facilities to quarantine women with venereal disease. However, soon thereafter, the Office of Defense Health and Welfare Services reviewed the situation and decided that it would be more appropriate to direct such assistance to the state rather than to a municipality. So Borland then contacted State Health Commissioner I. C. Riggin, who said that the state would apply for federal money to build a statewide facility for incarceration and treatment of these women. Though the federal grant was approved in early 1943, construction of the facility never began, reportedly because of shortages in construction material.[51]

At that point, Borland and state officials requested that either portable buildings from an old "demountable" Civilian Conservation Corps (CCC) camp be moved to the State Industrial Farm for Women to expand the capacity there or the federal government designate an abandoned CCC camp somewhere in the state for use as a quarantine site. Navy officials tried to help the city secure this assistance by writing to the surgeon general's office in support of the CCC camp proposal.[52] After much wrangling with federal officials, who resisted giving up any facilities that could possibly be used for military training, state officials announced that the Federal Works Agency (FWA) had donated a site in Prince Edward County, plus $105,000 for its renovation.[53]

Six weeks later, Governor Darden announced that he had canceled this plan, as the Prince Edward County camp had an inadequate water supply and many buildings that were beyond affordable repair. Darden noted that a shortage of doctors and nurses to staff the facility also contributed to his decision to call off the preparations.[54] The governor's public statements conflicted, however, with a PHS memo offering to detail a medical officer and nurses to the facility with the stipulation that the state pay the salaries of the nurses.[55]

The real problem may have been deeper conflicts in Virginia politics, not a staff shortage, as the governor reported. Virginia's long history of penurious government probably manifested itself as a reluctance to spend state money on such a facility. The federal government would take over the financing only if state leaders filed a statement "declaring themselves unwilling or unable to assume the responsibility."[56] State leaders failed to file such a statement, possibly fearing the political ramifications of such abdication of power to the federal government. Such resignation of local responsibility might have even triggered the imposition of the May Act in parts of the state.

Other cities across the nation had succeeded in transforming CCC camps and other abandoned federal sites into hospitals funded under the Lanham Act. Congress had passed this act in 1940 to allow FWA program money to be used to aid cities overcrowded by war-industry workers. When Virginia leaders applied for federal money for construction or renovation, they did so under the provisions of the Lanham Act. Three Florida cities, Sarasota, Ocala, and Wakulla, saw these camps converted into venereal disease treatment facilities by the end of 1942, as did Pontiac and Goldville in South Carolina. But in Virginia, disputes over how federal money should be spent impeded construction of a venereal disease detention/treatment facility. The federal government specified that Lanham Act funds could not be used to establish treatment centers that doubled as penal institutions.[57] The rapid treatment hospital in Richmond evaded this restriction by putting the occasional, particularly recalcitrant patient in quarantine, while keeping most of the patients there on an officially voluntary basis. But the state's grant proposal specified explicitly that the space would be for prisoners and would relieve prison overcrowding. The restrictions on the Lanham Act prevented the grant from being funded.[58]

While Borland was negotiating with federal officials, the military took its own steps toward curbing vice in the Hampton Roads area. In April 1942 the navy put forth a plan to control the movement of sailors by issuing an out-of-bounds order that covered key parts of the city, preventing them from entering a circumscribed region. Out-of-bounds orders had been used before in Norfolk, but since the war began they had usually targeted just particular businesses, not whole areas.[59] The wartime orders in Norfolk had previously covered "venereal disease sources," bars and hotels such as the Arab Tent Nite Club (placed out-of-bounds for six months in 1941), and restaurants that the navy judged unsanitary.[60]

This new, sweeping out-of-bounds order, given by the Fifth Naval District commander, Rear Admiral Manley H. Simons, blocked access to prostitution, gambling, and alcohol joints in the restricted area, mostly a portion of Main Street that had been notorious for vice. But all other businesses and activities in that district were now off-limits as well. The order authorized members of the shore patrol to enter these areas and arrest any servicemen who were in violation of the order.[61]

Six months later the navy, after consultation with Borland, established a permanent shore patrol in Norfolk, the first such force in the country.[62] Prior to this action, the shore patrol had no permanent staff, except a chief petty officer who handed out the daily assignments to the patrolmen. Commanders of individual ships whose seamen were visiting that day selected a certain number of them to serve on the shore patrol that evening. Two problems with this system had diminished the shore patrol's utility. First, officers served only a few days, so they developed no skill at the job. Second, shipmates were inclined to be lenient with each other, so the shore patrol frequently overlooked violations.[63]

The new, permanent shore patrol would be able to do a better job of enforcing the out-of-bounds order in the city, which, coupled with the previous year's closing of Norfolk's segregated district, had led to an explosion of vice just outside the city. Prostitutes relocated to "tourist cabins" — cheap hotels in the surrounding Norfolk County. On 18 October 1942, navy shore patrol and Norfolk city police conducted raids on three such businesses by the names of Shack's Cabins, Southern Cabins, and Timkin's Cabins, arresting fifty-three sailors, fifty women, and twelve nonmilitary men. Although the cabins were located in Norfolk County, the county police did not participate in the raid, but the reasons for the county's lack of participation would not be clear until another investigation two years later.[64] The raid was the biggest in the region's history, and even the *New York Times* reported on the event.[65]

Thirty-seven of the women arrested in the raid received twelve-month sentences to the State Industrial Farm for Women in Goochland.[66] Two of the three operators, one male and one female, received sentences of twelve months and fines of $500. Police turned the fifty-three navy men over to the shore patrol, where they were to be tried for violating an out-of-bounds order. According to military policy, they would also be tested and treated for venereal disease. Eight of the civilian men received fines ranging from $20 to $100, but none, save for the operator of Southern Cabins, was punished with incarceration.[67] Two days later some of the incarcerated women sought to be released on bail. The judge in the case refused their request, citing the newly passed legislation requiring that they be tested for venereal disease first.[68]

The outcome of this raid indicates the range of involvement by military, state, and local authorities in vice raids. It also demonstrates the differing fates of those arrested. Some women received jail time rather than a fine because they were repeat offenders. It is likely they worked regularly as prostitutes and were thus more prone to encounter the police than were the civilian men arrested the same day. There is no indication of how many of the women served a full sentence; given the overcrowding in the Goochland facility and the city jail, it is unlikely they all served a full twelve months. One history of Norfolk during the war suggests that these women probably did not serve their sentences owing to prison overcrowding but offers no documentary evidence to support this claim.[69] The civilian men arrested fared better than the women in front of the judge; not only did they all escape jail time (except for the one male operator) but they also did not encounter suspicion that they might have venereal disease and were not forced to be tested for the disease. Nonetheless, the sailors arrested by the shore patrol would have received mandatory testing and treatment for venereal disease as well as punishment for violating the out-of-bounds order.

The raid into Norfolk County proved only a temporary setback for the vice industry there. County leaders flatly rejected the prerogative of any other governing body to tell them what to do, ignoring federal demands and requests from the city of Norfolk to curb prostitution. The county's law enforcement system was corrupted by a political machine run by Judge A. B. Carney. Carney and the county sheriff's department allowed the operation of establishments for prostitution, gambling, and illegal liquor sales, provided that the business owners (except for those business owners who were police officers themselves) paid "Norfolk County Insurance" — simply put, a bribe — to public officials. Between 1942 and 1944, attempts by city, state, and military officials to curb the vice industry in the county and to curtail access by military personnel to these establishments met with entrenched resistance. These attempts included the literal invasion of the county by city and military officers in 1942, but Judge Carney held firm, insisting that the county had no problems with vice or corruption and blocking any attempts to challenge the operations of county officials. Finally, in March 1944 an investigation by a state legislative committee forced Carney's resignation. After this, corruption in the county abated somewhat, though the district's law enforcement problems continued to be exacerbated by a severe shortage of police officers.[70]

The different situations in Norfolk City and County are striking and suggest larger differences between the urban and rural South in this era. The

City of Norfolk was making an effort at venereal disease control; whatever the shortcomings of this project, there was no question that city leaders wanted the conflicts resolved and wanted the city to have a reputation of being hygienic and progressive. This was the urban South, and they were concerned with the city's image and economic development. Such questions did not seem to trouble the minds of Norfolk County's political leaders. There a group of powerful business leaders, police, and judicial officials were united in their common pursuit of personal gain. The modern focus on progress, hygiene, and image evident in the city was simply not an issue in the county.

Borland and other city officials felt that they had established that a lack of jail space hampered efforts to curb prostitution and treat venereal disease. They also believed that they knew the cure for this problem: state or federal assistance in building a new, bigger facility for incarceration and treatment. But all they got in 1942 was an enhanced shore patrol, out-of-bounds orders, and one raid in Norfolk County.

While city leaders waited for help with detention facility construction, federal officials decided to try their hand at diagnosing the problems in the city and the surrounding area. In 1943 Norfolk and the rest of the Hampton Roads area hosted two federal investigations, one under the auspices of the Army and Navy Munitions Board and one performed by the House Committee on Naval Affairs. Robert Moses led the first investigation. Moses worked as New York City's park commissioner and did consulting work for cities on public works and administration issues. After visiting Hampton Roads, Moses and his assistants would also check out San Diego and San Francisco, California, Newport, Rhode Island, and Portland, Maine.[71]

The Moses commission's report drew some damning conclusions about the situation in Norfolk. First, it argued that a lack of city services crippled the area. Norfolk needed to improve its public housing, water treatment, sewage facilities, garbage disposal, transportation, schools, recreation, and fire protection.[72] Moses also criticized vice control efforts in the area.

> It is urged that the present system of arresting prostitutes and confining them to the city jails without adequate facilities for treatment and with indeterminate sentences be abandoned and a more realistic approach be instituted. The only satisfactory method of handling this problem is to ascertain through the venereal disease clinics the names of those infected and to treat the whole situation as a medical problem instead of a policing matter.[73]

Moses criticized the closure of the red-light district on similar grounds, blaming federal officials for exacerbating the vice problem by trying to deny it existed.[74]

Moses used harsh language to describe federal and naval leadership in the region, saying they should bear much of the responsibility for problems well beyond the scope of local governments. Federal housing authorities had "bungled" their job, and he noted, "It is difficult to characterize past public housing activities in temperate language, or to see much evidence of initiative and energy on the part of the reshuffled National Housing Agency which inherited the mess."[75] As for the naval leadership in Norfolk, "the ranking official has little interest in the problem and does not have the combination of qualities which would enable him to bring order out of the existing confusion."[76]

A series of recommendations attached to the report called for a vast expansion of public services. Norfolk and the rest of Hampton Roads needed more public safety personnel, better public health programs and recreational facilities, and an expanded public infrastructure of water, sewer, and highways. Though the report recommended that some of the costs be taken on by local utility companies and operators, the area needed a significant increase in federal money.[77] "The public projects and the vital expanded wartime services to keep people working in the area can not be paid for by the local communities or the state, because the state and local government agencies do not have the money and can not raise it. This cost must be borne by the federal government." The projected price tag was $11.5 million.[78]

The military did not make the text of the Moses Report available during the war. Even Virginia's governor Darden never saw a copy, though the board summarized the report's findings and made them public. Phyllis Hall's article "Crisis at Hampton Roads: The Problem of Wartime Congestion, 1942–1944," tells the story of the report's suppression and concludes that its contents upset federal officials by criticizing their lack of leadership in Hampton Roads. The details of the report were elusive, but Virginia's citizens and leaders knew that Moses had criticized the city's conditions and the federal government's response.[79]

The enigmatic Moses Report moved federal officials not to action but to another study. In March the House Subcommittee Appointed to Investigate Vice Conditions in the Vicinity of Naval Establishments came to Hampton Roads for a two-day investigation under the leadership of Representative Edward Izac of California. One committee member, Margaret Chase Smith, a congresswoman from Maine, particularly attracted the attention of the local

press when she toured the women's quarters of the city jail.[80] The Izac committee's report made conclusions and recommendations that echoed the
Moses commission's findings closely, though its characterization of federal
policies in Norfolk was somewhat less scathing.[81]

Like Moses, Izac and his colleagues had ideas about how to alleviate a variety of Norfolk's problems. Although vice was the first and most extensively
examined issue, the report noted that "undue importance had been placed
on vice in the media."[82] The report's main conclusions regarding vice control can be summarized as follows: (1) Vice and venereal disease were "not
as widespread nor as serious as might have been expected"; (2) the cities in
Hampton Roads did a better job than Norfolk County of curbing prostitution; and (3) the City of Norfolk needed more jail and hospital space for the
"handling of girls and women who are found to be sources of infection."
Federal officials should immediately cease delaying the allocation of federal
funds for these projects.[83]

Two federal committees had now visited Hampton Roads and concluded—to no one's surprise—that the area had many problems, one of
which was vice and venereal disease control. Finally, in mid-1943 officials
began to do a better job of coordinating assistance to the area. A key step
was the creation of the Committee for Congested Production Areas, placed
under the direction of the Budget Bureau director, Harold Smith.[84] More
local change came when Admiral Herbert Fairfax Leary took over from Rear
Admiral Simons as the new commander for the Fifth Naval District. Leary
worked with Congress and the military to overcome the bureaucratic imped-
iments to change in Norfolk and the rest of Hampton Roads.[85]

In the next year local and federal officials would make major strides toward improving the region's problems by curbing food and housing shortages, building more schools, increasing the size of the shore patrol, and
improving train and bus service. The bulk of the funding for these projects
came from the federal government. Private groups also helped. The USO, the
YMCA, churches, and the Freemasons increased their offerings of "wholesome" recreation for servicemen in the summer and spring of 1943. The FWA
helped the USO renovate the old city hall building, and this large facility provided an entertainment venue for servicemen and civilians.[86] More federal
assistance helped the region address some public health problems—the
PHS assigned more doctors and nurses to the area and stopped drafting the
ones that were already there. By October 1943 the *Norfolk Ledger-Dispatch*
reported that only "six percent" of the Izac committee's recommendations
had yet to be carried out.[87]

Though the vice issue had brought investigators from all over the nation to Norfolk, the recommendations of Moses and Izac on this particular issue were only partly followed. Specifically, no federal funds were disbursed to the city, region, or state to build a detention/treatment center, to the almost unimaginable consternation of local leaders. In fact, federal officials sought to downplay the issue of vice in the area by, for example, changing the name of the "Subcommittee Appointed to Investigate Vice Conditions in the Vicinity of Naval Establishments" to the "Congested Areas Subcommittee."

Federal money never came through for a detention center, but a rapid treatment hospital did receive federal backing. The federal government finally allocated Lanham Act money for renovations to an existing structure, some dorms belonging to the federal National Housing Agency at Lambert's Point. Personnel from the FWA began the renovations needed to transform the facility, and the PHS assigned some medical personnel to staff the hospital.[88]

In the months after the Moses and Izac Reports, the district's naval commander, Admiral Leary, put forth some new efforts toward cutting venereal disease rates among sailors. These initiatives followed the earlier-established division of labor in which the military controlled the behavior of servicemen and left local officials to deal with female offenders. In May the navy doubled the size of the shore patrol to about six hundred men and included fifty African Americans in this newly enlarged force.[89] Leary expanded the areas from which servicemen were prohibited on 30 July 1943, restricting access to parts of Norfolk County where prostitution flourished. He did this immediately after the murder of a navy man in the county, but the order was largely in response to increasing evidence of corruption and mismanagement in the county police department.[90]

Then on 31 October 1943 Leary put a large section of the city, between Princess Anne Road and Main Street, under an out-of-bounds order, making the whole area off-limits to white military personnel between sunset and sunrise. Most of this district consisted of African American neighborhoods. Leary must have believed that white servicemen would only enter African American neighborhoods in search of prostitution or gambling, and therefore making this area off-limits would restrict their access to these illegal activities. But for unexplained reasons, the order also included a white section of East Main Street not known for vice that was home to the Masonic Service Center. The Masons provided recreational and support services for servicemen, services that local and naval leaders judged to be the kind of wholesome activities essential to curbing vice, so it was not at all clear why

Leary placed it out-of-bounds. He did not explain the reasons for this action and, in fact, departed office the next day, turning the job over to Rear Admiral David Le Breton, before the navy commanders had even made the new policy public.[91]

When Norfolk residents finally heard about the new policy a few days later, many reacted with skepticism and disappointment. Facing confused and frustrated local citizens, Police Chief John F. Woods gave a cryptic explanation for the draconian new policy: "While these restrictions are drastic, and they may appear to be even more drastic than they are, we feel that if citizens understood why they were imposed they would agree with us that they are necessary."[92]

While the white-owned *Norfolk Virginian-Pilot* tried to interpret the out-of-bounds order in a fairly positive light, saying that the shore patrol must have decided these areas were too vice-laden to control with its limited resources, the city's African American newspaper, the *Norfolk Journal and Guide*, reacted with outrage. This "harsh, hasty, inept, and uncalled for" order "puts all of Negro Norfolk outside the pale of decency, makes it suspect, and by inference labels it as unfit for contact by decent service men; that is, white wearers of uniforms." The paper concluded: "The Navy has given the Negroes of Norfolk, as such, a black eye. It has damned the good Negroes with the bad without distinction. It is making the innocent suffer along with the guilty. This is against the civilized conception of justice and equity. And it certainly does nothing to enhance good relations between the military services and the Negro citizens."[93] The reaction may have paid off. One history of the period reports, "At any rate, nothing more was ever heard of the order," suggesting that it was left on the books to give the navy greater authority over the black neighborhoods in case it were needed but was not enforced strictly.[94]

Expanding the out-of-bounds order compounded many local problems, while solving few. The shore patrol had enough trouble keeping soldiers out of the East Main Street area and the designated parts of the county. Now, with an enlarged area to monitor, it certainly could not effectively patrol this newly added sector. The sweeping out-of-bounds order also wreaked havoc on the local economy and the ability of military personnel to access all kinds of services. Placing hotels and rooming houses off-limits, for example, meant that service men and their families had even fewer places to stay in a region where such accommodations were already in short supply. Similarly, limiting access to the Masonic Services Center cut into already limited options for recreation. Sailors even found their access to grocery stores and barber shops hampered by these orders.[95] Despite the problems and inefficiencies posed in dealing with vice by simply trying to keep military personnel out of those areas, the out-of-bounds order comprised the main contribution the military made to solving the vice and venereal disease problems in the area. The shore patrol tried to keep sailors out of trouble, Admiral Simons wrote the occasional letter, and military hygiene officers promoted prophylaxis, check-ups, and treatment, but the military did little to help city officials incarcerate, rehabilitate, or treat female prostitutes or "pickup girls."

The interest of federal and military leaders in Norfolk's vice problems peaked in 1943, and little else happened on this front during the remainder of the war years. The new rapid treatment hospital opened at Lambert's Point on 15 June 1944, with room for forty-five white women, thirty African American women, nineteen white men, and sixteen African American men.[96] This facility was the fifth federally funded hospital to open in the state and the second such hospital in Virginia to treat venereal disease exclusively. Prior to the opening of the Lambert's Point hospital, the FWA and the PHS had worked with local officials in more than fifty other congested areas in the country to create these facilities, and in Norfolk's FWA region, Charlotte, Durham, Richmond, and South Charleston, West Virginia, already had them, but not Norfolk.[97] So, despite the fact that Norfolk was a critical military location and had experienced one of the greatest war-related population increases in the country, the city was comparatively slow to get a federally funded hospital.

The Lambert's Point operation combined elements of a detention facility, hospital, and rehabilitation center, thus allowing it to qualify for Lanham Act money since it was not simply a prison. City leaders worked out an agreement whereby individuals in jail could have their sentences suspended if they agreed to go directly to the hospital for treatment. Patients spent their time in recreational and educational activities. They watched films, some of which focused on venereal disease control, worked at jobs in the hospital for twenty cents an hour, and learned sewing and hairdressing. Press reports focused on the rehabilitation efforts directed at women in the facility, and it is not clear if male patients received similar care.[98] The hospital could not hold people there involuntarily, but patients could be threatened with incarceration under the state's quarantine laws if they left.[99]

After late 1943 neither federal nor local leaders put forth any new initiatives to control sexual behavior and thus venereal disease in Norfolk. The shore patrol continued to check the activities of servicemen, but city leaders increasingly recognized that their attempts to secure federal money for civilian venereal disease control work were futile.[100] Local efforts in 1944 and 1945 focused primarily on venereal disease education. The Office of Civilian Defense (OCD) began looking into venereal disease issues in the summer of 1943, following the suggestion of Dr. Raymond Kimbrough, the venereal disease control officer assigned to the region by the State Department of Public Health, that venereal disease could be considered an element of civilian defense.

The OCD formed a steering committee, led by local resident Alexander Bell, and initially involved itself with advocacy for and the planning of the Lambert's Point facility. After the hospital opened, Bell and his cohorts reformulated their group into the Norfolk Citizens Venereal Disease Control Committee in April 1944.[101] The most notable activity of this new organization was a public venereal disease control campaign held in November 1944. Workers in industrial plants received leaflets in their pay envelopes warning them of the dangers of venereal disease. Advertisements in newspapers, billboards, and placards on buses and streetcars encouraged citizens to undergo testing and treatment. Several downtown department stores hosted displays in their windows with messages such as "Invisible Killers: Syphilis and Gonorrhea" and "An examination is a wise investment in future health."[102]

The Venereal Disease Control Committee had a few African American members and directed its efforts toward citizens of both races. I have identified four African Americans among the committee's thirty-seven members, though there may have been more. P. B. Young Sr., the editor of the *Norfolk Journal and Guide*, and his son, P. B. Young Jr., both served on the Educational Committee. J. Eugene Diggs, a local black lawyer, was a member of the Social Protection Committee, as was Richard Bowling, pastor of the city's black First Baptist Church and an important leader of the black community.[103]

While the Venereal Disease Control Committee was organized for the sole purpose of addressing venereal disease, its African American members had a broader agenda for the group. The list of activities of the Social Protection Committee includes this item: "Prostitution problems. Negro policemen. Negro programs."[104] This offers an interesting insight into political activity by the city's black community. In 1939 a black Norfolk resident, Earnest Wright, applied to take the civil service exam to work as a police officer. After the Civil Service Commission informed him that he was barred from the job because of his race, Wright sued the city, and a circuit court judge agreed that his civil rights had been violated. The Civil Service Commission allowed

Wright to take the exam but still refused him the job. For the next six years, black civic leaders pushed for the hiring of black police officers, but the city refused, despite the severe shortages in personnel that wartime manpower problems generated.[105]

The agenda of the Social Protection Committee indicates that African Americans in Norfolk used the small amount of authority they possessed to promote change. In this case, the relatively powerless position of members of a subcommittee on venereal disease control became a way to advance the argument that black police officers were uniquely qualified to police the African American community. The fact that the navy had appointed black shore patrol members because of their usefulness in keeping black sailors in control, as well as the recommendation of local venereal disease expert Alexander Bell, must have bolstered the case of Diggs and others that the city would benefit from hiring black officers.[106] Finally, in November 1945 two African American men were appointed to the Norfolk police force, making them the city's first black police officers since Reconstruction.[107]

Why was it so difficult for Norfolk officials to discipline sexual behavior sufficiently to create the image of a well-governed city, as Richmond had? City and military leaders implemented most of the recommendations of the Izac Report that did not focus on prostitution and thus resolved most of the other troublesome issues in the city. Combining local and federal efforts had successfully addressed shortages in transportation, inadequate sewage treatment, and a lack of housing, so why did they fail to combat vice and venereal disease as well? The answer to this question has several elements, all of which highlight the unique issues raised when policy makers turn their attention to sexuality.

Virginia's historic attachment to business progressivism had endorsed spending money for infrastructure but not for health and welfare. In a city with few public welfare programs to begin with, leaders had few reasons to suddenly start spending a large amount of money on health care and job training for prostitutes. Even spending the funds to simply incarcerate this population had little support. Norfolk built a city farm during the First World War and had held some prostitutes there during that earlier crackdown on vice, but by 1940 the city had ceased to incarcerate any white women there at all.[108] The quarters for white women in the city jail, the local Florence Crittenton Home, and the brothel owners' quarantine facility (closed when the segregated district was disbanded) formed the area's best efforts to deal with delinquent white women. Expenditures of municipal funds for these facilities, however, ranged from minimal to none.

Compounding the reluctance of city leaders to fund prostitution and venereal disease control work was their conviction that the problems were not really local ones. Federal leaders had insisted that cities like Norfolk were wholly responsible for vice control, outraging Norfolk leaders who saw this as something that encompassed the region and the nation. The intractability of Norfolk County authorities increased Borland's reluctance to fund massive city-sponsored programs, since the county clearly contributed much to the city's high rate of venereal infection. The whole situation made the federal government less willing to accede to Borland's demands for funds to build a prison/treatment center. Military leaders must have questioned the strategy of partnering with corrupt and incompetent local governments. The fact that the county and city shared the same name did nothing to help the city's reputation.

Despite the PHS's patriotic appeals to stamp out venereal disease in the name of national security, neither the health of men who visited prostitutes nor the health of women involved in the sex trade was an important priority for the city's government. The military men who put themselves at risk for infection were usually not Norfolk citizens, and locals believed that the women who sold or traded sex were outsiders also. In addition, those who became infected received the infection through illegal and — in the eyes of local leaders — immoral activity. Norfolk's leaders were reluctant to fund efforts that made having sex with prostitutes safer, thereby countenancing this kind of behavior.

Convinced the venereal disease situation was not really a local issue, city leaders dug in their heels. When the antivice campaign of the 1940s began, Norfolk's citizens and leaders could accept some expansion of city responsibilities, but not to the degree envisioned by federal leaders. Even near the end of the war, the city council held fast to the position that city spending for vice control should be minimal or, better, nil. In August 1944 Alexander Bell, representing the city's Venereal Disease Control Committee, asked the council for an appropriation of $2,300 to aid the committee's efforts. Specifically, Bell sought funding for "the purpose of display cards to be used on street cars and buses, pamphlets, billboard advertising, needles, syringes, etc." Borland expressed his support for the request and pointed out that this would be a onetime appropriation, not the first of a series of annual appeals. However, the council balked at the allocation, with one member expressing concern that the appropriation "would be a new departure in city government."[109] In 1945, citing local opposition, the council turned down another plan to convert an old police building into a temporary detention facility for women.[110]

Not only did local, state, and federal leaders fail to decide if Norfolk was at fault for the high rate of venereal disease in soldiers and sailors there, they could not even agree on the extent of the problem or, in fact, if there was a problem at all. Throughout the war, city and military officials cited endlessly contradictory statistics, asserting variously that the city had the worst venereal disease problem in the nation, an average problem, or no problem at all. As was true of other diseases, documenting the prevalence of venereal disease required careful epidemiological studies, which health experts there had neither the time nor resources to conduct during the war. Lacking good data and analysis, they relied on scattered and incoherent evidence that they could easily manipulate to advance a particular claim.

Officials framed the local problem in a positive or a negative light, depending on the situation. City leaders cited evidence of a declining local infection rate when they needed to prove that they were doing a good job.[111] On other occasions they played up the venereal disease problem in the city to bolster their case for outside help and to raise concerns among the city's citizens about the disease.[112] Officials tended to base the optimistic claims about the local venereal disease control effort on military statistics, which indicated that military personnel usually became infected outside the city, as well as on the increasing number of people seeking treatment for venereal disease at the local health department.[113] They based the more pessimistic claims on the rate of venereal disease discovered among local men inducted for the draft or on the rate of infection among locally stationed military personnel.[114]

The dueling Moses and Izac Reports offer an excellent example of the confusion over the situation in Norfolk. In March 1943 the Moses commission labeled the local venereal disease problem "acute," but the next month the visiting Izac committee said the opposite — that the disease's prevalence in Norfolk was not as widespread or as severe as might have been expected.[115] Observing that venereal infections had dropped to "encouraging" levels and continued to decline, the committee concluded that "still further improvement is assured."[116]

This statistical uncertainty offers further explanation for why public policy that focused on sexual behavior differed from tasks other local officials undertook. It was not crystal clear whether Norfolk had a problem with venereal disease or not, whereas there was no question it needed more sewer treatment capacity, for example. Furthermore, the stigma attached to these diseases and the invasive examination required for their detection made charting their prevalence more difficult than quantifying the lack of roads or shortage of sewage treatment facilities.

The final, important difference between efforts to control sexual behavior and the other projects that federal, state, and local leaders took on in wartime Virginia was that the subjects of regulation resisted state discipline. The women who offered sexual access and the soldiers who sought it constantly defied the attempts of city leaders to constrain their movement. This is not atypical of sex workers and their clients in general, nor is it surprising to historians of sexuality who have shown how in other historical contexts sexually deviant individuals (i.e., people involved in prostitution, interracial sex, or homosexuality) often successfully eluded authority by slipping through the cracks in systems designed to constrain them. But this resistance added to the challenge facing local policy makers.[117]

The perceived needs of public health and national security built on a history of fears about unrestrained sexual behavior to make sexual regulation an imperative in wartime Norfolk. A similar combination of ideological and political concerns turned the focus of the local government to the regulation of female sexuality. The military's ability to discipline its own male personnel, coupled with federal insistence that local governments regulate women's behavior, made female sexual danger a prime concern. And Norfolk's leaders demonstrated the same tradition of parsimony that had shaped sexual regulation in previous decades.

These continuities with past forms of sexual regulation were overshadowed, however, by the clear differences in the changed political and social context of Norfolk during the Second World War. Local officials could no longer operate under a vision of government by and for the white upper class now that federal officials insisted that the priorities of the military and national security take precedence. And the clear distinction between governing and governed fell apart as city leaders expressed growing reluctance to devote local resources to governing individuals they perceived as outsiders. These Virginia leaders no longer had the degree of control necessary to construct a precise disciplinary state that targeted a clear segment of the disfranchised population. All this sealed Norfolk's reputation as a disorderly city.

Epilogue

While the war raged in Europe and Asia in early 1944, the postwar era had begun in the arena of venereal disease control. In September 1943 John Mahoney, a U.S. Public Health Service (PHS) physician, announced his discovery that the new antibiotic penicillin could effectively and rapidly cure most cases of syphilis. Soon after, other researchers found that penicillin also treated gonorrhea. By 1944 the engines of wartime production had taken on the task of making these drugs, and military doctors prescribed them regularly. After the war penicillin became available for the civilian population as well.[1]

The success in treating these diseases with penicillin combined with the end of the war to bring the crisis of venereal disease to a close. A weakening of the U.S. military by venereal disease could no longer bring about the end to democracy that the PHS once threatened it might. Nonetheless, those who had spent the past decade or more fighting venereal disease were reluctant to see the campaign end. After the war local and national health leaders sought briefly to keep the dream of a nationwide commitment to venereal disease control alive, before admitting the momentum for this work had passed.

On 1 May 1945, a few days before Germany's surrender but while fighting against Japan was still fierce, the Committee on Military Affairs of the U.S. House of Representatives met to weigh the future of the May Act. The committee considered three options: let the act expire; extend it for one more year (with the hope the war would end by then); or make it a permanent statute. All of the witnesses testifying supported the act's extension through the war's end, and two—Surgeon General Parran and Allen Johnstone of the American Social Hygiene Association (ASHA)—went on record supporting indefinite continuation. After listening to the testimony, the committee recommended the act remain in place until hostilities ceased but left open the question of what to do after that.[2]

Several months later, shortly after the war in the Pacific had ended as well, the Interdepartmental Committee on Venereal Disease met to plan the future of venereal disease control in the postwar period. On the table was a plan to indefinitely continue the May Act. The transcript of this committee's 12 September 1945 meeting is a remarkable document for a number of reasons. First, it is striking that at the close of the war officials from the FBI, the PHS, the War Department, and various service branches were seriously contemplating making such a measure permanent, given the fact that it so significantly enhanced federal authority at the expense of city and state governments. Extending the May Act would mean that any time the federal government felt that the health of service members was being insufficiently protected by local officials because of the persistence of prostitution in a particular locale, the FBI could enter that area and take over police functions. Given the number of military bases in the nation, this proposal could have dramatically augmented federal power and contracted local authority in a significant portion of the country, and it might have made the FBI a prominent fixture in many communities.[3]

This expansion of federal power into enforcement of prostitution statutes was part of a larger vision of greater federal influence that was considered, but ultimately rejected, in the postwar years. Other aspects of this vision that were never realized included universal military service and federal full-employment legislation.[4] The committee's meeting underscores the common threads that tied sexual regulation with this plan for an expanded federal role. A permanent May Act would have opened the door for greater federal policing authority. If postwar America were one in which all young men were called for service, this act would have covered a larger number of people and might have found wider support as Americans sought to protect their sons from immorality and disease. Thomas Devine, director of the Social Protection Division, offered a perspective on the connections between employment issues, venereal disease control, and the May Act during the meeting: "Of course, in your proposed full employment legislation you have what is really an expression of Federal concern for full employment. It occurred to me in some permanent legislation you might have something that was the equivalent of that with a Federal concern for prostitution."[5]

Devine saw the wartime federal venereal disease campaign as a model for a more powerful federal government in areas beyond public health. He argued that a federal call for full employment could establish a precedent that might solve the constitutional problems of a permanent May Act. Just as the federal government could support, but not mandate, full employment, it could formally express concern for venereal disease and underscore the value of efforts to control it, without officially mandating action.[6]

The committee's meeting ended with what can only be described as an existential crisis, and this crisis foreshadowed the fate of prostitution and venereal disease control policies nationwide in the coming years. The confusion began when a War Department representative explained that suppression of prostitution for purposes of venereal disease control was no longer a pressing issue for the military. At first this seemed irrelevant; the committee's purpose was to control venereal disease in the civilian population. But if venereal disease among civilians did not concern the military, then where was the rationale for extending the May Act? All present agreed that prostitution was a bad thing, but that was not enough to justify such sweeping federal powers. Suddenly, committee members were at a loss to explain why they were there: "I remember we discussed several months ago what the actual functions of this committee were, and I am not exactly sure yet what they are," noted Thomas Sternberg, a representative from the Army Medical Corps. William Snow, of the PHS, tried valiantly to keep efforts going: "What we want to do is carry that [success in repressing prostitution] on." But the moment had passed, and an era seemed to come to a close as the meeting did. Venereal disease did not and would not threaten national security and could no longer justify unconstitutional measures. A few minutes later, the meeting adjourned with no recommendation on the May Act.[7]

The ASHA had come to fame through its venereal disease control campaign, and its members had fought the disease single-mindedly since the eve of the war or, in some cases, even earlier. Given the continued prevalence of venereal disease, they saw no reason why the great war on the disease should end. This helps explain the uproar in Norfolk about the city's venereal disease problem that was produced by a visit to the city of an ASHA field agent a few years after the war ended.

ASHA agent Thomas Edwards came to Norfolk for eleven days in the fall of 1947 to study the venereal disease situation. Though the war was over, the military remained a significant presence, and Norfolk remained a busy and growing naval base. The new threat of Soviet military power justified continued expenditures in all branches of the military, including the navy.[8] As a result, the ASHA believed that the venereal disease rate in Norfolk remained a pressing concern. Edwards surveyed local data and conditions and, comparing his results with those found by other agents in other cities, he concluded that Norfolk had the highest venereal disease rate in the United States. He asserted that the city had fallen from its position during the war as a city with one of the lowest venereal disease rates in the nation (a claim that likely surprised many and relied on the rosiest statistics available from the war years) to the one with the highest. Edwards laid the blame for this on lax law enforcement in the postwar years that had allowed for a reexpansion of houses of prostitution; he found four such houses in operation. In addition, according to the field officer, girls working in downtown taverns often sold their sexual services.[9]

Responses to the report came from across the city. The Norfolk Council of Social Agencies, to whom Edwards had voiced his conclusions, appointed a committee to investigate further. The *Norfolk Virginian-Pilot* questioned the reliability of Edwards's statistics and suggested that a comparison of naval and civilian rates was in order. Naval officials, responding to an allegation by Edwards that city and military officials had failed to cooperate in matters of vice, defended the city's law enforcement efforts. The city's director of public safety launched his own investigation into prostitution in Norfolk.[10]

While many expressed outrage and concern, the only plan to address Edwards's concerns came from local tavern owners. Apparently troubled by the role of local civilian women in spreading the disease, they proposed the establishment of a private venereal disease clinic in which to examine waitresses. City leaders reacted with some confusion to the tavern owners' plan. Either these businessmen were assuming that their waitresses were likely to have sex with their customers, which troubled public safety officials, regardless of whether the women had venereal disease, or tavern owners were clinging to the old fallacy that food handlers could pass on venereal disease through the food. Playing it safe, City Manager C. A. Harrell carefully distanced himself from the plan, saying he neither approved nor disapproved of it.[11]

The furor calmed when the ASHA representative clarified that the high venereal disease rate applied only to service personnel. A Norfolk Council of Social Agencies report also helped defuse the situation by asserting that the city's venereal disease rate had, in fact, decreased and that enforcement of prostitution laws was not lax.[12] Norfolk officials avoided undertaking any new venereal disease control work.

This incident in Norfolk was the last episode in the war on venereal disease waged during the Second World War. On one level, the ASHA representative was right: the people of Norfolk, citizens and officials alike, did, in fact, care less about venereal disease in 1947 and were doing less to control it than in previous years. The problem for the ASHA was that this was not really a crisis any longer. The venereal disease campaign came to a close in

Virginia and across the nation despite efforts on a number of fronts to continue significant involvement by state authorities in the control of venereal disease and, by extension, prostitution.

The new availability of antibiotics allowed for a downsizing of the health infrastructure aimed at venereal disease. By 1946 physicians could treat gonorrhea with one injection rather than a series of three, so testing and treatment could occur in one visit to the clinic.[13] The rapid treatment hospital in Richmond closed in July 1947 because the PHS cut its funds for the facility, and the state and city would have had to more than triple their contribution to the hospital for it to remain in operation. Henceforth, city health officials would send any patients who needed residential treatment (those with particularly severe infections) to the Hampton Roads rapid treatment center.[14] By 1950 the state decided to cease funding all residential facilities for syphilis patients, as the vast majority of cases could be treated on a walk-in basis. Gone were the days of trying to find space to house people receiving treatment. Instead, the state provided penicillin for venereal disease to physicians at no cost for private patients, and poor or indigent patients could be treated for free at county health departments.[15] Also gone were efforts at "social uplift" of women and girls arrested for prostitution and found to have venereal disease. In July 1946 the Richmond welfare department withdrew its social workers from the venereal disease clinic at the municipal hospital because the duration of the women's stay for treatment was so short that there was no time to offer other programs aimed at their moral betterment.[16]

The fate of venereal disease control in Virginia demonstrates that, in the changing scientific and political context of postwar America, some of the logic behind the sexual regulations conceived in earlier decades began to erode. This is not to suggest that concern about sexual danger passed or that state interest in disciplining it had ended. Indeed, new kinds of sexual danger seemed to threaten America in the postwar era, most notably sexual danger embodied in the figures of the homosexual and the sexual psychopath.[17] But these new sexual projects were the product of the new postwar era. The regulations examined in this work were closely tied to the particular political, social, and intellectual context of interwar and wartime Virginia. In the 1950s, as the politics of race was transformed in the South, as eugenics became increasingly suspect, as discourses of progress and modernization changed, and as constructions of gender and class shifted, the policies enacted between 1920 and 1945 came under challenge.

At first it appeared that Virginia's eugenic laws would be able to with-

stand the growing worldwide hostility toward such laws that resulted from
the eugenic policies of Nazi Germany. Within the United States, ideological
changes — including a new sensitivity to human rights, increased calls for
racial justice, and a rejection of Nazi eugenic policies — brought strength
to antieugenic arguments. Despite this, some policy makers in Virginia
not only defended the state's sterilization policies in the postwar years but
sought to expand them. In a 1949 article in the *American Journal of Mental
Deficiency*, Dr. W. I. Prichard, the superintendent of the Petersburg State Colony, called for an expansion of sterilization in Virginia. Prichard suggested
that between 1 and 2 percent of the population was feebleminded and thus
should be targeted for sterilization. He warned that if the wartime decline in
sterilizations continued — a decline he attributed to a lack of medical personnel to perform the procedure — society would "deteriorate." The article
concluded by appealing for an expansion of eugenic sterilization in Virginia,
asking that a new law permitting "extramural sterilization" be passed. This
proposal would have extended the authority of the government to sterilize
people to those not residing in state facilities. Prichard hoped it would benefit the state by saving the cost of institutionalization and help patients avoid
the "stigma" of institutionalization. Though Prichard's plan did not become
law, it is clear other Virginia medical leaders agreed that sterilization should
continue. The number of individuals sterilized in Virginia increased after
the war's end. After dropping to 131 surgeries in 1944, Virginia's sterilization rate inched up in the next decade, peaking at 195 in 1954.[18]

Virginia's leaders continued the state's prohibition of interracial marriage in the postwar years, though the application of the Racial Integrity Act
changed with the retirement and death of Walter Plecker. Many of the violations of the Racial Integrity Act described by journalists in the postwar years
stemmed from reports by family members, such as in the Purcell/Rhoton
and Hamilton/Hammond cases discussed in Chapter 2, rather than from
the aggressive investigative tactics that had marked Plecker's tenure. Even
in the landmark *Naim v. Naim* case, the accusation of interracial marriage
came from Mrs. Naim while attempting to divorce her husband, Ham Say
Naim.[19]

As the Second World War receded into the past, the South was on the brink
of a dramatic transformation. Like other southern states, Virginia's government underwent unprecedented changes in the late 1950s and 1960s. A
combination of factors, many of them with origins in the Civil Rights Movement, significantly undermined the political formations and policies of the
past era. Following pressure from civil rights activists and their legal allies,

voting restrictions, segregation, and legal discrimination ceased to rule political and social relations. Those seeking such changes pressured for more
federal involvement in matters traditionally left to states, and the Supreme
Court responded with a number of decisions that overturned racially biased
state laws. In Virginia, legislative reapportionment and African American
voting helped break the Byrd machine and, with it, the state's staunch commitment to low taxes and minimal public services.[20] In his successful campaign for governor in 1965, Mills Godwin promised to expand public services in the commonwealth, including education at all levels, mental health
facilities, environmental protections, and cultural programs.[21] To pay for
this, he proposed and successfully lobbied for a statewide sales tax. With
its passage, the Byrd era closed for good, and state leaders went on record,
finally, as supporting a functioning government over low taxes.[22]

In addition, economic changes, coupled with new techniques to promote
industrial development, made obsolete the earlier generation's vague attempts to mark the state as modern and progressive. Southern states turned
to more tangible and substantial measures to attract businesses, such as
industrial development bonds and tax incentives, and many of them established industrial development corporations and state development agencies
to encourage industrial expansion.[23] With these broad changes came significant revisions in the policies designed to police sexual behavior under discussion here, particularly those with origins in racial bias and paternalism.

In the 1950s and 1960s, involuntary sterilization, including the sterilization of those judged mentally incompetent, declined across the United
States. The legal history of the undoing of sterilization laws is complex, because it involved a variety of different state statutes, disputes on the federal
level (over whether involuntary sterilizations should be paid for with federal
funds or by the institutions that performed them), and questions of both
the right to voluntary sterilization and protection from involuntary sterilization. Though many legal and public health leaders agreed that involuntary
sterilizations were both legally and ethically problematic, a clear judicial
condemnation of the procedure was slow to come. Furthermore, many "voluntary" sterilizations involved a degree of coercion, particularly for women
who had no other options available. As late as 1976, a U.S. district court in
Raleigh, North Carolina, upheld a law allowing the involuntary sterilization
of some individuals.[24]

Ultimately, two events brought the practice to a halt. In 1978 the Department of Health, Education, and Welfare published new, strict standards for
funding the sterilization of the retarded, mentally ill, uneducated, or poor,

aimed at curtailing all procedures except those done with fully informed consent.[25] Then in 1980 a suit was filed by a woman who had been sterilized without her consent in 1949 at the Lynchburg Training School, when she was fourteen. A U.S. district court agreed to hear the case, *Poe v. Lynchburg*, which was attracting considerable attention since it challenged the statute upheld in *Buck v. Bell*. A settlement under which the state agreed to identify, inform, and compensate all persons involuntarily sterilized brought the case to a close. In 2001 the Virginia General Assembly passed a resolution formally expressing regret for the state's eugenic program, and the following year Governor Mark Warner apologized on behalf of the state on the seventy-fifth anniversary of the decision in *Buck v. Bell*.[26]

Movie censorship in Virginia ended in the 1960s, again the product of national developments. After thirty-seven years of rejecting the notion that the principle of free speech applied to motion pictures, the Supreme Court reversed its course with the case of *Burstyn v. Wilson* in 1952.[27] This decision, known as the *Miracle* decision because it concerned a film by Federico Fellini with that title, opened the gates to challenges to state censorship boards. In 1965 the Court found in *Freedman v. Maryland* that the licensing procedure, the process also used by Virginia to censor films, violated the constitution. Soon the Virginia State Board of Censors disbanded.[28]

Another Supreme Court decision, this one a direct challenge to a Virginia statute, curtailed the state's interracial marriage ban. In 1959 two Virginians, Richard Loving and Mildred Jeter, went to the District of Columbia to be married. Upon returning to Virginia, they were convicted of leaving the state to evade its miscegenation laws and sentenced to a year each in jail. A judge suspended their sentences under the condition they leave the state and not return for twenty-five years. At first, the couple complied, but in 1963 they filed a motion to vacate the judgment against them. When the state supreme court of appeals upheld the sentence, the couple's lawyers brought the case to the U.S. Supreme Court. In 1967 the Court decided in *Loving v. Virginia* that legally denying marriage solely on the basis of racial classification violated the equal protection clause of the fourteenth amendment. In striking down this law, the Court also invalidated similar laws in fifteen other states, all southern or border states.[29]

Thus, a number of the policies regulating sexual behavior in the prewar years disintegrated in the face of changes after 1960. In contrast, the fight against venereal disease did not end, but it did take on new characteristics in the succeeding decades. Federal funding for and national concern about venereal disease decreased dramatically during the 1950s, and this was soon followed by an increase in venereal disease rates later in the decade. Despite the effective remedy of antibiotics, cases of gonorrhea tripled in the United States between 1965 and 1975, and with the advent of AIDS venereal disease took on added significance.[30] In Virginia the General Assembly repealed the premarital venereal disease testing law in 1984. Several attempts in the 1990s to reinstate the requirement failed to become law.[31]

Though this work has told the story of a particular kind of regulation—sexual regulation—in a specific historical period, some aspects of the philosophy of government that Virginia's leaders articulated between 1920 and 1945 remain influential in Virginia as well as other states. Today, many states disfranchise individuals who are incarcerated, on probation, or on parole, and in some states even individuals who have completed all court-ordered punishment are still prevented from voting.[32] The disfranchisement of current and former felons reflects the continuing belief that those who make the laws are a distinct group from those who are punished by the law. The policy makers studied in this work also demonstrated a belief that race and class influenced an individual's danger to society. Similar ideas still prevail in Virginia, as the state has recently allowed judges to weigh risk factors for recidivism when they sentence offenders. Judges may punish convicted criminals differently based on personal characteristics. For nonviolent offenders, the state considers the risk for recidivism to be higher in young, male, and jobless individuals. In the case of sex offenders, courts may also take into account the level of education and marital status. Such policies mean that low-income individuals and young people are judged to be more dangerous and are more likely to be incarcerated. Correlations between race, income, and education in the United States mean that African Americans on average receive stiffer penalties. A final, persistent attribute in the history of Virginia's government helped motivate this new approach to sentencing—a lack of money. Incarceration rates have soared in recent decades, and lawmakers have found that offender risk-assessment has helped alleviate prison overcrowding and thus reduce prison costs.[33]

Notes

Abbreviations

The following abbreviations are used throughout the notes.

Acts of the General Assembly

      Commonwealth of Virginia, *Acts of the General Assembly of the Commonwealth of Virginia*

AW   Alexander Weddell Papers, Virginia Historical Society, Richmond

DMPC   Records of the Virginia Division of Motion Picture Censorship, Library of Virginia, Richmond

ICA   House Committee on Naval Affairs, *Investigation of Congested Areas, Part I, Hampton Roads*

JRF   Papers of the Julius T. Rosenwald Fund, Fisk University, Nashville

NCF   Norfolk Central Files, Library of Virginia, Richmond

NDSE5   Records of Naval Districts and Shore Establishments, 5th Naval District, RG 181, National Archives Mid-Atlantic Region, Philadelphia

NJG   *Norfolk Journal and Guide*

NVP   *Norfolk Virginian-Pilot*

NWHC   Norfolk World War II History Commission Papers, Norfolk Records Management Division, Norfolk, Va.

RDPS   City of Richmond, *Annual Report of the Department of Public Safety*

RDPW   City of Richmond, *Annual Report of the Department of Public Welfare*

RNL   *Richmond News Leader*

RTD   *Richmond Times-Dispatch*

TINC   *Tuskegee Institute News Clipping File*

USPHS   Records of the United States Public Health Service, Group 3: States 1936–1944, RG 90, National Archives, College Park, Md.

UVSC   The Albert and Shirley Small Special Collections Library, Alderman Library, University of Virginia

VDH   Commonwealth of Virginia, *Annual Report of the Department of Health*

Introduction

1. *Acts of the General Assembly* 1922, ch. 257; *Acts of the General Assembly* 1924, chs. 371 and 394; *Acts of the General Assembly* 1940, ch. 102, sec. 5073.

2. "Elite" is both a useful as well a problematic term. I use it throughout this work to emphasize that the economic and social position of a certain segment of the white population gave it political privileges and divergent political interests from other whites. This class was by no means homogenous. Differences of gender, geography, religion, and ideology produced disagreements and divergent agendas within the white elite class, and identifying these differences is an important part of this study. J. Douglas Smith's work on Virginia during this period uses the term in a similar way to "refer to those persons whose opinions, whether because of wealth, social prestige, occupation, political office or appointment, made the most difference in shaping the commonwealth's political, social, economic, and cultural climate." J. Douglas Smith, *Managing White Supremacy*, 9.

3. On historical constructions of African Americans as sexually dangerous and lacking self-control, see Brundage, *Lynching in the New South*, 58–71; Davis, *Women, Race, and Class*, 172–201; Fredrickson, *Black Image in the White Mind*, 174, 276–82; Terry, *American Obsession*, 81–82, 94, 204–5, 242–43; and D. White, *Ar'nt I a Woman?*, 27–61. On the belief that white working-class and poor southern women were sexually dangerous, see Cahn, "Spirited Youth or Fiends Incarnate." On class and sexual danger, see Terry, *American Obsession*, 34–35, 52–53, 78–79, 87–90. On the political and cultural interpretations of the gender and sexuality of working-class and poor women, see Peiss, *Cheap Amusements*; Enstad, *Ladies of Labor*; and Kunzel, *Fallen Women*.

4. See, for example, Gordon, *Pitied but Not Entitled*; Koven and Michel, *Mothers of a New World*; Mink, *Wages of Motherhood*; and Piven and Cloward, *Regulating the Poor*.

5. Elna Green notes the absence studies of the South in this literature and outlines her efforts at rectifying this imbalance in *This Business of Relief*, 2.

6. The quote is usually attributed to Thomas Jefferson. On the limited nature of southern government in this era, see Black and Black, *Politics and Society in the South*, 27–64; and Link, *Paradox of Southern Progressivism*, 3–159. On Virginia, see Heinemann, *Harry Byrd*.

7. Heinemann, *Depression and the New Deal*, 137.

8. See Foucault, *History of Sexuality*, especially 85–86.

9. Somerville, *Queering the Color Line*, 1–9.

10. Although elite-run governments emphasized the sexual dangers posed by certain parts of the population, African Americans and lower-class whites were thought to be predisposed to criminality and a general threat to the social order. For example, William Link writes, "Most reformers expressed what can be described as, at best, uneasiness with majoritarian democracy. To many of them, working-class and rural whites had become a dangerous, uncontrollable element in the South's new social mix." Southern reformers also believed that African American criminality was on the rise in the Progressive Era, as morals in the black community declined. Link, *Paradox of Southern Progressivism*, 59.

11. Of course, the rape of white women by black men was considered a public

act with political implications, but such assaults (imagined or real) were considered manifestations of black sexuality that violated white sexual traditions. In contrast the rape of black women by white men was seen as private and nonpolitical, and it was not constructed as rape at all by white elites.

12. Foucault outlines the formation of the disciplinary society in *Discipline and Punish*. Recent historical works about sexuality and the state that employ this expanded notion of a state include Briggs, *Reproducing Empire*; Chauncey, *Gay New York*; Odem, *Delinquent Daughters*; and Reagan, *When Abortion Was a Crime*.

13. Key, *Southern Politics*, 19–20.

14. Kousser, *Shaping of Southern Politics*, 180–81, 240; Key, *Southern Politics*, 20. On Virginia's 1901–2 constitutional convention, see Perman, *Struggle for Mastery*, 195–223.

15. Bell, "Biological Relationship," 731; Plecker, "Racial Improvement," 489.

16. J. Douglas Smith, *Managing White Supremacy*, 5–8, 40–75.

17. On class relations within the African American community, see Gaines, *Uplifting the Race*, 1–17. J. Douglas Smith finds that upper-class African American community leaders in Virginia were primarily male, in contrast to findings in other southern states. Smith also rejects the label "elite" for this group, noting that they had "significantly less wealth and lacked the political power of white elites," in *Managing White Supremacy*, 10.

18. On gender's role in demarcating boundaries of race and class in the wider Western historical context, see Bederman, *Manliness and Civilization*, 1–44; Cott, "Passionlessness"; and Welter, "Cult of True Womanhood." On the South in particular, see Bynum, *Unruly Women*, 35–58; Gilmore, *Gender and Jim Crow*; and Hewitt, *Southern Discomfort*.

19. Stoler, *Carnal Knowledge and Imperial Power*; Gilman, *Difference and Pathology*. On the United States, see Hodes, *White Women, Black Men*; and Mumford, *Interzones*.

20. The threats that white elites perceived to their dominance is demonstrated in J. Douglas Smith, *Managing White Supremacy*, 40–75.

21. Link, *Paradox of Southern Progressivism*, 3–159.

22. Heinemann, *Harry Byrd*, 60–64.

23. Tindall, *Emergence of the New South*, 224–38; Grantham, *South in Modern America*, 99–101. A number of works have discussed the drive for economic development in southern states in the decades after the 1920s. Among them are Cobb, *Selling of the South*; and Goldfield, *Promised Land*, 27–33. On Richmond, see Silver, *Twentieth-Century Richmond*, 22–93.

24. Grantham, *South in Modern America*, 97; Link, *Paradox of Southern Progressivism*, 248–62; Sosna, *In Search of the Silent South*.

25. Brundage, *Lynching in the New South*, 178–80; Heinemann, *Harry Byrd*, 63; Link, *Paradox of Southern Progressivism*, 58–61. Christopher Silver's work on Richmond indicates that efforts at government reform and urban planning in Richmond were inspired by the logic of business progressivism as well, and he argues that reformers saw city growth, government reform, and "the formulation of a stable biracial society" as part of this progressive agenda. Silver, *Twentieth-Century Richmond*, 52, 53–93.

26. Ownby, *Subduing Satan*, 167–92; Ullman, *Sex Seen*.

27. Describing Virginia's electorate with this degree of specificity is important, and in this respect my argument here echoes the work of Elna Green in *Southern Strategies*, xiv–xvi, 36–45. See also Greenwood, *Bittersweet Legacy*, 128.

28. Bartley, "The Era of the New Deal as a Turning Point in Southern History," in Cobb and Namorato, *New Deal and the South*, 137.

29. Freidel, *F.D.R. and the South*, 23; Bartley, "Era of the New Deal," 138; Douglas L. Smith, *New Deal in the Urban South*, 1–44, 128–64; Grantham, *South in Modern America*, 116–38.

30. Heinemann, *Depression and the New Deal*, 8–10; Heinemann, *Harry Byrd*, 119.

31. Heinemann, *Depression and the New Deal*, 138–39.

32. Heinemann, *Harry Byrd*, 160.

33. Ibid., 165.

34. Ibid., 167–72.

35. Ibid., 265–67.

36. Grantham, *South in Modern America*, 172. A comparative analysis of southern cities in the war years can be found in Daniels, "Going among Strangers."

37. Heinemann, *Harry Byrd*, 58.

Chapter One

1. *Acts of the General Assembly* 1922, ch. 257.

2. *Acts of the General Assembly* 1924, ch. 371.

3. Ibid., ch. 394.

4. For information on Progressive Era antiprostitution efforts in the South, see Sims, *Power of Femininity*, 68–77; Link, *Paradox of Southern Progressivism*, 117–23; and McArthur, *Creating the New Woman*, 83–87.

5. On health and welfare programs in Virginia in the 1920s, see Link, *Paradox of Southern Progressivism*, 223–31; Heinemann, *Harry Byrd*, 58–84; and Grantham, *South in Modern America*, 88–115.

6. Gregory Michael Dorr argues that similar motivations explain the concurrent passages of the Racial Integrity Act and eugenic sterilization laws in 1924. He writes that both "resonated with dominant cultural themes of southern living"; in particular, hierarchies of race, class, and gender. He also connects support for eugenics in Virginia and efforts to move the state into the forefront of progressive reform. G. Dorr, "Assuring America's Place," 257–94. See also G. Dorr, "Segregation's Science." Lisa Lindquist Dorr has argued that the two laws "reflected fears of changing gender roles and increasing female sexual agency and independence" in "Arm in Arm," 150. See also Sherman, "'Last Stand,'" 69–92.

7. J. Douglas Smith calls attention to the local base that supporters of eugenics drew on, particularly in Richmond, in *Managing White Supremacy*, 82–85.

8. Lombardo, "Eugenic Sterilization in Virginia," 69–70.

9. For a brief historical overview of the definition of mental retardation, see Noll, *Feeble-Minded in Our Midst*, 2–4.

10. Trent, *Inventing the Feeble Mind*, 60–183.

11. Noll, *Feeble-Minded in Our Midst*, 33–36, 110–12. In the case of Virginia, see, for instance, Darden, "Moral Subnormality." Johanna Schoen also concludes that "patients' sexual misbehavior provides another indication of mental disease or deficiency" and that feebleminded individuals threatened to degrade the gene pool. Schoen, *Choice and Coercion*, 92–95.

12. Noll, *Feeble-Minded in Our Midst*, 24–25.

13. Ibid., 110–112; *Acts of the General Assembly* 1918, ch. 300.

14. Several historians have made similar observations about Priddy's surgical record. See G. Dorr, "Segregation's Science," 413–15. Lombardo discusses Priddy's record of surgery in this era in "Eugenic Sterilization in Virginia," 133–34. See also Smith and Nelson, *Sterilization of Carrie Buck*, 30–34.

15. Smith and Nelson, *Sterilization of Carrie Buck*, 34–37.

16. Lombardo, "Eugenic Sterilization in Virginia," 131–35.

17. Ibid., 131; G. Dorr, "Segregation's Science," 428. Laughlin was the director of the Eugenics Records Office at the Cold Spring Harbor Laboratory in New York and a leading advocate of eugenics.

18. G. Dorr, "Segregation's Science," 422–26.

19. For a discussion of the rationale for southern eugenic policies, see Larson, *Sex, Race, and Science*, 40–84. See also Arnold, "Eugenic Sterilization"; and Darden, "Moral Subnormality."

20. *Acts of the General Assembly* 1924, ch. 394.

21. Letter from J. S. DeJarnette to Aubrey Strode, 24 July 1939, cited in Smith and Nelson, *Sterilization of Carrie Buck*, 241–42.

22. For a full discussion of this issue, see L. Dorr, "Arm in Arm," 150.

23. A. S. Priddy, quoted in Laughlin, *Legal Status of Eugenical Sterilization*, 28.

24. Quoted in Noll, *Feeble-Minded in Our Midst*, 75–76.

25. See also the comment of G. Dorr, in "Segregation's Science," 414–15: "Gender, not disease, was the crucial factor controlling Priddy's sterilization decisions."

26. Noll, *Feeble-Minded in Our Midst*, 68–69.

27. Strode, a participant in the drafting of the sterilization statute, describes the legal considerations that went into writing the bill in "Sterilization of Defectives."

28. Noll, *Feeble-Minded in Our Midst*, 69–71.

29. A. S. Priddy, quoted in the Deposition of Harry Laughlin in the Circuit Court of Amherst County in the case of *Buck v. Bell*, in Laughlin, *Legal Status of Eugenical Sterilization*, 17.

30. Smith and Nelson, *Sterilization of Carrie Buck*, 5–6.

31. Noll, *Feeble-Minded in Our Midst*, 102; Larson, *Sex, Race, and Science*, 54, 106; Trent, *Inventing the Feeble Mind*, 177.

32. See Beardsley, *History of Neglect*, especially 11–41; and S. Smith, *Sick and Tired*, 4.

33. The close, and arguably sinister, relationships between these men is described in detail in Smith and Nelson, *Sterilization of Carrie Buck*, 65–88.

34. Noll, *Feeble-Minded in Our Midst*, 70.

35. *Buck v. Bell*, 274 US 200 (1927).

36. Reilly, *Surgical Solution*, 87.

37. "Birth Control in Virginia," editorial, *Virginia Medical Monthly* 61 (December 1934): 552–53.

38. James Trent traces the development of arguments for eugenic sterilization, explaining that the procedure was originally envisioned as a way to strengthen institutional order (sexually sterilized inmates might be less volatile) and improve the genetic stock of the nation. As a range of factors increased the number of people considered "feeble-minded," it became clear that institutions could never meet this capacity. Sterilization was put forth as a means of institutional population control. "[S]terilization, now out of favor as a means of eugenic control, took on a new life. Sterilization could be linked with another growing interest of the superintendents: inmate parole and discharge to communities." Trent, *Inventing the Feeble Mind*, 192–202.

39. Reilly, *Surgical Solution*, 111–27.

40. Carrington, "Sterilization of Habitual Criminals, with Report of Cases"; Carrington, "Sterilization of Habitual Criminals."

41. Noll, *Feeble-Minded in Our Midst*, 77–79. Noll cites Stephen J. Gould on the *Buck v. Bell* case. Gould wrote that opponents of the Virginia Sterilization Statute were "conservative Virginia Christians who held, according to eugenical modernists, antiquated views about individual preferences and 'benevolent' state power." Gould, "Carrie Buck's Daughter," 14–18.

42. For a review of the history of these laws in Virginia, see Wadlington, "*Loving* Case"; Pascoe, "Miscegenation Law"; Finkelman, "Crimes of Love"; and Wallenstein, "Race Marriage and the Law of Freedom."

43. *Acts of the General Assembly* 1924, ch. 394.

44. Ibid.; Sherman, "'Last Stand,'" 77–78.

45. G. Dorr, "Segregation's Science," 379–80. Nineteen twenty-four was also the year that the U.S. Congress passed an immigration act that reflected eugenic ideology as well.

46. For a discussion of the impact of the national eugenics movement on the proponents of the Racial Integrity Act, see Sherman, "'Last Stand,'" 71–72; and G. Dorr, "Segregation's Science," 262–65.

47. For more on Cox's anthropology career, see G. Dorr, "Segregation's Science," 463–73. On the ASCOA and the Racial Integrity campaign in general, see also Sherman, "'Last Stand,'" 69–72; and J. Douglas Smith, *Managing White Supremacy*, 76–100.

48. L. Dorr, "Arm in Arm," 155–56.

49. See, for example, "Powell Paints Lurid Picture of Depravity of White Virginians," *NJG*, 13 March 1926, 1, 9.

50. Link labels this the "social efficiency state" in *Paradox of Southern Progressivism*, 203–4.

51. See, for example, T. C. Leonard, "'More Merciful and Not Less Effective.'" On the South in particular, see Larson, *Sex, Race, and Science*, 60–61, 66, 68. Larson notes that "Southern legislatures never demonstrated a sufficient appreciation of the sup-

posed economic and social calculus of eugenics to adequately fund eugenic segregation efforts" (91). Evidence from Virginia confirms that these efforts were underfunded and motivated by more than economics.

52. Sherman, "'Last Stand,'" 78.

53. Ibid.

54. Quoted in ibid., 78.

55. *Acts of the General Assembly* 1924, ch. 394.

56. "Racial Integrity and Propinquity," undated editorial in *NVP*, reprinted in *NJG*, 3 December 1924, 8.

57. "Virginia 'Nordic Blood' Purists Reveal Their Scheme to J. A. Rogers," *NJG*, 6 March 1926, 1, 7; "Powell Paints Lurid Picture," 1, 9; "Powell's Revelations of Race Intermixing Further Reviewed," *NJG*, 20 March 1926, sec. 2, p. 8.

58. For more on UNIA's relationship to Powell, see Bair, "Remapping the Black/White Body"; see also G. Dorr, "Segregation's Science," 543–47.

59. Editorial, *Richmond Planet*, 24 February 1924, 4.

60. "The Nordic Craze," *NJG*, 14 February 1925, 12.

61. Ibid.

62. Note the scarcity of articles listed under the heading "Amalgamation—1924—Virginia" in reel 20, *TINC*.

63. Paul Lombardo has written about this case involving Atha Sorrells in "Miscegenation, Eugenics, and Racism," 440–43.

64. "Indian Warfare Starts over Race Classification," *NJG*, 11 July 1925, 1.

65. "He's an Indian and Can Marry a White Woman," *St. Louis Argus*, 18 December 1925, in reel 22, *TINC*. Plecker used the term "self-styled Indian" in "Eugenics or Race Deterioration," 287.

66. "Indian Warfare Starts over Race Classification," 1; "Racial Integrity Bill Is Defeated," *Baltimore Sun*, 14 February 1928, 1, in reel 30, *TINC*; "The Racial Bills," *RNL*, 8 February 1926, 7.

67. "Says Social Fabric of State Would Totter under Integrity Law Amendment," *NJG*, 6 February 1926, 1, 6; "Racial Integrity Bill Is Defeated"; "Substitute Bill Being Sought by Its Opponents," *NJG*, 8 February 1930, 1, 7. The Virginia General Assembly meets biennially.

68. "Says Social Fabric of State Would Totter," 1, 6.

69. "Words Fly in Racial Purity Wrangle in Va," *St. Louis Argus*, 10 February 1928, in reel 30, *TINC*.

70. "Racial Integrity Bill Defeated in the Virginia Legislature," *Newport News Star*, 16 February 1928, in reel 30, *TINC*.

71. "Fight over Race Bill," Associated Press report in unidentified newspaper, in reel 30, *TINC*; "Words Fly in Racial Purity Wrangle"; "Race Villified before Solons," *Richmond Planet*, 7 February 1926, 4.

72. "Race Villified before Solons," 4.

73. "Bill Brands 63 'First Families' of VA. 'Colored,'" *RNL*, 9 February 1926, 1.

74. "The Racial Bills," *RNL*, 8 February 1926, 4.

75. "Substitute Bill Being Sought," 1, 7.

76. "Best Families Suffer under VA. Race Law," *Baltimore Afro-American*, 13 August 1927, in reel 27, *TINC*; "Caucasian Superiority," *Kansas City Call*, 9 September 1927, in reel 27, *TINC*.

77. "The 1930 Virginia Legislature," *NJG*, 15 March 1930, in reel 35, *TINC*.

78. "Fight over Race Bill."

79. "With Eyes Open," undated editorial, *RTD*, in reel 30, *TINC*. The *Newport News Daily Press* also expressed veiled support for strict racial standards by rebutting an *NVP* editorial on the subject with the views of Earnest Sevier Cox, one of the Racial Integrity Act's most public supporters. See "The 'Massenburg Nostrum,'" *Newport News Daily Press*, 9 February 1926, 6.

80. For a thorough history of the Public Assemblages Act, see J. Douglas Smith, *Managing White Supremacy*, 107–29.

81. "The Leading White Citizens Make Protest," *Richmond Planet*, 20 February 1926, 1; "Not the Virginia Way," *RNL*, 9 February 1926, 8.

82. "Color Psychology Amazingly Revealed in State Legislature," *NJG*, 27 February 1926, 1.

83. J. Douglas Smith, *Managing White Supremacy*, 125. Byrd's misgivings about the Public Assemblages Act did not, of course, amount to serious opposition to it. Nonetheless, the bill was sufficiently troublesome that he treated it differently than other bills and failed to sign it.

84. "Va. 'Racial Integrity Bill' Is Now Law, Separates Races," *Chicago Defender*, 21 June 1930, in reel 35, *TINC*.

85. "Racial Integrity Act of 1924," *VDH* 1928, 47. No author is given, but it is likely that Plecker wrote this portion of the report.

86. Plecker credited Earnest Sevier Cox's book *White America* as the source of his understanding that only two solutions to the "race problem" existed, in "Racial Improvement," 489.

87. J. David Smith, *Eugenic Assault on America*, 63.

88. "Virginia 'Nordic Blood' Purists Reveal Their Scheme to J. A. Rogers," *NJG*, 6 March 1926, 1, 7; "Powell Paints Lurid Picture of Depravity of White Virginians," *NJG*, 13 March 1926, 1, 9; "Powell's Revelations of Race Intermixing Further Reviewed," *NJG*, 20 March 1926, sec. 2, p. 8.

89. Pascoe, "Miscegenation Law."

90. Plecker, "Eugenics or Race Deterioration," 283–87; Plecker, "New Family and Racial Improvement."

91. Plecker, "Eugenics or Race Deterioration," 285.

92. Reilly, "Virginia Racial Integrity Act Revisited," 486.

93. In fact, Harry Laughlin worked in support of both the Virginia law and the 1924 Immigration Act. Noll, *Feeble-Minded in Our Midst*, 39, 173n60.

94. "Discuss Measure at Public Hearing before Delegates," *RTD*, 27 February 1922, 1. J. Douglas Smith points out that the National Association for the Advancement of Colored People had initiated an effort to censor Griffith's *Birth of a Nation*. The issue came to Virginia when an NAACP staffer wrote to Governor Westmoreland Davis, asking him to stop the showings of the film in Virginia. These events presumably con-

tributed to Griffith's opposition to censorship and his interest in participating in the debate in Virginia. J. Douglas Smith, "Patrolling the Boundaries of Race." Smith dates the first censorship proposal to 1918, though the *RTD* article, written in 1922, stated that the bill had first been considered and rejected in 1920. Since Smith cites a 1918 letter from Dixon to Governor Davis, I am assuming his dating of this proposal is the correct one.

95. Mary Gray Peck, "Report on State Censorship in Virginia," 27 January 1920, box 118, National Board of Review Records, New York Public Library. I am indebted to Nancy J. Rosenbloom for calling my attention to Peck's report and for providing me with a copy of it.

96. Ibid. For more information about the National Board of Review and its involvement in the politics of censorship, see Rosenbloom, "From Regulation to Censorship."

97. Peck, "Report on State Censorship."

98. "Novelist Has Tilt with Dr. M'Daniel at House Hearing," *RTD*, 28 February 1922, 1, 2.

99. Ibid.

100. "The Autocracy of Censorship," *RTD*, 26 February 1922, 6.

101. "Novelist Has Tilt with Dr. M'Daniel," 1, 2. A Richmond rabbi, E. N. Calisch, cited the failure of Prohibition to stop people from drinking and, somewhat paradoxically, critiqued the efforts of reformers to enforce a particular moral viewpoint. "Calisch Condemns Strict Censorship," *RTD*, 4 March 1922, 1, 5.

102. "Salaries of $2,400 to Come from Fees," *RTD*, 12 March 1922, sec. 2, p. 4; "Censorship," editorial, *RTD*, 9 March 1922, 6; "No Morals by Legislation," editorial, *RTD*, 21 March 1922, 6.

103. "The Censors To-Be," editorial, *NVP*, 16 March 1922, 8. Virginia's leading African American paper, the *NJG*, did not comment on the legislation but did object to the board's ban on Oscar Micheaux's *Birthright* in 1926. "Birthright Banned," editorial, *NJG*, 8 March 1926, 12.

104. "Movies and Books," editorial, *Norfolk Ledger-Dispatch*, 10 March 1922, 8.

105. "Calisch Condemns Strict Censorship," 1. The censorship effort in New York had been tinged somewhat with anti-Semitism, and this may have also been a factor in Calisch's opposition. Rosenbloom found that "The fear of an unregulated and increasingly powerful industry, perceived as dominated by Jews, many of foreign birth, provided the context for the passage of the bill," in "From Regulation to Censorship," 389.

106. "National Censorship of Films Proper Plan," *RTD*, 13 March 1922, 3.

107. Jowett, "'Significant Medium,'" 267–71.

108. "Divorce Product of Indecent Dress," *RTD*, 20 February 1922, 3.

109. "Filibuster Threat Furnishes Scare to Bill's Backers," *RTD*, 10 March 1922, 1.

110. *Acts of the General Assembly* 1922, ch. 257.

111. "Filibuster Threat Furnishes Scare," 1.

112. The Florida law did not establish a censorship board but instead required that the New York censors or the National Board of Review pass films before theaters

could show them in Florida. Sklar, *Movie-Made America*, 78–79, 126–32; Jowett, "'Significant Medium.'"

113. Trent, *Inventing the Feeble Mind*, 185–86.

114. A. S. Priddy, quoted in the Deposition of Harry Laughlin in the Circuit Court of Amherst County in the case of *Buck v. Bell*, in Laughlin, *Legal Status of Eugenical Sterilization*, 17.

115. Arnold, "Eugenic Sterilization," 45.

116. Lombardo, "Eugenic Sterilization in Virginia," 155.

117. I have no evidence to suggest that the testimony of Native Americans before the General Assembly on the revision of this act was orchestrated in any way by white legislators, but it seems entirely possible that those concerned with the impact on white elites of eliminating the Pocohontas exception actively recruited Native Americans to bolster their case.

118. Gregory Michael Dorr and J. Douglas Smith make similar observations about upper-class critics of Plecker's legislative agenda, but their focus is different. Dorr argues that the Massenburg bill and the plan to eliminate the Pocohontas exception met with controversy for their impact on "prominent" whites. Smith also concludes that other members of Virginia's white elite did not share the "extremism" of Plecker but adds that they were also concerned that "saddling" African Americans with "humiliating laws" would upset the relative racial calm in the state, for which white elites claimed credit. I would add to these interpretations the importance of considering competing views of the state. Plecker envisioned a more expansive government, a regulatory state that reached into the lives of elites and nonelites alike. Plecker's enthusiasm for state intervention may well have come from the vast authority he claimed for himself as an agent of the state—director of the Bureau of Vital Statistics. See G. Dorr, "Segregation's Science," 550; and J. Douglas Smith, *Managing White Supremacy*, 123–29.

Chapter Two

1. All statistics on sterilization cited here represent officially reported numbers unless otherwise indicated. It is quite likely that some surgeries in Virginia, as in the nation, were not reported. One other Southern state, North Carolina, performed a comparable number of sterilizations. For the period between 1909 and 1953, North Carolina performed over 8,000 sterilizations, more than Virginia and second only to California nationally. Prichard, "Sterilization of the Mentally Deficient," 545; Reilly, *Surgical Solution*, 94, 129–30, 137–38, 157–58; Woodside, *Sterilization in North Carolina*, 20; Schoen, *Choice and Coercion*, 82.

2. See, for example, Darden, "Moral Subnormality"; Garnett, "Birth Control"; and Arnold, "Eugenic Sterilization."

3. Garnett, "Birth Control."

4. See, for example, the procedures followed when Emma Buck, Carrie Buck's mother, was committed in 1920 in Smith and Nelson, *Sterilization of Carrie Buck*, 7–15.

5. "Virginia State Now Regrets Sterilising the 'Feebleminded,'" *Independent* (Lon-

don), 16 February 2001, 17; Michael Ollove, "The Lessons of Lynchburg," *Baltimore Sun*, 6 May 2001, 7F.

6. Bishop, "Sterilization Survivors Speak Out." Mary Odem's work on state attempts to control juvenile delinquents, *Delinquent Daughters*, explores in more detail the interactions between families and the state in such circumstances. She finds many cases in which family members reported adolescent girls for delinquency in her California case-study and argues that families sometimes sought the help of law enforcement in controlling young female family members. On social workers and families in North Carolina sterilization procedures, see Schoen, *Choice and Coercion*, 85–90.

7. "Virginia State Now Regrets," 17; Ollove, "Lessons of Lynchburg," 7F; Bishop, "Sterilization Survivors Speak Out." Schoen concludes that in North Carolina, "most clients of eugenic sterilization programs were poor." *Choice and Coercion*, 90–92.

8. Bell, "Biological Relationship."

9. Arnold, "Brief Review."

10. G. Dorr, "Segregation's Science," 631; Himmstedt, "Not for Their Own Good," 29.

11. Plecker, "Racial Improvement," 488.

12. For a longer discussion of the sterilization of African Americans in Virginia at Central State Hospital, see Himmstedt, "Not for Their Own Good," 26–45.

13. Ibid., 22–27; G. Dorr, "Segregation's Science," 375–449.

14. Bishop, "Sterilization Survivors Speak Out"; "Virginia State Now Regrets," 17; Ollove, "Lessons of Lynchburg," 7F.

15. Commonwealth of Virginia, *Annual Report of Central State Hospital, 1940*, 16.

16. The General Assembly defined the procedure physicians would follow for commitment and sterilization in the sterilization statute. See *Acts of the General Assembly 1924*, ch. 394.

17. Mary Odem discusses how families sometimes used the juvenile justice system to control rebellious daughters in *Delinquent Daughters*, 157–84. For another discussion of family responses to sterilization, see Schoen, *Choice and Coercion*, 84–98.

18. Nationally, women comprised 58 percent of the officially reported sterilizations performed before 1949.

19. Reilly, *Surgical Solution*, 98.

20. Woodside, *Sterilization in North Carolina*, 65–67. In this section, Woodside is specifically referring to opposition to voluntary sterilization, but such attitudes would also have been present when individuals or families were giving their opinion on involuntary sterilization.

21. Ladd-Taylor, "Saving Babies and Sterilizing Mothers"; Schoen, *Choice and Coercion*, 132–57.

22. Philip Reilly comments on these gender disparities in Virginia and other states, noting that women were sterilized more often than men, in *Surgical Solution*, 98. He is correct but fails to note that the rate of male sterilizations actually increased after the 1924 law was passed.

23. Prichard, "Sterilization of the Mentally Deficient," 545.

24. Joseph DeJarnette, "Mendel's Law: A Plea for a Better Race of Men," quoted in Lombardo, "Involuntary Sterilization in Virginia," 19.

25. Woodside, *Sterilization in North Carolina*, 194–95.

26. Studies of eugenic sterilization in other locations include Schoen, *Choice and Coercion*; and Gallagher, *Breeding Better Vermonters*.

27. James, *State Becomes Social Worker*, 64.

28. Ibid., 79–80.

29. James, *Virginia's Social Awakening*, 16, 200–201.

30. James, *State Becomes Social Worker*, 209.

31. "Nazi Virginians Separate Man and Ofay Wife," *Baltimore Afro-American*, 18 June 1938, in reel 57, *TINC*; "3 Couples Run Afoul of Racial Purity Laws," *NJG*, 18 June 1938, in reel 57, *TINC*.

32. "Youth Puzzled over His Race Is Held by Police," *NJG*, 4 June 1938, in reel 57, *TINC*; "3 Couples Run Afoul."

33. "First Test Case under New Race Integrity Law," *NJG*, 28 August 1926, 1; "First Case in VA. under Interracial Act," *Washington Tribune*, 20 August 1926, in reel 25, *TINC*. The assertion that the case was the first under the law may not be true. In November 1924 a judge in Richmond ruled that there was insufficient evidence to prove that Atha Sorrells was part "Negro," due to her having a grandmother listed as such in 1856. "Grandma Negro, Virginian Weds Just the Same," *Baltimore Afro-American*, 24 November 1924, in reel 20, *TINC*. The Dove case was probably the first in which an individual was convicted under the act.

34. "Miscegenation Charge Here Dismissed," *RTD*, 4 February 1949, 2.

35. "Salem Court Suspends Term of Negro, 20, on Race Count," *RTD*, 5 March 1949, 3.

36. "Woman Charges Mate with Being Colored When She Finds Marital Ship on the Rocks," *Pittsburgh Courier*, 12 September 1925, in reel 20, *TINC*; "Says Husband Is Colored after Marital Ship Capsizes," *Louisville News*, 22 August 1925, in reel 20, *TINC*; *Naim v. Naim*, 350 U.S. 985 (1956).

37. "Virginia Race Integrity Law May Be Tested," *Baltimore Herald Commonwealth*, 7 December 1929, in reel 33, *TINC*; "Moved from Phoebus Jail When Crowd Gathers with Spreading of News," *NJG*, 23 November 1929, in reel 33, *TINC*. Umlauf and Whitehead were acquitted by a jury that cited a failure by prosecutors to prove the couple had left the state in order to marry. However, the judge ordered them to leave the area upon release. J. Douglas Smith, *Managing White Supremacy*, 221.

38. Newspaper accounts of violations of the Racial Integrity Act are useful in demonstrating the variety of ways that the law functioned, but there is no way to draw any quantitative conclusions from them, as it is not clear if they are a representative sample of the cases actually prosecuted. The newspaper accounts I have gathered suggest that prosecutions of African American men for marrying white women may have been more common, but the Umlauf and Dove cases demonstrate that prosecutions of white men for marrying nonwhite women did occur. It also appears that men, regardless of race, seem to have been more likely than their wives to serve time in jail for these offenses.

39. G. Dorr, "Segregation's Science," 493; J. Douglas Smith, *Managing White Supremacy*, 90–91.

40. Walter Plecker to Local Registrars, Physicians, Health Officers, Nurses, School Superintendents, and Clerks of Courts, January 1943, MSS 10972, UVSC.

41. G. Dorr, "Segregation's Science," 370–448.

42. Walter Plecker to Mary Gildon, quoted in J. Douglas Smith, *Managing White Supremacy*, 91.

43. Walter Plecker to Mrs. Robert Cheatham, quoted in ibid.; an unnamed but identical letter is quoted in Smith and Nelson, *Sterilization of Carrie Buck*, 62.

44. Plecker, "Racial Improvement," 488.

45. "Negroid Baby Registry as White Noted," *RTD*, 29 September 1931, 1; "Plecker Claims Racial Integrity Statute Is Violated in Virginia," *RTD*, 10 April 1931, 16.

46. Plecker to Local Registrars, Physicians, [etc.], January 1943, UVSC.

47. "Grandma Negro, Virginian Weds Just the Same," *Baltimore Afro-American*, 24 November 1924, in reel 20, *TINC*. For a complete account of this case, see J. Douglas Smith, *Managing White Supremacy*, 92–94. See also G. Dorr, "Segregation's Science," 498–500.

48. "Urges That Race Law Be Modified," *RNL*, 30 December 1931, 1.

49. Plecker, "Eugenics or Race Deterioration," 287.

50. "Plecker Claims Racial Integrity Statute," 16.

51. Ibid.

52. G. Dorr, "Segregation's Science," 498.

53. Ibid., 527.

54. "Substitute Bill Being Sought by Its Opponents," *NJG*, 8 February 1930, 1, 7.

55. Gregory Michael Dorr interprets Plecker's clashes with other white political leaders from a different perspective. He writes that Plecker's opponents agreed with his eugenics agenda but believed in taking a less vicious approach, fearing that extreme measures would exacerbate racial tensions. G. Dorr, "Segregation's Science," 526–28. J. Douglas Smith makes a similar argument, saying that Plecker and other advocates of racial integrity were "excessive," "extremists" who, many believed, could injure "otherwise harmonious race relations," in *Managing White Supremacy*, 78, 97. I agree with this analysis in general, but I believe the conflicting views of government and the state played a central role in these disagreements.

56. "Evan Chesterman Assured of Movie Censorship Position," *RTD*, 17 March 1922, 1.

57. Arnold, "Eugenic Sterilization," 46.

58. *Acts of the General Assembly* 1922, ch. 257.

59. Board of Censors, *Annual Report, 1965*, 3, series 10, box 48, folder 3, DMPC. Though the number of films censored or banned was relatively low, I do not believe that this was due to laxity on the part of the censors. Rather, an awareness of what would and would not pass censorship boards such as Virginia's likely dissuaded filmmakers and marketers from wasting money on the licensing fee for a film that they thought might be rejected.

60. Board of Censors reports on *Girls of the Underworld*, 18 September 1930, series

15, box 53, folder 20, and *The Miracle of Life*, 18 February 1926, series 15, box 54, folder 32, DMPC.

61. Board of Censors report on *The Last Man on Earth*, 29 October 1924, series 15, box 54, folder 52, DMPC.

62. Board of Censors report on *Odor in the Court*, 18 July 1934, series 15, box 54, folder 71, DMPC.

63. Board of Censors report on *The Pace That Kills*, 2 August 1929, series 15, box 54, folder 78, DMPC.

64. Board of Censors report on *After Bedtime*, 16 March 1923, series 15, box 55, folder 3, DMPC.

65. Board of Censors report on *The New Aunt*, 2 May 1929, series 15, box 54, folder 66, DMPC.

66. J. Douglas Smith points out that the board "censored far more films for sexual reasons than racial ones" because far more films "dealt with sexual subjects than racial ones." Nonetheless, the censors monitored films with racial subjects with great care when they did encounter them. J. Douglas Smith, "Patrolling the Boundaries of Race," 273–91.

67. Board of Censors report on *A Son of Satan*, 22 July 1924, series 15, box 55, folder 4, DMPC. For more on Micheaux's dealings with the Board of Censors, see J. Douglas Smith, "Patrolling the Boundaries of Race," 278–87.

68. Board of Censors report on *White Cargo*, 19 June 1930, series 15, box 56, folder 17, DMPC. J. Douglas Smith also reports on the censors' reaction to *White Cargo* in "Patrolling the Boundaries of Race," 285–87.

69. Board of Censors report on *Cracked Wedding Bells*, 5 October 1923, series 15, box 53, folder 90, DMPC. J. Douglas Smith also discusses the mixed views of the censors with regard to *Cracked Wedding Bells* in "Patrolling the Boundaries of Race," 277–79.

70. Board of Censors reports on *The Primrose Path*, 27 September 1930, series 15, box 54, folder 84, and *Three Women*, 4 September 1924, series 15, box 55, folder 19, DMPC.

71. Board of Censors, *Annual Report, 1928–1929*, series 10, box 48, folder 3, DMPC.

72. Board of Censors, *Annual Report, 1965*, 3, series 10, box 48, folder 3, DMPC. The Board of Censors was not the only department in Virginia that brought in funds to the state coffers. Many of the institutions developed under the auspices of the State Board of Charities and Corrections in pre–New Deal Virginia were largely self-supporting, while others provided valuable services to state government. The state benefited from prison labor in the industrial department of the State Farm (where convicts made license tags for Virginia and several other states as well as furniture), the State Convict Road Force, and the State Convict Lime Grinding Plant. Some of these institutions turned profits. Children's homes functioned as industrial schools, bringing in a steady income, and the State Convict Road Force saved the state a significant amount of money by providing low-cost road construction and repair. State leaders paid close attention to the bottom line in these operations. In fact, when the

State Industrial Farm for Women failed to become self-supporting in its early years and its director requested a small share of the annual profits produced by the State Farm for Defective Misdemeanants to round out the budget at the women's institution, state authorities contemplated closing the women's facility because it could not support itself. James, *State Becomes Social Worker*, 53–58, 64–65, 174.

73. Board of Censors, *Annual Report, 1929–1930*, series 10, box 48, folder 3, DMPC.

74. Ibid. The board's papers and reports do not indicate if they passed the films that they could not view. Some films could be screened without the audio, and if the distributor could furnish a script, the censors read the script aloud to each other while they watched the silent film.

75. J. Douglas Smith characterizes those who helped enforce the work of the censors across the state a "vast network of unpaid spies" in "Patrolling the Boundaries of Race," 280.

76. Evan Chesterman to Davis Lee, 25 October 1924, and Davis Lee to Evan Chesterman, 28 October 1924, series 15, box 55, folder 4, DMPC. J. Douglas Smith also mentions Davis Lee's assistance in "Patrolling the Boundaries of Race," 282. The board was disbanded in 1966 after a series of anticensorship decisions by the U.S. Supreme Court, culminating in *Freedman v. Maryland*, 380 U.S. 51, 56 (1965), which set stringent requirements for state licensing procedures. See Jowett, "'Significant Medium,'" 267–71. The last annual report for the Virginia board that I have been able to locate was the one ending in 1965, so I suspect they disbanded without issuing a final report.

77. "Salaries of $2,400 to Come from Fees," *RTD*, 12 March 1922, 1.

78. "Evan Chesterman Assured of Movie Censorship Position," *RTD*, 17 March 1922, 1.

79. A movement for the establishment of these bureaus had formed in the South in the late nineteenth century, though many states failed to develop well-functioning statistics-gathering activities until the 1920s. Link, *Paradox of Southern Progressivism*, 19–23, 223.

80. Sherman, "'Last Stand,'" 70–71.

81. *VDH* 1921, 9; *VDH* 1926, 13.

82. Prichard, "Sterilization of the Mentally Deficient," 545.

Chapter Three

1. O. Anderson, "Progress in the Control of Venereal Diseases," 80–81. Emerging after 1900, the social hygiene movement introduced a new approach to venereal disease control. The earlier movement for social purity had emphasized the moral failure represented by prostitution and worked to reform the women who had fallen into its trap. The growing popularity of eugenic ideology sidelined the purity movement's emphasis on environmental causes of immorality in favor of hereditary explanations. In the new era of social hygiene, prostitutes were considered criminals who threatened public health by their propensity to spread venereal disease. Renaming the Division of Venereal Disease Control reflected this new perspective to the extent that

the social hygiene movement focused more on public education than on repressing particular behaviors. For a full discussion of these two contrasting approaches, see Pivar, *Purity and Hygiene*.

2. O. Anderson, "Progress in the Control of Venereal Diseases."

3. *VDH* 1941, 47–50; "Progress of Venereal Disease Control in Virginia," copy in UVSC.

4. For a full account of venereal disease prevention activities during the First World War, see Bristow, *Making Men Moral*.

5. O. Anderson, "Progress in the Control of Venereal Diseases," 77–78.

6. *VDH* 1931, 44–45; O. Anderson, "Progress in the Control of Venereal Diseases," 77–78.

7. O. Anderson, "Progress in the Control of Venereal Diseases," 79. Edward H. Beardsley points out that venereal disease control experienced similar fates in the 1920s in South Carolina, Georgia, and North Carolina in *History of Neglect*, 171–74.

8. Allan Brandt has noted the apparent conflict in these two trends of increased sexual freedom coupled with decreased discussion of venereal disease. He concludes that Victorian sensibilities persisted to the extent that peacetime discussions of the "unseemly" subject of venereal disease were judged unacceptable, in *No Magic Bullet*, 128–29.

9. Ibid., 123–31; Bristow, *Making Men Moral*, 190–93.

10. Mumford, *Interzones*, 20.

11. "Virginia Health Officer Brands Colored Races as Incapable of Attaining Highest Civilization," *NJG*, 14 February 1925, 1; Richard Bowling, "Entering Wedges of Caste," editorial, *NJG*, 20 February 1925, 12.

12. *VDH* 1929, 35.

13. *VDH* 1927, 23.

14. Jones, *Bad Blood*, 48–49.

15. *VDH* 1927, 23.

16. Ibid., 27.

17. *VDH* 1929, 35.

18. *VDH* 1930, 65–66; *VDH* 1931, 34. The sales to physicians did not cost the state any money and was thus paid for out of the revolving fund.

19. *VDH* 1930, 65.

20. A hint at some disagreement between Williams, Flannagan, and the Board of Health appears in *VDH* 1931, 34–35: "Dr. Flannagan has always been in charge of such social hygiene work as has been attempted by the health department. This work has never had the whole-hearted support of Dr. Williams." Then the report quotes Flannagan: "'This bureau is now the vestigal remains of a once highly developed functioning bureau combating venereal disease by all approved methods. . . . My view is that [the] educational work of the bureau should be restored as soon as possible, as a preliminary to comprehensive attack on the venereal diseases as soon as the opportunity is propitious.'"

21. Thomas Leonard makes this argument in "What Is Virginia Doing to Curb Venereal Disease?," 596–97: "The reason [for ignoring the venereal disease problem]

may be that state officials are sometimes guided by political considerations to some extent, and it is part of the creed of politicians to pass up unpopular campaigns."

22. On the AMA's concern about public health programs, see Brandt, *No Magic Bullet*, 145; Barney, *Authorized to Heal*, 122–51; and Starr, *Social Transformation of American Medicine*, 193–94.

23. "Resolution [1930]"; "Resolution [1939]."

24. *VDH* 1929, 35.

25. Paul Erlich began to successfully treat syphilis with Salvarsan in 1910, and other successful — though potentially dangerous — treatments were soon developed, including mercury and arsenic-based drugs. Brandt, *No Magic Bullet*, 101.

26. Ibid., 130–31.

27. "News Notes," *Virginia Medical Monthly* 55 (November 1928): 589.

28. See, for example, Ransone, "Prevention of Syphilis"; Clark, "Syphilis Problem"; T. Leonard, "What Is Virginia Doing?"; McGinnes and Corpening, "Laboratory Diagnosis of Syphilis"; D. Smith, "Prevention of Syphilis"; Usilton and Riley, "Venereal Disease Prevalence"; and Williams, "Social Significance of Syphilis."

29. Ransone, "Prevention of Syphilis," 83.

30. Brandt, *No Magic Bullet*, 136.

31. D. Smith, "Prevention of Syphilis."

32. Flannagan, "Discussion of Venereal Disease," 31.

33. Ransone, "Prevention of Syphilis," 82.

34. For more on racist framings of venereal disease and the phrase "syphilis-soaked race," see Jones, *Bad Blood*, 16–29.

35. Ibid., 29.

36. Flannagan, "Devil's Masque," 252–55.

37. Ibid., 254.

38. Beardsley, *History of Neglect*, 114–15.

39. Ennion Williams to Mr. Junius [*sic*] Rosenwald, 21 May 1928, box 224, folder 5, JRF.

40. Ibid. For more on the role of the Negro Organization Society of Virginia in local and national health campaigns, see S. Smith, *Sick and Tired*, 36–39.

41. Edwin R. Embree to Ennion Williams, 29 September 1928, box 224, folder 5, JRF.

42. Beardsley describes the political agenda of the Rosenwald Fund (and the Duke Endowment) in *History of Neglect*, 114: "Although each organization chose, perhaps wisely, to work for change within the confines of segregation, both challenged the racial status quo at key points and thus helped prepare the South for the demolition of its segregated health and medical system in the post-war period."

43. Bousfield's travel diary, in which he recorded his experiences traveling through the South while in the employment of the Rosenwald Fund, offers insights into his racial views. See box 9, folder 100, JRF.

44. Williams to Embree, 27 August 1929, box 224, folder 5, JRF.

45. Warren Draper to S. L. Smith, 1 September 1932, and Mary Mastin to Warren Draper, 29 August 1932, box 224, folder 5, JRF. For more on Rosa Taylor and a discus-

sion of the role of African American women in promoting public health in the black community, see S. Smith, *Sick and Tired*, 71–75.

46. Riggin, "Effects upon Virginia," 131–34.

47. "Public Health Activities in Virginia."

48. A. J. Aselmeyer to M. O. Bousfield, 23 October 1940, box 153, folder 1, USPHS.

49. Ibid.

50. Ibid.

51. R. A. Vonderlehr to Taliaferro Clark, 7 April 1932, box 231, folder 10, JRF.

52. Undated letter from Joint Health Department and Rosenwald study, no recipient specified, box 231, folder 10, JRF.

53. Vonderlehr to Michael Davis, 27 April 1934, box 231, folder 10, JRF. Virginia's government sold the drugs at cost to physicians but did not distribute them for free.

54. *VDH* 1929, 35.

55. Clark to Dr. M. M. Davis, 18 November 1930, box 231, folder 10, JRF.

56. Keith Wailoo discusses the connections between politics and growth of a health care system in Memphis, noting how important having access to diseased patients was in furthering the reputations of doctors and medical institutions, in *Dying in the City of the Blues*, 29–40.

57. Garnett, "Syphilis."

58. Vonderlehr, "Syphilis and Gonorrhea."

59. Williams, "Social Significance of Syphilis," 361.

60. *VDH* 1939, 45.

61. Clark to Davis, 26 May 1932, box 231, folder 10, JRF. Though the quote is from Taliaferro Clark, he was communicating how Albemarle County physicians described the benefits of this study.

62. Clark, "Syphilis Problem," 525. Gregory Michael Dorr has pointed out an important connection between advocates of eugenics and venereal disease control in Virginia. Taliaferro Clark and Raymond Vonderlehr were both alumni of the University of Virginia and closely tied to the eugenics movement. They both studied under advocates of eugenics at the University of Virginia Medical School. G. Dorr, "Assuring America's Place," 263–64, 264n20.

63. Clark to Davis, 18 November 1930, box 231, folder 10, JRF.

64. "Results of Rosenwald Demonstrations in the Treatment of Syphilis," unpublished PHS study, 1935, box 153, folder 1, JRF.

65. If hookworm was the "germ of laziness," it stood to reason that laziness itself might function like a germ and be contagious, especially since many whites believed blacks to be predisposed to laziness anyway.

66. For a discussion of the racial and economic correlates of venereal disease infection during the 1910s and 1920s, see Brandt, *No Magic Bullet*, 116–17, 129.

67. James Jones finds that economic arguments often factored into campaigns for venereal disease control in *Bad Blood*, 34.

68. Williams, "Social Significance of Syphilis."

69. Ransone, "Prevention of Syphilis," 79.

70. *VDH* 1938, 45.

71. Brandt, *No Magic Bullet*, 138–44.

72. Jones, *Bad Blood*, 67.

73. A. J. Aselmeyer to M. O. Bousfield, 23 October 1940, describing unpublished PHS study "Results of Rosenwald Demonstrations," box 153, folder 1, JRF.

74. O. Anderson, "Progress in the Control of Venereal Diseases," 80–81; "Report of the Committee of the Medical Society."

75. "State Venereal Drive Is Ready," *RNL*, 27 January 1937, 15.

76. *VDH* 1939, 43.

77. O. Anderson, "Progress in the Control of Venereal Diseases," 80.

78. Surgeon General Thomas Parran to I. C. Riggin, 9 October 1938, box 293, USPHS.

79. Usilton and Vonderlehr, "Prevalence and Incidence of Venereal Diseases," 304.

80. Horsley, "Politics and Medicine"; Barney, *Authorized to Heal*, 59–60.

81. "Progress in the Control of Venereal Disease in Virginia."

82. Riggin, "Syphilis and the Contact Case," 499.

83. O. Anderson, "Progress in the Control of Venereal Diseases," 81–83; "Virginia—Venereal Disease Control Activities as of October 1, 1936," report attached to I. C. Riggin to R. A. Vonderlehr, Assistant Surgeon General, 8 October 1936, box 293, USPHS; "Moral Code Violators to Face Tests," *RNL*, 16 May 1938, 1.

84. Brandt, *No Magic Bullet*, 136.

85. "Syphilis Treatments Show Big Gain," *RTD*, 20 August 1937, 1.

86. Usilton and Vonderlehr, "Prevalence and Incidence of Venereal Diseases."

87. Burney and Vonderlehr, "Venereal Disease Program in Richmond."

88. "Tax Problem 'Alarming' Says Bright, Syphilis Fight Less of a Worry," *RTD*, 4 November 1937, 1.

89. Ibid.

90. Silver, *Twentieth-Century Richmond*, 56–58.

91. "Dr. Upshur to Have Charge of Venereal Control in the City," *RTD*, 1 April 1938, 3; "Report of Venereal Disease Control," *RDPW* 1940, 39.

92. Burney and Vonderlehr, "Venereal Disease Program in Richmond," 311.

93. In 1934 DuPont implemented this program at all its facilities across the nation. Brandt, *No Magic Bullet*, 134; comments of Dr. W. L. Weaver in "Industry vs. Venereal Disease," 90–93; Burney and Vonderlehr, "Venereal Disease Program in Richmond," 311.

94. Comments of Weaver in "Industry vs. Venereal Disease," 90–93.

95. Brandt writes that "City and state health departments continued to pass ordinances requiring the examination for venereal disease of domestics and food handlers, although it was well-known that infections were rarely, if ever, transmitted without intimate sexual contact." Brandt, *No Magic Bullet*, 156.

96. *RDPW* 1938, 85.

97. Ibid., 83; "Plan Employee Health Tests," *RNL*, 22 April 1939, 1, 2.

98. Putting a rosy spin on this situation, Upshur told the *RNL* that the majority of the "servants" found to have venereal disease had been allowed to continue their jobs. "Plan Employee Health Tests," 1, 2.

99. City of Norfolk, *Civic Affairs* (1940 annual report), 52.

100. "Supplemental Report from Division of Venereal Disease Control."

101. Sturkie, "Syphilis in Industry."

102. "Elks Health Week Speaker Wages Fight on Disease," *NJG*, 4 April 1927, 5.

103. For more on African American health organizing, see Gamble, *Making a Place for Ourselves*. Susan L. Smith writes that "Black health activists turned National Negro Health Week into a vehicle for social welfare organizing and political activity in a period where the vast majority of African Americans were without formal political and economic power." S. Smith, *Sick and Tired*, 36–39, 58–71.

104. "Dread Disease," *NJG*, 15 January 1916, in reel 5, *TINC*.

105. For more on this case, see Leavitt, *Typhoid Mary*.

106. Quoted in Manning, "Byrd, David Wellington," 453.

107. S. Smith, *Sick and Tired*, 40–42.

108. A number of documents refer to testing domestic workers in Richmond. The 1938 annual report of the city's venereal disease control officer specifies that "housewives" were expected to oversee this household task. "Report of Venereal Disease Control," *RDPW* 1938, 85.

109. Brandt, *No Magic Bullet*, 156–57.

110. "Report of Venereal Disease Control," *RDPW* 1938, 85.

111. Ibid.

112. T. Leonard, "What Is Virginia Doing?," 599.

113. "Report of Venereal Disease Control," *RDPW* 1938, 83.

114. Conrad, "Discussion of Papers."

115. "Report of Venereal Disease Control," *RDPW* 1938, 87–89; "Report of Venereal Disease Control," *RDPW* 1939, 81–83; "Report of Venereal Disease Control," *RDPW* 1940, 39–44.

116. Burney and Vonderlehr, "Venereal Disease Program in Richmond," 313–14.

117. See, for example, Bynum, *Unruly Women*.

118. The number of individuals who passed through the city jail each year, tabulated by race and sex, is unavailable. But the approximate number of people arrested each year in Richmond during this era numbered around 30,000; on average, about 700 people per year underwent venereal disease testing at the jail or at the request of the police or juvenile courts between 1938 and 1940. Though this data is incomplete and sketchy, it does demonstrate that more African American men underwent testing than any other group. For data on race and gender of arrests, see, for example, *RDPS* 1940, 16.

Chapter Four

1. J. Douglas Smith documents such conflicts around race in Virginia in these decades and documents their connection to challenges to elite rule in *Managing White Supremacy*.

2. F. C. Smith to Thomas Parran, 2 October 1936, box 293, USPHS.

3. Manning, "Byrd, David Wellington."

4. Smith to Parran, 2 October 1936.

5. On private funding for African American health programs in the South in this period, see Beardsley, *History of Neglect*, 101–27.

6. The record is unclear as to the racial background of the city nurse and the WPA worker.

7. Smith to Parran, 2 October 1936.

8. Manning, "Byrd, David Wellington," 453; D. W. Byrd to R. A. Vonderlehr, 22 July 1937, box 293, USPHS.

9. W. R. L. Taylor to Thurston [*sic*] Parran, 21 September 1936, and F. C. Smith to "The Surgeon General," 14 September 1936, box 293, USPHS.

10. Thomas Parran to J. R. Waugh, 12 July 1938, box 295, USPHS.

11. Public Clinic, 1937 annual report and February 1938 monthly report to the Works Progress Administration of Virginia, box 215, folder 1, JRF.

12. Parran to Waugh, 12 July 1938.

13. Thomas Parran to Otis Anderson, 15 June 1938, box 295, USPHS.

14. Robert Olesen to I. C. Riggin, 5 July 1938, box 293, USPHS. Riggin's letter to Olesen is not available, but Olesen wrote Riggin saying he was replying to Riggin's earlier letter in which he cited the problems in "methods of disbursement."

15. The political opinions of PHS officials varied, of course, but Vonderlehr was privately critical of southern white racism. If Virginia's white medical establishment knew of his racial views, that may have fueled their distrust of his intentions in helping Byrd. Vonderlehr discussed his racial views, in particular his opposition to Virginia's interracial marriage law, in a letter to O. C. Wenger, 6 June 1940, box 295, USPHS.

16. "Colored Doctors Claim Unfair Attitude of the City's Health Bureau," *NJG*, 26 January 1924, 1; "Health Clinic Will Be Closed First of May," *NJG*, 19 April 1924, 1.

17. On the relationship between the PHS and the NMA, as well as for a broader discussion of the political ramifications of African American health activism, see S. Smith, *Sick and Tired*, especially 58–81.

18. Thomas Parran to D. W. Byrd, 19 February 1938, box 215, folder 1, JRF.

19. D. W. Byrd to M. O. Bousfield, 10 March 1938, box 215, folder 1, JRF; Manning, "Byrd, David Wellington," 453.

20. Bousfield to A. W. Dumas, 12 July 1940, box 215, folder 4, JRF.

21. A study by an all-white MSV committee that year charged with studying the "problems of negro physicians" concluded that (1) African American physicans did not face barriers to receiving malpractice insurance; (2) African American physicians could attend meetings of the medical society's local branches if these local societies wished to allow this, but they were not welcome in the state-wide group; and (3) access for African Americans to postgraduate work and medical libraries was adequate and slated to improve. "Proceedings, Joint Meeting," 571.

22. Ibid.

23. Virginius Dabney, "The 'Barber Bill' Is with Us Again," *RTD*, 11 February 1934, 5; "No Compromise on This Bill," *RNL*, 21 January 1930, 8.

24. Dabney, "'Barber Bill,'" 5; "Barbers and Health," *RTD*, 21 February 1940, 8.

25. Supporters of the bill later denied making such statements and having such

motivations, according to a 1940 editorial, "Barbers and Health," 8; Dabney, "'Barber Bill,'" 5.

26. "Want Law Stop Race Barbers Serving Whites," *NJG*, 6 February 1926, 1.

27. Dabney, "'Barber Bill,'" 5.

28. Ibid.; "Barbers and Health," 8.

29. "Report of Committee on Legislation and Public Health," 539.

30. Dabney, "'Barber Bill,'" 5.

31. *Acts of the General Assembly* 1918, ch. 300, sec. 5088-a.

32. "Premarital Syphilis Test Bill Tabled," *RTD*, 3 March 1938, 1.

33. "Premarital Test Bill Is Passed by House," *RNL*, 3 February 1940, 1.

34. "Premarital Syphilis Test Bill Tabled," 1; "Report of Committee on Syphilis Control."

35. *Acts of the General Assembly* 1940, ch. 102, sec. 5073-a; Riggin and Holmes, "Evaluation of the Operation"; Holmes, "New Premarital Law."

36. O. Anderson, "Progress in the Control of Venereal Diseases," 86–88; "Report of Committee on Syphilis Control"; "Premarital Syphilis Test Bill Tabled," 1, 4.

37. Riggin and Holmes, "Evaluation of the Operation," 98.

38. Kentucky and Tennessee had also passed such laws by 1940. "Progress in State Legislation," 358–59.

39. Riggin and Holmes, "Evaluation of the Operation."

40. The state health department had begun to expand contact tracing in 1940–41, just as the premarital testing law was passed. O. Anderson, "Progress in the Control of Venereal Diseases," 81–82, 88; *VDH* 1941, 47–50.

41. T. Leonard, "What Is Virginia Doing?," 598.

42. On southern elites and opposition to lynching, see Link, *Paradox of Southern Progressivism*, 58–61.

Chapter Five

1. "News Notes," *Birth Control Review*, May 1924, 153; A. T. McAtee, "Virginia Anti-Birth Control Bill," *Birth Control Review*, June 1924, 182.

2. Dennett, *Birth Control Laws*, 85; McAtee, "Virginia Anti-Birth Control Bill," 182.

3. Dennett, *Birth Control Laws*, 85.

4. For more on "black market" birth control, see Tone, *Devices and Desires*, 67–90.

5. Statement of Paul J. Zentay of the Maternal Health Association, 12 May 1932, Senate Committee on the Judiciary, *Birth Control Hearings*. I have been unable to verify these statistics from Zentay's testimony.

6. Gordon, *Woman's Body, Woman's Right*, 274–76.

7. Plecker, "Racial Improvement."

8. Ibid., 489–90.

9. Ibid., 489.

10. Ibid., 488–89; "Blames Birth Decline on Propaganda," *RNL*, 18 June 1935, 1, 15.

11. Tucker, "Subject of Birth Control."

12. Congress never passed the doctors-only bill. McCann, *Birth Control Politics*, 69–72.

13. Wright Clarkson to Carter Glass, 5 May 1934, reel 82, *Margaret Sanger Papers* (microfilm collection).

14. "State Survey Results."

15. "Woman Physician Advocate of Scientific Birth Control," *RNL*, 22 June 1935, 1, 3.

16. Koste, "Baughman, Mary Barney," 394–96.

17. Ibid., 395. On connections between Virginia eugenic advocates and the Cold Spring Harbor Laboratory, a national center for eugenics research, see G. Dorr, "Segregation's Science," 141–42.

18. "Experts Disagree on Extent of Abortions in Virginia," *RTD*, 7 March 1937, 4.

19. Ibid.

20. Reagan, *When Abortion Was a Crime*, 36–37.

21. "Experts Disagree on Extent," 4.

22. Ibid.

23. Ibid.

24. McCann, *Birth Control Politics*, 101, 106–11.

25. "Virginia Birth Control League Organizes," *Birth Control Review*, July–August 1932, 219; "Here in Interest of Birth Control," *RNL*, 3 February 1933, 16.

26. "Governor Not to Stop Birth Control Talk," *RNL*, 16 May 1933, 1.

27. "Birth Control Fight Leader Will Speak," *RTD*, 14 May 1933, 1.

28. Statement of Paul Zentay, Senate Committee on the Judiciary, *Birth Control Hearings*.

29. "Va. Labor Endorses Control Legislation,"1 *RNL*, 16 May 1933, 1, 13.

30. "1500 Hear Talk on Birth Control," *RNL*, 18 May 1933, 1; "Predicts Clinics on Birth Control Soon in Virginia," *RNL*, 17 May 1933, 1. It is not clear how Sanger concluded that the state's birth rate was increasing, but she did not get this information from the state's Vital Statistics Bureau. According to Plecker, the bureau's director, the birth rate in the state had steadily declined between 1921 and 1929, then remained stationary until 1933, whereupon it began again to decline. See "Blames Birth Decline on Propaganda," *RNL*, 18 June 1935, 1, 15.

31. Harrison, "Quality of Life," 3, copy in UVSC.

32. "Club Women Favor Birth Control Plan," *RTD*, 11 May 1935, 1; "Soldiers' Best Friend," *RTD*, 8 November 1932, 6.

33. "Virginia Committee for Planned Parenthood Is Organized," *RTD*, 31 January 1940, 13.

34. Bagby, "Public Health and Planned Parenthood," 7–8, copy in UVSC.

35. Harrison, "Quality of Life," 1–4.

36. "The Birth Control Report," *RNL*, 21 March 1931, 8.

37. Excerpts from "National Committee on Federal Legislation for Birth Control, Reports on Interviews with Representatives and Senators, 1931–36," reprinted in "Birth Control and the Good Old Boys." The report mistakenly identified Burch as "Birch."

38. "Club Women Favor Birth Control Plan," 1. See also "Birth Control Body to Meet," *RNL*, 13 November 1935, 2.

39. Others across the nation made similar arguments for birth control during the Depression. In fact, birth control pioneer Clarence Gamble opposed New Deal public relief efforts and argued that public money should instead be spent on birth control programs. Critchlow, *Intended Consequences*, 34.

40. Bagby, "Public Health and Planned Parenthood," 5, 7.

41. Hazel Moore, "Meeting Notes, Harry Flood Byrd," 27 April 1934; Carter Glass to "Mrs. Beck", January 1935, quoted in Hazel Moore, "Meeting Notes, Carter Glass"; and Harry F. Byrd to R. W. Garnett, 19 May 1934, all in reel 82, *Margaret Sanger Papers*.

42. *Newsletter of the Virginia League for Planned Parenthood*, December 1941, n.p., copy in UVSC; Harrison, "Quality of Life," 18.

43. C. White, *Roanoke*, 87.

44. Cynthia Addington Boatwright Papers (Ms90-070), Special Collections, Digital Library and Archives, University Libraries, Virginia Polytechnic Institute and State University.

45. Adair, "Letters," 265–66.

46. Martin-Perdue, *Talk about Trouble*, 440n62.

47. Virginia Nursing Organizations: History, <http://www.library.vcu.edu/tml/speccoll/nursing/vnaexdir.html> (accessed 15 November 2005).

48. *Newsletter of the Virginia League for Planned Parenthood*, December 1941, n.p.

49. "Birth Control Centers in the United States," *Birth Control Review*, March 1936, 8. Number of clinics in other southern states: Georgia, four; Arkansas, three; North Carolina, Kentucky, and Tennessee, two each; South Carolina and Alabama, one each; none in Louisiana or Mississippi.

50. "Work of the Virginia League for Planned Parenthood," copy in UVSC.

51. See, for example, Bagby, "Public Health and Planned Parenthood," 5; and Harrison, "Quality of Life," 2.

52. On the Newport News clinic and three other Virginia League for Planned Parenthood clinics in Richmond, Hampton, and Salem in 1931, see Harrison, "Quality of Life," 5.

53. Schoen, "Fighting for Child Health."

54. Harrison, "Quality of Life," 3; Bagby, "Public Health and Planned Parenthood," 3.

55. "Report — Hazel Moore — 1937," box 65, folder 3, and "A Public Health Child-Spacing Program Survey and Analysis of Virginia," by the Birth Control Federation of America, 2 September 1941, box 48, folder 4, Papers of the Planned Parenthood Federation of America, Sophia Smith Collection, Smith College. I am indebted to Johanna Schoen for calling my attention to these documents.

56. "Reports for House of Delegates [1942]"; "Proceedings of the Medical Society [1942]," 695.

57. "Reports for House of Delegates [1946]"; H. Hudnall Ware Jr., "Annual Report, 1946," Virginia League for Planned Parenthood, 1–2; I am indebted to Johanna Schoen for calling my attention to this document.

58. "Public Health Child-Spacing Program Survey."

59. *Newsletter of the Virginia League for Planned Parenthood*, December 1941, n.p. On Garnett, see Chapter 3; on Aubrey Strode, see Chapter 1; on Bagby, see Chapter 6.

60. Bagby, "Public Health and Planned Parenthood"; Plecker, "Racial Improvement," 489.

61. Schoen, "Fighting for Child Health"; Rodrique, "Black Community."

Chapter Six

1. Lutz, *Richmond in World War II*, 38, 59, 67; Dabney, *Richmond*, 328–33; "City Seeking Federal Funds to Attack Venereal Diseases," *RTD*, 18 March 1943, 1, 9.

2. Sims, *Power of Femininity*, 68–70; D'Emilio and Freedman, *Intimate Matters*, 152–54.

3. Sims, *Power of Femininity*, 74–75.

4. Link, *Paradox of Southern Progressivism*, 119–20.

5. D'Emilio and Freedman, *Intimate Matters*, 202–5.

6. Link, *Paradox of Southern Progressivism*, 119–20.

7. Regulating prostitution in this way had its origins in nineteenth-century France. See Corbin, *Women for Hire*.

8. Link, *Paradox of Southern Progressivism*, 121–23; James, *Virginia's Social Awakening*, 114–16; "Probes Point to 120 Houses of Vice in Richmond," *RNL*, 2 March 1915, 1.

9. James, *Virginia's Social Awakening*, 115.

10. Ibid., 116.

11. The new statute allowed civil courts to act against houses of ill fame with injunctions and contempt proceedings. Formerly, only criminal courts could intervene. James, *Virginia's Social Awakening*, 113; "Byrd Arraigns Attackers of His Character," *RNL*, 10 July 1925, 1. Thirty-two states passed "red light abatement laws" between 1909 and 1917. D'Emilio and Freedman, *Intimate Matters*, 210–11.

12. "Mapp Defends Attack on Byrd's Senate Record," *RNL*, 9 July 1925, 1, 3.

13. "Byrd Arraigns Attackers," 1, sec. 2, p. 17; "In the Name of Fair Play," *RNL*, 10 July 1925, 8.

14. For more on the CTCA's moral reform and social hygiene efforts, see Bristow, *Making Men Moral*.

15. Storey, "American Communities," 4.

16. Meyer, *Creating GI Jane*, 101.

17. Brandt, *No Magic Bullet*, 162; Parran and Vonderlehr, *Plain Words about Venereal Disease*, 88–89.

18. Parran and Vonderlehr, *Plain Words about Venereal Disease*, 2, 68.

19. Magee et al., "Relationships of the Army and Navy"; Hegarty, "'Patriots, Prostitutes, Patriotutes,'" 23.

20. "Dr. Bagby Heads Group to Fight Venereal Ills," *RTD*, 2 January 1941, 8.

21. "Bagby Calls for Venereal Disease Drive," *RNL*, 12 March 1941, 1.

22. "Dr. Bagby Heads Group," 8. See also Walter Clarke, "Syphilis, Gonorrhea, and National Defense I."

23. "Bagby Calls for Venereal Disease Drive," 1.

24. "No Syphilis Found among Whites Here," *RNL*, 1 April 1941, 2.

25. Lutz, *Richmond in World War II*, 20; "140 Richmond Men Barred by Syphilis," *RNL*, 15 March 1941, 1. The racial demographics of the original pool of 2,384 draftees is not noted in reports.

26. "No Syphilis Found," 2.

27. 1942 Code of Virginia, sec. 4548f.

28. "Prostitution Bill Change Is Passed," *RTD*, 1 October 1942, 4.

29. Meyer, *Creating GI Jane*, 100–104.

30. K. Anderson, *Wartime Women*, 104–5.

31. Manley H. Simons to Gov. Colgate Darden, 25 September 1942, General Correspondence Files, 1940–43, box 87, NDSE5.

32. *RDPS* 1941, 14; *RDPS* 1942, 16; *RDPS* 1943, 15; *RDPS* 1944, 15; *RDPS* 1945, 17. These records do not tabulate arrests for each crime by gender.

33. K. Anderson, *Wartime Women*, 104–5.

34. Meyer, *Creating GI Jane*, 101–4.

35. I have been unable to locate arrest statistics tabulated by crime and gender, so I do not know the gender of those arrested for prostitution and sex offenses. Over the course of the war years, the arrests for "sex offenses" outstripped those for "prostitution and commercialized vice" for reasons I cannot fully explain. I suspect that police found sex offense charges held up better in court. See *RDPS* 1941, 14; *RDPS* 1942, 16; *RDPS* 1943, 15; *RDPS* 1944, 15; *RDPS* 1945, 17.

36. Treatment protocols for venereal diseases changed frequently during the war years, and different doctors employed different protocols, so it is difficult to know exactly how long patients were held in Richmond facilities. In 1943 the most rapid treatment for syphilis utilized arsenicals and lasted several weeks—perhaps as long as ten weeks, by some methods. Gonorrhea required just a few days of treatment. Scientists recognized during the war that penicillin could cure venereal diseases, but it was not available for widespread use until after 1945. Brown et al., *Syphilis and Other Venereal Diseases*, 14–16.

37. Keve, *History of Corrections in Virginia*, 69, 89–91.

38. Keve asserts this connection between Trinkle's advocacy for women and Youell's request in ibid., 140.

39. Commonwealth of Virginia, *Annual Report of the Penitentiary, 1923*, quoted in Keve, *History of Corrections in Virginia*, 141.

40. James, *State Becomes Social Worker*, 174–75; Hoffer, Mann, and House, *Jails of Virginia*, 126.

41. *Brief Summary of the Work*, 86.

42. Lutz, *Richmond in World War II*, 280; "City Seeking Federal Funds to Attack Venereal Diseases," *RTD*, 18 March 1943, 1, 9; "Hanson Disapproves Use of City Home as Venereal Treatment Center," *RNL*, 24 March 1943, 3,

43. Myrtle Cohen and Alice Harman, "Report on the Richmond, Virginia Labor Market Area," 23, 33, Papers of the Federal Security Agency, Community War Services Region IV, box 215, Records of the Office of Community War Services, Social Protection Division, RG 215, National Archives, College Park, Md.; R. A. Vonderlehr to "The Surgeon General," 20 March 1943, box 293, USPHS.

44. J. R. Heller to Thomas Parran, 31 July 1944, box 293, USPHS; *RDPS* 1941, 14; *RDPS* 1942, 16; *RDPS* 1943, 15; *RDPS* 1944, 15.

45. *RDPS* 1941, 14; *RDPS* 1945, 17. This is not to suggest that the nature of the encounter between African American women and law enforcement did not change. It is likely that more African American women were forced to undergo venereal disease testing, which would have made the arrest experience different from the prewar period.

46. Commonwealth of Virginia, *Annual Report of the Penitentiary, 1939*, 66–67, *Annual Report of the Penitentiary, 1940*, 28, *Annual Report of the Department of Corrections, 1943*, 82–84, *Annual Report of the Department of Corrections, 1945*, 14.

47. Schlegel, *Conscripted City*, 300.

48. The pickup girl campaign echoed a similar panic during the First World War, when public health officials charged that young women had sex with soldiers, spreading venereal disease. Bristow, *Making Men Moral*, 113–19.

49. Marilyn Hegarty argues that wartime venereal disease control measures, coupled with a more general fear of the disorderly potential of female sexuality, led policy makers to collapse the distinction between professional prostitute and sexually active young women, in "'Patriots, Prostitutes, Patriotutes'"; K. Anderson, *Wartime Women*, 104–5.

50. "Official Says Va. Prostitution Costs Navy 18,000 Lost Man Days," *RNL*, 15 October 1942, 1.

51. "Survey Shows 'Amateurs' to Blame in 65%–73% of Army, Navy Venereal Cases," *RNL*, 3 August 1943, 3, 6.

52. "Young Girls Here Drop Moral Standards When They See Uniform, Records Reveal," *RTD*, 21 February 1943, 5.

53. K. Anderson, *Wartime Women*, 96. Marilyn Hegarty also questions the accuracy of wartime statistics on venereal disease and sexual behavior in "'Patriots, Prostitutes, Patriotutes,'" 10–14.

54. "Disease Here Is Due Mainly to 'Pickups,'" *RTD*, 6 August 1943, 5.

55. Meyer, *Creating GI Jane*, 101–6; Gordon, *Heroes of Their Own Lives*, 220. Marilyn Hegarty makes a similar argument about the discipline of middle-class women's sexuality in her study of pickup girls, "'Patriots, Prostitutes, Patriotutes,'" 199–200.

56. For a discussion of the experience of women with the increased scrutiny and discipline of this period, see Hegarty, "'Patriots, Prostitutes, Patriotutes,'" 156–97.

57. "Disease Here Is Due Mainly to 'Pickups,'" 5.

58. "Young Girls Here Drop Moral Standards," 5.

59. "War's Mark on Youth," editorial, *RTD*, 9 October 1942, 12; "Young Girls Here Drop Moral Standards," 5.

60. Elmwood Street, "War and Community, No. 20: The Story of the Brookfield Home for Girls" and "War and Community, No. 21: The Story of the Family Service Society of Richmond," radio broadcasts, WMBG, Richmond, Va., 12 July and 2 August 1942, transcripts in box 37, AW.

61. "Young Girls Here Drop Moral Standards," 5.

62. Virginia Department of Public Welfare, "Annual Report on Social Protection,"

Richmond, Va., July 1943–July 1944, Subject Classification Files, 1944–46, box 215, Records of the Office of Community War Services, Social Protection Division, RG 215, National Archives.

63. "War's Mark on Youth," 12.

64. "Patient Jailed for Refusing Treatment," *RNL*, 17 May 1941, 2.

65. *Opinions of the Attorney General, 1942–1943*, 179–80.

66. "War's Mark on Youth," 12.

67. Elmwood Street, "War and Community, No. 48: The Story of the Phyllis Wheatley Branch YWCA," radio broadcast, WMBG, Richmond, Va., 2 May 1943, transcript in box 37, AW.

68. On racial disparities in health care in the South, see Beardsley, *History of Neglect*, especially 11–41.

69. Lutz, *Richmond in World War II*, 119, 244.

70. Richmond had a bicameral city government until 1947, when a charter revision replaced the thirty-two-member council with a nine-member body. Silver, *Twentieth-Century Richmond*, 177–81.

71. Lutz, *Richmond in World War II*, 244.

72. Karen Anderson points out that law enforcement officials in some other cities across the country were "less than enthusiastic" about juvenile curfew laws because they were "so difficult to enforce consistently," in *Wartime Women*, 103.

73. See, for example, "Mental Hygiene Activities [August 1942]"; and "Mental Hygiene Activities [November 1942]."

74. "Mental Hygiene Activities [April 1942]."

75. "Parenthood Discussed," *RTD*, 26 September 1942, 5.

76. Lutz, *Richmond in World War II*, 184.

77. On the history of the Mosque, see ibid., 22. On community-sponsored dances, see "Welcome Mat Out for Soldiers," *RTD*, 14 February 1943, sec. 4, p. 4; and E. J. Keyes, "Outline of Richmond's Hospitality Program to Members of the Armed Forces," 12 January 1944, 1–7, Richmond War and Community Fund Papers, box 37, AW.

78. Lewis Chewning, Chairman of the Richmond Community Recreation Association, to The Honorable and Mrs. Alexander W. Weddell, July 9, 1943, Executive Committee Minutes, 28 June 1943, Richmond War and Community Fund Papers, box 37, AW.

79. "Welcome Mat Out for Soldiers," 4; Keyes, "Outline of Richmond's Hospitality Program," 3. On gender, sexuality, class, and race in USO senior and junior hostess programs in the United States, see Winchell, "Good Food, Good Fun, and Good Girls."

80. "City Seeking Federal Funds to Attack Venereal Disease," *RTD*, 18 March 1943, 1, 9.

81. "VD Work Expanded by City," *RNL*, 22 July 1943, 1.

Chapter Seven

1. Social Protection Section of the Office of Defense Health and Welfare Services, "Safeguards plus Salvage."

2. Van Urk, "Norfolk," 146; "Norfolk, VA."

3. Parramore, *Norfolk*, 295–96.

4. Wertenbaker, *Norfolk*, 318.

5. Rabinowitz, *First New South*, 120–21.

6. James, *Virginia's Social Awakening*, 109–19.

7. Parramore, *Norfolk*, 332; "Main Street Conditions Are Protested by Navy," *NVP*, 8 November 1940, 12.

8. H. G. Parker to Charles Borland, 1 April 1941, box 136, NCF.

9. Wertenbaker, *Norfolk*, 324–25.

10. Brandt, *No Magic Bullet*, 35–37. See also Bailey, *First Strange Place*.

11. James, *Virginia's Social Awakening*, 114.

12. For a discussion of these issues, see Hodes, *White Women, Black Men*.

13. Schlegel, *Conscripted City*, 184.

14. "White slavery" traditionally referred to the sale of women for prostitution. It came into popularity in the United States in the early twentieth century, entering the legal code with the 1910 White Slave Traffic Act, also known as the Mann Act. See Haag, *Consent*, 63–93.

15. "Authorities Still Silent on Vice Report," *NVP*, 9 May 1936, 16. An *NVP* article from 1940 notes that "Abolition of segregated districts in the city has been tried and ordered before and they have been abolished, theoretically, in previous years." "Segregated District to Go, Borland," *NVP*, 8 November 1940, 12. However, I have come across no evidence of such efforts, except the events of 1936, and I am suspicious that these vague claims may have been simply part of the rhetoric used by opponents of the district's abolition.

16. Schlegel, *Conscripted City*, 11–12.

17. "Segregated District to Go," 12.

18. Brandt, *No Magic Bullet*, 166–67.

19. "Segregated District to Go," 12; Statement of John J. Hurley, *ICA*, 345.

20. "Vice — Regulation of," editorial, *NVP*, 8 November 1940, 7.

21. "Raids Are Made on East Main Street Houses," *NVP*, 14 January 1941, 1.

22. Edwin James Cooley, the Federal Security Agency's regional representative in Seattle, reported on this issue in a letter to Eliot Ness, director of the Social Protection Section. Cooley to Ness, 8 July 1943, General Records, 1942–56, box 4, Records of the Office of Community War Services, Social Protection Division, RG 215, National Archives.

23. "Norfolk, VA"; Davenport, "Norfolk Night"; Van Urk, "Norfolk," 148.

24. "Norfolk, Sinful Place? What of It? It Queries," *NVP*, 22 March 1942, sec. 2, p. 1.

25. "Norfolk: Enemy Hasn't Raided Us but Out of Town Writers Have," *NVP*, 27 June 1942, 16.

26. "Norfolk: Enemy Hasn't Raided Us"; "Norfolk, Sinful Place?," 1.

27. "Reaction Here Divided on Magazine Article," *NVP*, 19 June 1942, sec. 2, p. 12.

28. "Prostitution Fight Pledged in This Area," *NVP*, 9 July 1942, 20.

29. ComFive, Fifth Naval District, memorandum to "All Activities," 8 July 1944, Past Director's Activities, box 10, NDSE5.

30. Social Protection Section, "Safeguards plus Salvage," 44. Italics in original.

31. "Jail Room to Hold 45 Women Now Has 110 Confined in It," *NVP*, 17 July 1942, sec. 2, p. 18.

32. "Prostitution Fight Pledged," 20.

33. For example, in a letter dated 21 May 1941, the Norfolk chief of police, John F. Woods, wrote the following to City Manager Borland about suspended sentences: "I took this subject up at a recent conference with the City Manager and explained to him that I had requested Judge Jacob to use whatever means he possibly could to cut down the increase in the number of women in the City Jail and by imposing suspended sentences and the Judge, with a few exceptions, has complied with my request." Woods to Charles Borland, 21 May 1941, box 136, NCF.

34. The SPD criticized this approach in print and said the division and the FBI sought to stop cities from doing this. Social Protection Section, "Safeguards plus Salvage," 43.

35. "Prostitution Problem Put before State," *NVP*, 26 June 1942, 11. Newspapers claimed that this worked—that few women were rearrested after this. However, there is no evidence to support this claim and some to refute it, such as reports that many of the women arrested in the October 1942 raid in Norfolk County had been arrested before. "52 Tourist Cabin Vice Raid Cases Draw $2,060 in Fines, 438 Months in Sentences," *NVP*, 20 October 1942, 20.

36. The SPD opposed the tactic of expelling accused prostitutes from the city in "Safeguards plus Salvage," 43.

37. Charles Borland to C. L. Vickers, 7 September 1944, box 169, NCF.

38. H. G. Parker to Borland, 1 April 1941, box 135, NCF.

39. James, *Virginia's Social Awakening*, 118–19.

40. Estelle Freedman discusses the expansion of women's prisons during the First World War and notes that less than half of the women's prisons established during the war remained open after 1920, in *Their Sister's Keepers*, 147. Nicole Hahn Rafter observes that southern states and cities were more likely to use temporary facilities to jail women, facilities that could close or move as the situation necessitated and funding allowed, in *Partial Justice*, 97–98.

41. Borland to Parker, 29 March 1941, box 136, NCF.

42. Parker to Borland, 1 April 1941, box 135, NCF.

43. Memorandum on meeting held in the office of Norfolk city manager, 1 November 1944, box 169, NCF.

44. Parker to Borland, 1 April 1941.

45. Borland to Parker, 29 March 1941.

46. Schlegel, *Conscripted City*, 333–34.

47. "Use of Old Jail Quarters City's Aim until New Plant Is Built at Welfare Center," *NVP*, 11 July 1945, 18.

48. In 1942 I. C. Riggin reported at a conference in Norfolk that the venereal disease infection rate in the city had dropped consistently since 1939. "Prostitution Fight Pledged in This Area," *NVP*, 9 July 1942, 20.

49. Carter, "New Patterns of Venereal Disease Control," 214.

50. Borland to Gov. Colgate Darden, 29 July 1942, box 163, NCF.

51. "Vice Attacked in Other Navy Ports as Washington's Concern Increases, Norfolk Will Welcome Federal Help," *NVP*, 24 February 1943, sec. 2, p. 1; "A New Climax of Futility," editorial, *NVP*, 20 March 1943, 14.

52. W. F. Draper to Rear Admiral Manley H. Simons, 12 May 1943, box 293, USPHS.

53. "New Climax of Futility," 14.

54. Ibid.; R. A. Vonderlehr to "The Surgeon General," 20 March 1943, box 293, USPHS; Statement of John J. Hurley, *ICA*, 347–48.

55. "New Climax of Futility," 14; Schlegel, *Conscripted City*, 131; R. A. Vonderlehr to Director of District No. 2, 17 September 1942, box 293, USPHS. See also Statement of Hurley, 347–48; and Testimony of Manley H. Simons, *ICA*, 25.

56. W. F. Draper to Manley H. Simons, 22 May 1943, box 293, USPHS.

57. Draper to Simons, 22 May 1943; Hegarty, "'Patriots, Prostitutes, Patriotutes,'" 66–67, 100–101.

58. The PHS "disapproved the application on the ground that the facility was corrective rather than medical." Statement of Hurley, 347.

59. Portions of the city were placed out of bounds in the 1930s. See, for example, Fifth Naval District Order No. 11, 5 August 1933, and Fifth Naval District Order No. 13, 12 July 1934, General Correspondence Files, 1926–40, box 95, NDSE5.

60. Memorandum to the Commandant, Fifth Naval District, from the District Naval Officer, 10 June 1941; Fifth Naval District Order No. 27, 19 June 1941; Fifth Naval District Order No. 2 [correction to], 1 March 1943, Past Director's Activities, box 10, NDSE5. See also Correspondence, 1940–43, box 87, and Records of the Newport News Shipyard, Correspondence, 1941–46, box 186, NDSE5.

61. Schlegel, *Conscripted City*, 323.

62. "Shore Patrol Seen Improving Navy Relations," *NVP*, 7 November 1942, 2; Statement of Hurley, 345–46.

63. Schlegel, *Conscripted City*, 232–33.

64. Ibid., 234; "Total of 115 Persons Arrested as Police and Navy Authorities Stage Sudden Raids in County," *NVP*, 19 October 1942, 14. The investigation would reveal the vast corruption in the county that rendered the police all but inactive in vice control.

65. "Navy, Police Nab 115 in Raid near Norfolk," *New York Times*, 19 October 1942, 6.

66. "Total of 115 Persons Arrested," 14.

67. As for the fates of the three other civilian men arrested, one, an African American employee of one establishment, received a $500 fine; a second was released, along with his female consort, when they proved they were married; and the judge set the third free when he proved he was a taxi driver delivering sandwiches to a customer. Some of the women unaccounted for above were fined—those who had never been arrested before were more likely to get this more lenient treatment—and others were released for various reasons. "52 Tourist Cabin Vice Raid Cases Draw $2,060 in Fines, 438 Months in Sentences," *NVP*, 20 October 1942, 20.

68. "Bail Refused Appellants in Vice Roundup," *NVP*, 21 October 1942, 20.

69. Schlegel, *Conscripted City*, 234.

70. "When Law Enforcement and Politics Mix," *NVP*, 4 March 1944, 10; Parramore, *Norfolk*, 342–43; Schlegel, *Conscripted City*, 324–425.

71. Hall, "Crisis at Hampton Roads," 411.

72. Robert Moses, "Covering Report," in Andrews and Skidmore, *Survey of Congested War Production Areas*, 9–10, Army and Navy Munitions Board Secret and Confidential Correspondence, 1922–45, entry 5, box 47, RG 225, National Archives, College Park, Md., 14–17. I am indebted to Phyllis Hall for providing me with a copy of this document.

73. W. Earle Andrews and Louis Skidmore, "Survey of Congested Areas of War Production, Norfolk, Virginia, Area," in Andrews and Skidmore, *Survey of Congested War Production Areas*, 17.

74. Moses, "Covering Report," 2.

75. Ibid.

76. Ibid., 4.

77. Ibid., 4–17.

78. Ibid., 17.

79. Hall, "Crisis at Hampton Roads."

80. "Girls behind Norfolk Jail Bars Visited by Congresswoman, Cells Found Clean but Crowded," *NVP*, 27 March 1943, 20.

81. Naval Affairs Investigating Committee, *Investigation of Congested Areas*, 643–45.

82. Ibid.

83. Ibid.

84. Hall, "Crisis at Hampton Roads," 425.

85. "Federal Area Post Is Given to Hummell," *NVP*, 22 May 1943, 16; "Leary Given Command of Navy District," *NVP*, 23 May 1943, sec. 2, p. 1.

86. Testimony of Charles Borland, *ICA*, 3.

87. The one specific item that federal and local officials failed to implement was the establishment of mess halls for servicemen in the downtown area. However, as I discuss, the recommendations regarding venereal disease were only partly followed. Schlegel, *Conscripted City*, 255–63; Parramore, *Norfolk*, 338–40; "Thanks to the Izac Committee," *Norfolk Ledger-Dispatch*, 12 October 1943, 6. Hall gives more detail on the improvements made in Norfolk in the ensuing years in "Crisis at Hampton Roads," 425–31.

88. W. F. Draper to Rear Admiral Manley H. Simons, 12 May 1943, box 293, USPHS.

89. Schlegel, *Conscripted City*, 256. Some African American men may have been part of the shore patrol earlier, according to one history of the city, but the addition of fifty men in 1943 was the first time a significant number of African Americans were involved. "Virginia Belles," typescript, n.d., reel 12, NWHC.

90. Schlegel, *Conscripted City*, 274–78.

91. Ibid., 322–33.

92. Ibid., 323.

93. Article in *NJG*, 13 November 1943, quoted in ibid., 323.

94. Ibid., 324.

95. Ibid., 274.

96. Ibid., 300.

97. "Five State Medical Centers Now Operating in Drive against Venereal Disease," *RTD*, 18 June 1944, sec. 2, p. 1.

98. Ibid.

99. Council of Social Agencies, "The Venereal Disease Control Program of Norfolk [1944]," reel 6, NWHC.

100. "Use of Old Jail Quarters City's Aim until New Plant Is Built at Welfare Center," *NVP*, 11 July 1945, 18; "Five State Medical Centers," 1.

101. Minutes, meeting of Norfolk Citizens Venereal Disease Control Committee, 9 April 1944, reel 6, NWHC.

102. Schlegel, *Conscripted City*, 341; undated list of committee assignments and activities, Papers of the Norfolk Citizens Venereal Disease Control Committee, reel 6, NWHC. Some pictures of the displays appear in Bell and Pariser, "Norfolk Faces an Issue," 422–25.

103. Undated list of committee assignments and activities. On Diggs and Bowling, see Lewis, *In Their Own Interests*, 38, 70–71.

104. Undated list of committee assignments and activities.

105. Lewis, *In their Own Interests*, 154–55.

106. Bell and Pariser, "Norfolk Faces an Issue," 429.

107. Lewis, *In their Own Interests*, 154–55, 197. For more accounts of African Americans using health activism to further the struggle for civil rights, see S. Smith, *Sick and Tired*.

108. James, *Virginia's Social Awakening*, 118; Schlegel, *Conscripted City*, 333–34.

109. "Council Defers Decision on VD Publicity Fund," *Norfolk Ledger-Dispatch*, 30 August 1944, 8.

110. "Use of Old Jail Quarters City's Aim until New Plant Is Built at Welfare Center," *NVP*, 11 July 1945," 18.

111. For example, in July 1942 the state health commissioner asserted that the venereal disease infection rate in Norfolk had dropped 33 percent since 1939. "Prostitution Fight Pledged in This Area," *NVP*, 9 July 1942, 20. In 1943 Manley H. Simons, the commander of the Fifth Naval District, said that vice in Norfolk was no worse than in other similar communities. "Vice Here Held No Worse than in Other Ports," *NVP*, 25 February 1943, 22.

112. For example, in an editorial in the *NVP* calling for greater anti–venereal disease efforts, the paper cited a naval official's claim that Virginia had the worst record in the nation for spreading venereal disease among troops. "The Raid on the Assignation Cabins," *NVP*, 21 October 1942, 6. Alexander Bell wrote that the city was experiencing an "alarming increase in the number of infectious cases of venereal disease."

Alexander Bell to Richard Marshall, coordinator of the Office of Civilian Defense, 1 April 1944, Papers of the Norfolk Citizens Venereal Disease Control Committee, reel 6, NWHC.

113. On decreasing numbers of infections occurring in Norfolk, see Carter, "New Patterns of Venereal Disease Control," 213. Alexander Bell pointed to increasing applications for venereal disease treatment in "Norfolk Faces an Issue," 9.

114. In 1944 a local physician told a group of officials that syphilis cases in the city had increased 31 percent and gonorrhea by 185 percent between 1932 and 1943. Schlegel, *Conscripted City*, 301. A 1945 navy report found that one-half of venereal infections among servicemen in that naval district were contracted in the Norfolk area. "Historical Analysis of the District Medical Officer for the Period 1 September 1945 to 1 October 1946," History of the Fifth Naval District and Naval Base Activities, 1939–46, box 3, NDSE5.

115. Moses, *Survey of Congested War Production Areas*, 7; House Naval Affairs Investigating Committee, *Investigation of Congested Areas*, 644.

116. House Committee, *Investigation of Congested Areas*, 644.

117. See Mumford, *Interzones*; Hodes, *White Women, Black Men*; and Chauncey, *Gay New York*.

Epilogue

1. Brandt, *No Magic Bullet*, 170–71.

2. House Committee on Military Affairs, *Hearings*, 1 May 1945.

3. Minutes, Interdepartmental Committee on Venereal Disease, 12 September 1945, transcript in Committee Meetings, box 2, Records of the Office of Community War Services, Social Protection Division, RG 215, National Archives.

4. For more on plans for full employment after the war, see Brinkley, *End of Reform*, 227–64.

5. Minutes, Interdepartmental Committee on Venereal Disease, 25–26.

6. Ibid., 38–41.

7. Ibid.

8. Parramore, *Norfolk*, 354.

9. "Norfolk Rates Worst in V.D., Was 3rd Best," *NVP*, 9 November 1948, 28; "V.D. Control Efforts Win Full Backing," *NVP*, 10 November 1948, 28; "The Edwards Report on Norfolk's V.D. Rating," *NVP*, 11 November 1948, 6, 28; "High V.D. Rate Pertained to Men in Navy," *NVP*, 12 November 1948, 40. For a discussion of the varied statistics concerning the city's venereal disease rate, see Chapter 7.

10. "Norfolk Rates Worst in V.D.," 28; "Edwards Report," 6, 28; "High V.D. Rate," 40.

11. "Tavern Owners Here Organize Joint V.D. Clinic," *NVP*, 26 November 1948, 28; "City Disavows Any Sanction of V.D. Clinic," *NVP*, 27 November 1948, 18; "Let the Tavern Owners Think Up Something Better," editorial, *NVP*, 27 November 1948, 6.

12. "Venereal Infections Only in Small Degree Traceable to Organized Prostitution, Declares Report, Which Cites Navy Figures on 'Pick-ups,'" *NVP*, 28 November 1948, 1, sec. 2, p. 2.

13. City of Richmond, *Annual Report of the Department of Public Health, 1946*, 36.

14. "V.D. Center Faces Slash in U.S. Funds," *RNL*, 13 February 1947, 1B; "V.D. Hospital Closes, Staff Transferred," *RNL*, 1 July 1947, 19.

15. *VDH* 1950, 45.

16. "Social Uplift of V.D. Girls Given Up Here," *RNL*, 29 July 1946, 1B.

17. See, for example, Freedman, "'Uncontrolled Desires'"; Johnson, *Lavender Scare*; and Friedman, "Sadists, Sissies."

18. Prichard, "Sterilization of the Mentally Deficient"; Reilly, *Surgical Solution*, 128–29, 185.

19. G. Dorr, "Principled Expediency"; *Naim v. Naim*, 350 U.S. 985 (1956).

20. Reapportionment followed a 1964 Supreme Court decision, *Reynolds v. Sims*, 377 U.S. 533 (1964), which held that seats of state legislatures must be apportioned on a population basis. In Virginia this decision brought more electoral power to urban areas where the Byrd machine had been historically weak. Wilkinson, *Harry Byrd and the Changing Face of Virginia Politics*, 248–49.

21. In 1962 Virginia still had the lowest gross tax burden in the nation, and a study the previous year found that Virginia's expenditures per pupil for schools in relation to per capita income placed the state last among the forty-eight states surveyed. Wilkinson, *Harry Byrd*, 241.

22. Ibid., 273–301.

23. Goldfield, *Promised Land*, 28–31.

24. Reilly, *Surgical Solution*, 150.

25. Ibid., 148–52.

26. Ibid., 152–57; "Va. Apologizes to the Victims of Sterilizations," *Washington Post*, 3 May 2002, B01.

27. *Burstyn v. Wilson*, 343 U.S. 495 (1952).

28. Jowett, "'Significant Medium'"; *Freedman v. Maryland*, 380 U.S. 51 (1965).

29. Wadlington, "*Loving* Case"; *Loving v. Virginia*, 388 U.S. 1 (1967). The other states whose laws the decision invalidated were Alabama, Arkansas, Delaware, Florida, Georgia, Kentucky, Louisiana, Mississippi, Missouri, North Carolina, Oklahoma, South Carolina, Tennessee, Texas, and West Virginia.

30. Brandt, *No Magic Bullet*, 174.

31. Repeal of the premarital venereal disease test is *Acts of the General Assembly* 1984, ch. 140. HB 1135 Marriage Blood Test was introduced 25 January 1994 by Delegate Harry R. Purkey of Virginia Beach.

32. Fellner and Mauer, *Losing the Vote*. In 2003 Virginia passed legislation that permits circuit courts to restore voting rights to ex-offenders who petition for their restoration. I would argue that this process still presents a significant obstacle to reinfranchisement for many Virginians. Furthermore, restoration of voting rights depends on the court's judgment that the individual has demonstrated "civil responsibility." In short, reinfranchisement is both cumbersome and capricious. *Acts of the General Assembly* 2003, ch. 946, states: "[The] court may approve the petition for restoration to the person of his right if the court is satisfied from the evidence presented that the petitioner has completed, five or more years previously, service of any sentence and

any modification of sentence including probation, parole, and suspension of sentence; that the petitioner has demonstrated civic responsibility through community or comparable service; and that the petitioner has been free from criminal convictions, excluding traffic infractions, for the same period."

33. Bazelon, "Sentencing by the Numbers"; *Opinions of the Attorney General of Virginia*, Opinion 01–002, 24 April 2001, <http://www.oag.state.va.us/media%20center/Opinions/2001opns/apr01ndx.htm> (accessed 25 October 2005); Kern and Farrar-Owens, "Sentencing Guidelines."

Bibliography

Manuscript Collections
Charlottesville, Virginia
University of Virginia, Alderman Library
  The Albert and Shirley Small Special Collections Library

College Park, Maryland
National Archives at College Park
  Records of the United States Public Health Service, Group 3: States 1936–1944,
    RG 90
  Records of the Office of Community War Services, Social Protection Division,
    RG 215

Nashville, Tennessee
Fisk University, John Hope and Aurelia E. Franklin Library
  Papers of the Julius T. Rosenwald Fund

Norfolk, Virginia
Norfolk Records Management Division
  Norfolk World War II History Commission Papers, microfilm

Philadelphia, Pennsylvania
National Archives Mid-Atlantic Region
  Records of Naval Districts and Shore Establishments, Fifth Naval District,
    Norfolk, Va., RG 181

Richmond, Virginia
Library of Virginia
  Norfolk Central Files
  Records of the Virginia Division of Motion Picture Censorship, RG 53
Richmond Public Library
  City Records Center/Archives
Virginia Historical Society
  Alexander Weddell Papers

Manuscript Collections on Microfilm

Bureau of Social Hygiene. *The Bureau of Social Hygiene Project and Research Files, 1913–1940: A Collection of the Rockefeller Archive Center of the Rockefeller University*. Wilmington, Del.: Scholarly Resources, 1980.

The Margaret Sanger Papers: Collected Documents Series. Edited by Esther Katz, Cathy Moran Hajo, and Peter C. Engelman. Bethesda, Md.: University Publications of America, 1996.

Tuskegee Institute News Clippings File. Edited by John W. Kitchens. Carver Research Foundation, Tuskegee Institute. Sanford, N.C.: Microfilming Corp. of America, 1981.

Newspapers and Journals

Birth Control Review
Independent (London)
Newport News Daily Press
New York Times
Norfolk Journal and Guide
Norfolk Ledger-Dispatch
Norfolk Virginian-Pilot
Richmond News Leader
Richmond Planet
Richmond Times-Dispatch
Virginia Medical Monthly

Government Documents

Andrews, W. Earle, Louis Skidmore, and Madigan-Hyland, under the direction of Robert Moses. *Survey of Congested War Production Areas for the Army and Navy Munitions Board*. 15 January 1943.

A Brief Summary of the Work of the Several Departments of Government. Printed as an Addition to the Address of Governor Colgate W. Darden. Delivered before the General Assembly of the Commonwealth of Virginia, 9 January 1946.

City of Norfolk. *Annual Reports of the City Manager*. Norfolk, 1939–46.

City of Richmond. *Annual Reports of the Department of Public Health*. Richmond, 1942–46.

———. *Annual Reports of the Department of Pubic Safety*. Richmond, 1940–45.

———. *Annual Reports of the Department of Public Welfare*. Richmond, 1935–41.

Commonwealth of Virginia. *Acts of the General Assembly of the Commonwealth of Virginia*. Richmond: Division of Purchase and Printing, 1918–2003.

———. *Annual Report of Central State Hospital, 1940*. Richmond: Division of Purchase and Printing, 1941.

———. *Annual Reports of the Department of Corrections*. Richmond: Division of Purchase and Printing, 1943–45.

———. *Annual Reports of the Department of Health*. Richmond: Division of Purchase and Printing, 1921–50.

————. *Annual Reports of the Department of Public Welfare*. Richmond: Division of Purchase and Printing, 1943–44.

————. *Annual Reports of the Penitentiary*. Richmond: Division of Purchase and Printing, 1939–40.

————. *Opinions of the Attorney General and Report to the Governor of Virginia*. Richmond: Division of Purchase and Printing, 1943.

Laughlin, Harry. *The Legal Status of Eugenical Sterilization*. Supplement to the Annual Report of the Municipal Court of Chicago. Chicago, 1929.

U.S. Congress. House. Committee on Military Affairs. *Hearings before the Committee on Military Affairs*. 79th Cong., 1st sess., 1 May 1945.

————. Committee on Naval Affairs. *Investigation of Congested Areas, Part I, Hampton Roads: Hearings before a Subcommittee of the Committee on Naval Affairs*. 78th Cong., 1st sess., 24–27 March 1943.

————. Naval Affairs Investigating Committee. Subcommittee Appointed to Investigate Vice Conditions in the Vicinity of Naval Establishments. *Investigation of Congested Areas, I: Report on Hampton Roads Area*. 78th Cong., 1st sess., 1943.

————. Senate. Committee on the Judiciary. *Birth Control Hearings before the Subcommittee of the Committee on the Judiciary*. 72nd Cong., 1st sess., 1932.

Federal Court Cases

Buck v. Bell, 274 U.S. 200 (1927).

Loving v. Virginia, 388 U.S. 1 (1967).

Naim v. Naim, 197 Va. 80, 87 S.E. 2d 749 (Virginia Supreme Court, 1955), vacated and remanded, 350 U.S. 891 (U.S. Supreme Court 1955), reinstated and affirmed, 197 Va. 734, 90 S.E. 2d 849 (Virginia Supreme Court), appeal dismissed, 350 U.S. 985 (U.S. Supreme Court 1956).

Primary Source Articles, Reports, and Pamphlets

Anderson, Otis. "Progress in the Control of Venereal Diseases in Virginia." *Venereal Disease Information* 224 (March 1941): 79–87.

Arnold, G. B. "A Brief Review of the First Thousand Patients Eugenically Sterilized at the State Colony for Epileptics and Feebleminded." *Proceedings of the American Association on Mental Deficiency*, no. 43 (1938): 56–63.

————. "Eugenic Sterilization of the Epileptic and Mentally Deficient." *Virginia Medical Monthly* 67 (January 1940): 45–47.

Bagby, Bathurst B. "Public Health and Planned Parenthood." Pamphlet produced by the Virginia League for Planned Parenthood, n.d. (c. 1941).

Bell, Alexander, and Harry Pariser. "Norfolk Faces an Issue: A Progress Report on Social Hygiene Efforts in a 'War Congested' Area." *Journal of Social Hygiene* 31 (October 1945): 420–30.

Bell, J. H. "The Biological Relationship of Eugenics and the Development of the Human Race." *Virginia Medical Monthly* 57 (February 1931): 727–33.

Burney, L. E. and R. A. Vonderlehr. "The Venereal Disease Program in Richmond with Recommendations for Suggested Changes." *Virginia Medical Monthly* 64 (September 1937): 307–16.

Carrington, Charles V. "Sterilization of Habitual Criminals, with Report of Cases." *Virginia Medical Semi-Monthly* 13 (December 11, 1908): 379–80.

———. "Sterilization of Habitual Criminals." *Virginia Medical Semi-Monthly* 14 (December 24, 1909): 421–22.

Carter, T. J. "New Patterns of Venereal Disease Control as Seen by the Navy Medical Officer." *Journal of Social Hygiene* 29 (April 1943): 210–19.

Clark, Taliaferro. "The Syphilis Problem." *Virginia Medical Monthly* 60 (December 1933): 524–31.

Clarke, Walter. "Syphilis, Gonorrhea, and National Defense I." *Journal of Social Hygiene* 26 (November 1940): 341–43.

Conrad, C. E. "Discussion of Papers by Drs. Smith, Newcomb, Coleman, and Ransone in Symposium on Syphilis." *Virginia Medical Monthly* 58 (May 1931): 84.

Darden, O. B. "Moral Subnormality as an Expression of Mental Unsoundness." *Virginia Medical Monthly* 58 (March 1932): 773–76.

Davenport, Walter. "Norfolk Night." *Collier's Weekly*, 28 March 1942, 17–18.

Federal Works Agency, Work Projects Administration for the District of Columbia. *Slave Narratives: A Folk History of Slavery in the United States from Interviews with Former Slaves.* Project Gutenberg Etext number 13847, <http://www.gutenberg.org/etext/13847>.

Flannagan, Ray. "The Devil's Masque — a Dream." *Virginia Medical Monthly* 52 (July 1925): 252–55.

———. "Discussion of Venereal Disease Prevalence in Virginia." *Virginia Medical Monthly* 54 (April 1927): 31.

Garnett, R. W. "Birth Control, a Social and Economic Need." *Virginia Medical Monthly* 61 (May 1934): 106–8.

———. "Syphilis — a Major Social Problem." *Virginia Medical Monthly* 63 (February 1937): 653–56.

Harrison, Mrs. Carter H. "The Quality of Life." Pamphlet produced by the Virginia League for Planned Parenthood. Reprinted in *Virginia Club Woman*, April 1941, 1–4.

Holmes, E. M. "The New Premarital Law." In *Papers and Addresses, Annual Conference of State Health Workers*, 46–50. Richmond: Virginia State Department of Health, 1940.

Horsley, J. Shelton. "Politics and Medicine." *Virginia Medical Monthly* 52 (April 1925): 56–58.

"Industry vs. Venereal Disease: A Program — of Education and Action Offered in Connection with the 73rd Annual Meeting of the American Public Health Association." *Journal of Social Hygiene* 31 (February 1945): 83–100.

Leonard, Thomas. "What Is Virginia Doing to Curb Venereal Disease?" *Virginia Medical Monthly* 61 (January 1935): 596–97.

Magee, James, Ross McIntire, Charles P. Taft, Thomas Parran, and William Snow.

"Relationships of the Army and Navy, the U.S. Public Health Service, the Office of Defense Health and Welfare Services, and the American Social Hygiene Association." *Journal of Social Hygiene* 29 (February 1943): 100–105.

McGinnes, G. F., and Adah Corpening. "Laboratory Diagnosis of Syphilis." *Virginia Medical Monthly* 57 (December 1930): 584–86.

"Mental Hygiene Activities." *Virginia Medical Monthly* 69 (April 1942): 214–15.

"Mental Hygiene Activities." *Virginia Medical Monthly* 69 (August 1942): 455.

"Mental Hygiene Activities." *Virginia Medical Monthly* 69 (November 1942): 631–32.

Newsletter of the Virginia League for Planned Parenthood. December 1941.

"Norfolk, VA: 'Confusion, Chicanery, Ineptitude.'" *Architectural Forum* 76 (June 1942): 366–72.

Plecker, W. A. "Eugenics or Race Deterioration — Which?" *Virginia Medical Monthly* 52 (August 1925): 282–88.

———. "The New Family and Racial Improvement." Pamphlet produced by the Bureau of Vital Statistics. Richmond, 1928.

———. "Racial Improvement." *Virginia Medical Monthly* 52 (November 1925): 486–90.

Prichard. W. I. "Sterilization of the Mentally Deficient in Virginia." *American Journal of Mental Deficiency* 53 (April 1949): 542–45.

"Proceedings, Joint Meeting, Medical Society of Virginia and West Virginia State Medical Association." *Virginia Medical Monthly* 67 (September 1940): 570–75.

"Proceedings of the Medical Society of Virginia Annual Meeting, 1942." *Virginia Medical Monthly* 69 (December 1942): 683–97.

"Progress in State Legislation to Protect Marriage from Syphilis." *Journal of Social Hygiene* 34 (November 1948): 355–80.

"Progress in the Control of Venereal Disease in Virginia." *Virginia Medical Monthly* 66 (January 1939): 52–53.

"Progress of Venereal Disease Control in Virginia." *Study Bulletin: Devoted to the Fight against Syphilis* (March 1941): 3–4.

"Public Health Activities in Virginia as Affected by Recent Federal Appropriations." *Health* 24 (April 1934): 1.

Ransone, C. B. "Prevention of Syphilis." *Virginia Medical Monthly* 58 (May 1931): 79–85.

"Report of Committee on Legislation and Public Health." Reports for the 1932 Annual Session of the Medical Society of Virginia. *Virginia Medical Monthly* 58 (December 1932): 539.

"Report of Committee on Syphilis Control." *Virginia Medical Monthly* 67 (July 1940): 440.

"Report of the Committee of the Medical Society of Virginia to Review the Question of Syphilis Control." *Virginia Medical Monthly* 64 (April 1937): 42–46.

"Reports for House of Delegates, Medical Society of Virginia, 1942 Annual Session." *Virginia Medical Monthly* 69 (September 1942): 415.

"Reports for House of Delegates, Medical Society of Virginia, 1946 Annual Session." *Virginia Medical Monthly* 73 (October 1946): 470.

"Resolution," House of Delegates of the Medical Society of Virginia, 1930 meeting. Reprinted in *Virginia Medical Monthly* 57 (December 1930): 610–11.

"Resolution," House of Delegates of the Medical Society of Virginia, 1939 meeting. Reprinted in *Virginia Medical Monthly* 67 (December 1939): 610–11.

Riggin, I. C. "Effects upon Virginia of the Medical Provisions in the Federal Social Security Act." *Virginia Medical Monthly* 63 (June 1936): 131–34.

———. "Syphilis and the Contact Case." *Virginia Medical Monthly* 67 (August 1939): 499–550.

Riggin, I. C., and E. M. Holmes. "An Evaluation of the Operation of the Premarital Legislation in Virginia." *Virginia Medical Monthly* 69 (February 1942): 96–100.

Smith, Dudley C. "The Prevention of Syphilis." *Virginia Medical Monthly* 54 (April 1927): 28–32.

Social Protection Section of the Defense Health and Welfare Services. "Safeguards plus Salvage." *Journal of Social Hygiene* 28 (January 1942): 40–48.

"State Survey Results." *Virginia Medical Monthly* 61 (March 1935): 993.

Storey, Thomas A. "American Communities Face a New Challenge." *Journal of Social Hygiene* 27.1 (January 1941): 1–9.

Strode, Aubrey E. "Sterilization of Defectives." *Virginia Law Review* 11 (February 1925): 296–99.

Sturkie, S. D. "Syphilis in Industry." *Study Bulletin: Devoted to the Fight against Syphilis* (December 1940): 3–4.

"Supplemental Report from Division of Venereal Disease Control, State Department of Health." Reprinted in *Virginia Medical Monthly* 68 (December 1941): 711.

Tucker, Byron R. "The Subject of Birth Control." *Virginia Medical Monthly* 52 (October 1925): 464.

Usilton, Lida, and W. D. Riley. "Venereal Disease Prevalence in Virginia." *Virginia Medical Monthly* 57 (September 1930): 389–97.

Usilton, Lida J., and R. A. Vonderlehr. "Prevalence and Incidence of Venereal Disease in Richmond, Virginia — with Recommendations." *Virginia Medical Monthly* 64 (September 1937): 299–306.

Van Urk, J. Blan. "Norfolk — Our Worst War Town." *American Mercury* (February 1943): 146–51.

Virginia League for Planned Parenthood. "The Work of the Virginia League for Planned Parenthood." Broadside, 1941.

Virginia Nursing Organizations: History, <http://www.library.vcu.edu/tml/speccoll/nursing/vnaexdir.html>.

Vonderlehr, R. A. "Syphilis and Gonorrhea as a Major Public Health Problem." *Virginia Medical Monthly* 63 (September 1936): 366–70.

Ware, H. Hudnall, Jr. "Annual Report, 1946." Virginia League for Planned Parenthood.

Williams, Ennion S. "The Social Significance of Syphilis." *Virginia Medical Monthly* 63 (September 1936): 360–64.

Secondary Sources

Adair, Cornelia. "Letters Addressed to Dr. J. A. C. Chandler, for the Contemplated Celebration of His Fifteen Years Service as President of William and Mary College." *William and Mary College Quarterly Historical Magazine* 14 (October 1934): 265–88.

Anderson, Karen. *Wartime Women: Sex Roles, Family Relations, and the Status of Women during World War II.* Westport, Conn.: Greenwood Press, 1981.

Bailey, Beth, and David Farber. *The First Strange Place: The Alchemy of Race and Sex in World War II Hawaii.* New York: Free Press, 1992.

Bair, Barbara. "Remapping the Black/White Body: Sexuality, Nationalism, and Biracial Antimiscegenation Activism in 1920s Virginia." In *Sex, Love, Race: Crossing Boundaries in North American History*, edited by Martha Hodes, 399–419. New York: New York University Press, 1999.

Barney, Sandra Lee. *Authorized to Heal: Gender, Class, and the Transformation of Medicine in Appalachia, 1880–1930.* Chapel Hill: University of North Carolina Press, 2000.

Bartley, Numan. *The New South, 1945–1980.* Baton Rouge: Louisiana State University Press, 1995.

Bazelon, Emily. "Sentencing by the Numbers." *New York Times Magazine*, 2 January 2005, 18–19.

Beardsley, Edward H. *A History of Neglect: Health Care for Blacks and Mill Workers in the Twentieth-Century South.* Knoxville: University of Tennessee Press, 1987.

Bederman, Gail. *Manliness and Civilization: A Cultural History of Gender and Race in the United States, 1880–1917.* Chicago: University of Chicago Press, 1995.

"Birth Control and the Good Old Boys in Congress." *Margaret Sanger Papers Project Newsletter* 26 (Winter 2000–2001): 2–5.

Bishop, Mary. "Sterilization Survivors Speak Out." *Southern Exposure* (Summer 1995): 12–17.

Black, Earl, and Merle Black. *Politics and Society in the South.* Cambridge: Harvard University Press, 1987.

Brandt, Allan M. *No Magic Bullet: A Social History of Venereal Disease in the United States since 1880.* New York: Oxford University Press, 1985.

Briggs, Laura. *Reproducing Empire: Race, Sex, Science, and U.S. Imperialism in Puerto Rico.* Berkeley: University of California Press, 2003.

Brinkley, Alan. *The End of Reform: New Deal Liberalism in Recession and War.* New York: Vintage Books, 1996.

Bristow, Nancy K. *Making Men Moral: Social Engineering during the Great War.* New York: New York University Press, 1996.

Brown, William J., James F. Donohue, Norman W. Avanick, Joseph H. Blount, Neal H. Ewen, and Oscar G. Jones. *Syphilis and Other Venereal Diseases.* Cambridge: Harvard University Press, 1970.

Brundage, W. Fitzhugh. *Lynching in the New South: Georgia and Virginia, 1880–1930.* Urbana: University of Illinois Press, 1993.

Bynum, Victoria. *Unruly Women: The Politics of Social and Sexual Control in the Old South*. Chapel Hill: University of North Carolina Press, 1992.

Cahn, Susan. "Spirited Youth or Fiends Incarnate: The Samarcand Arson Case and Female Adolescence in the American South." *Journal of Women's History* 9 (Winter 1998): 152–80.

Chauncey, George. *Gay New York: Gender, Urban Culture, and the Making of a Gay Male World, 1890–1940*. New York: Basic Books, 1994.

Cobb, James C. *Industrialization and Southern Society, 1877–1984*. Chicago: Dorsey Press, 1984.

———. *The Selling of the South: The Southern Crusade for Industrial Development, 1936–1980*. Baton Rouge: Louisiana State University Press, 1982.

Cobb, James C., and Michael V. Namorato, eds. *The New Deal and the South*. Jackson: University Press of Mississippi, 1984.

Corbin, Alain. *Women for Hire: Prostitution and Sexuality in France after 1850*. Translated by Alan Sheridan. Cambridge: Harvard University Press, 1990.

Cott, Nancy. "Passionlessness: An Interpretation of Victorian Sexual Ideology, 1790–1850." *Signs* 4 (1978): 219–36.

Couvares, Francis G., ed. *Movie Censorship and American Culture*. Washington, D.C.: Smithsonian Institution Press, 1996.

Critchlow, Donald T. *Intended Consequences: Birth Control, Abortion, and the Federal Government in Modern America*. New York: Oxford University Press, 1999.

Dabney, Virginius. *Richmond: The Story of a City*. Garden City, N.Y.: Doubleday, 1976.

———. *Virginia: The New Dominion*. Charlottesville: University Press of Virginia, 1971.

Daniels, Pete. "Going among Strangers: Southern Reactions to World War II." *Journal of American History* 77 (December 1990): 886–911.

Davis, Angela. *Women, Race, and Class*. New York: Random House, 1981.

D'Emilio, John. *Sexual Politics, Sexual Communities: The Making of a Homosexual Minority in the United States, 1940–1970*. Chicago: University of Chicago Press, 1983.

D'Emilio, John, and Estelle Freedman. *Intimate Matters: A History of Sexuality in America*. New York: Harper and Row, 1988.

Dennett, Mary Ware. *Birth Control Laws: Shall We Keep Them, Change Them, or Abolish Them?* New York: Grafton Press, 1926.

Dorr, Gregory Michael. "Assuring America's Place in the Sun." *Journal of Southern History* 66 (May 2000): 257–96.

———. "Principled Expediency: *Naim v. Naim* and the Supreme Court." *American Journal of Legal History* 42 (April 1998): 119–59.

———. "Segregation's Science: The American Eugenics Movement and Virginia, 1900–1980." Ph.D. diss., University of Virginia, 2000.

Dorr, Lisa Lindquist. "Arm in Arm: Gender, Eugenics, and Virginia's Racial Integrity Acts of the 1920s." *Journal of Women's History* 11 (Spring 1999): 143–66.

Duggan, Lisa. *Sapphic Slashers: Sex, Violence, and American Modernity*. Durham, N.C.: Duke University Press, 2000.

Enstad, Nan. *Ladies of Labor, Girls of Adventure: Working Women, Popular Culture, and Labor Politics at the Turn of the Twentieth Century*. New York: Columbia University Press, 1999.

Fellner, Jamie, and Marc Mauer. *Losing the Vote: The Impact of Felony Disenfranchisement Laws in the United States*. Washington, D.C.: Human Rights Watch and the Sentencing Project, 1998.

Finkelman, Paul. "Crimes of Love, Misdemeanors of Passion: The Regulation of Race and Sex in the Colonial South." In *The Devil's Lane: Sex and Race in the Early South*, edited by Catherine Clinton and Michele Gillespie, 124–35. New York: Oxford University Press, 1997.

Foucault, Michel. *Discipline and Punish: The Birth of the Prison*. Translated by A. Sheridan. New York: Vintage Books, 1979.

———. *The History of Sexuality. Volume I: An Introduction*. Translated by Robert Hurley. New York: Vintage Books, 1990.

Fredrickson, George M. *The Black Image in the White Mind: The Debate on Afro-American Character and Destiny, 1817–1914*. New York: Harper and Row, 1971.

Freedman, Estelle. *Their Sister's Keepers: Women's Prison Reform in America, 1830–1930*. Ann Arbor: University of Michigan Press, 1981.

———. "'Uncontrolled Desires': The Response to the Sexual Psychopath, 1920–1960." *Journal of American History* 74 (June 1987): 199–225.

Freidel, Frank. *F.D.R. and the South*. Baton Rouge: Louisiana State University Press, 1965.

Friedman, Andrea. "Sadists, Sissies, and the American Way of Life: Anti-Pornography Campaigns in Cold War America." *Gender and History* 15 (August 2003): 201–27.

Gaines, Kevin. *Uplifting the Race: Black Leadership, Politics, and Culture in the Twentieth Century*. Chapel Hill: University of North Carolina Press, 1996.

Gallagher, Nancy L. *Breeding Better Vermonters: The Eugenics Project in the Green Mountain State*. Hanover, N.H.: University Press of New England, 1999.

Gamble, Vanessa. *Making a Place for Ourselves: The Black Hospital Movement, 1920–1945*. New York: Oxford University Press, 1995.

Gilman, Sander. *Difference and Pathology: Stereotypes of Sexuality, Race, and Madness*. Ithaca, N.Y.: Cornell University Press, 1985.

Gilmore, Glenda Elizabeth. *Gender and Jim Crow: Women and the Politics of White Supremacy in North Carolina, 1896–1920*. Chapel Hill: University of North Carolina Press, 1996.

Goldfield, David. *Promised Land: The South since 1945*. Arlington Heights, Ill.: Harlan Davidson, 1987.

Gordon, Linda. *Heroes of Their Own Lives: The Politics and History of Family Violence, Boston, 1880–1960*. New York: Viking, 1988.

———. *Pitied but Not Entitled: Single Mothers and the History of Welfare, 1890–1935*. New York: Free Press, 1994.

———. *Woman's Body, Woman's Right: A Social History of Birth Control in America*. New York: Grossman, 1976.

Gould, Stephen J. "Carrie Buck's Daughter." *Natural History* 93 (1984): 14–18.

Grantham, Dewey. *Southern Progressivism: The Reconciliation of Progress and Tradition*. Knoxville: University of Tennessee Press, 1983.

———. *The South in Modern America: A Region at Odds*. New York: Harper Collins, 1994.

Green, Elna C. *Southern Strategies: Southern Women and the Woman Suffrage Question*. Chapel Hill: University of North Carolina Press, 1997.

———. *This Business of Relief: Confronting Poverty in a Southern City, 1740–1940*. Athens: University of Georgia Press, 2002.

Greenwood, Janette. *Bittersweet Legacy: The Black and White 'Better Classes' in Charlotte, 1850–1910*. Chapel Hill: University of North Carolina Press, 1994.

Haag, Pamela. *Consent: Sexual Rights and the Transformation of American Liberalism*. Ithaca, N.Y.: Cornell University Press, 1999.

Hale, Grace Elizabeth. *Making Whiteness: The Culture of Segregation in the South, 1890–1940*. New York: Pantheon, 1998.

Hall, Phyllis A. "Crisis at Hampton Roads: The Problems of Wartime Congestion, 1942–1944." *Virginia Magazine of History and Biography* 101 (July 1993): 405–32.

Hegarty, Marilyn E. "'Patriots, Prostitutes, Patriotutes': The Mobilization and Control of American Women's Sexuality during World War II." Ph.D. diss., Ohio State University, 1998.

Heinemann, Ronald L. *Depression and the New Deal in Virginia: The Enduring Dominion*. Charlottesville: University Press of Virginia, 1983.

———. *Harry Byrd of Virginia*. Charlottesville: University Press of Virginia, 1996.

Hewitt, Nancy. *Southern Discomfort: Women's Activism in Tampa, Florida, 1880s–1920s*. Urbana: University of Illinois Press, 2001.

Himmstedt, Erin Kathleen. "Not for Their Own Good: African-American Mental Health and Eugenic Sterilization Programs in Virginia." MA thesis, University of Virginia, 1995.

Hodes, Martha. *White Women, Black Men: Illicit Sex in the Nineteenth-Century South*. New Haven: Yale University Press, 1997.

Hoffer, Frank William, Delbert Martin Mann, and Floyd Nelson House. *The Jails of Virginia: A Study of the Local Penal System*. Charlottesville, Va.: Institute for Research in the Social Sciences, 1933.

James, Arthur W. *The State Becomes Social Worker: An Administrative Interpretation*. Richmond, Va.: Garrett and Massie, 1942.

———. *Virginia's Social Awakening: The Contribution of Dr. Mastin and the Board of Charities and Corrections*. Richmond, Va.: Garrett and Massie, 1939.

Johnson, David K. *The Lavender Scare: The Cold War Persecution of Gays and Lesbians in the Federal Government*. Chicago: University of Chicago Press, 2003.

Jones, James. *Bad Blood: The Tuskegee Syphilis Experiment*. New York: Free Press, 1993.

Jowett, Garth. "'A Significant Medium for the Communication of Ideas': The *Miracle* Decision and the Decline of Motion Picture Censorship, 1952–1968." In

Movie Censorship and American Culture, edited by Francis G. Couvares, 258–76. Washington, D.C.: Smithsonian Institution Press, 1996.

Kennedy, N. Brent. *The Melungeons: The Resurrection of a Proud People*. Macon, Ga.: Mercer University Press, 1997.

Kern, Richard P., and Meredith Farrar-Owens. "Sentencing Guidelines with Integrated Offender Risk Assessment." *Federal Sentencing Reporter* 16 (February 2004): 165–69.

Keve, Paul. *The History of Corrections in Virginia*. Charlottesville: University Press of Virginia, 1986.

Key, V. O., Jr. *Southern Politics*. New York: Vintage Books, 1949.

Koste, Jodi L. "Baughman, Mary Barney." *Dictionary of Virginia Biography*, vol. 2, edited by Sara B. Bearss, John T. Kneebone, J. Jefferson Looney, Brent Tarter, and Sandra Gioia Treadway, 394–96. Richmond: Library of Virginia, 2001.

Kousser, J. Morgan. *The Shaping of Southern Politics: Suffrage Restriction and the Establishment of the One-Party South, 1880–1910*. New Haven: Yale University Press, 1974.

Koven, Seth, and Sonya Michel, eds. *Mothers of a New World: Maternalist Politics and the Origins of Welfare States*. New York: Routledge, 1993.

Kunzel, Regina G. *Fallen Women, Problem Girls: Unmarried Mothers and the Professionalization of Social Work, 1890–1945*. New Haven: Yale University Press, 1993.

Ladd-Taylor, Molly. "Saving Babies and Sterilizing Mothers: Eugenics and Welfare Politics in the Interwar United States." *Social Politics* 4 (Spring 1997): 147–49.

Larson, Edward J. *Sex, Race, and Science: Eugenics in the Deep South*. Baltimore: Johns Hopkins University Press, 1995.

Leavitt, Judith Walzer. *Typhoid Mary: Captive to the Public's Health*. Boston: Beacon, 1997.

Leonard, Thomas C. "'More Merciful and Not Less Effective': Eugenics and American Economics in the Progressive Era." *History of Political Economy* 35.4 (2003): 709–34.

Lewis, Earl. *In their Own Interests: Race, Class, and Power in Twentieth-Century Norfolk, Virginia*. Berkeley: University of California Press, 1991.

Link, William. *The Paradox of Southern Progressivism, 1880–1930*. Chapel Hill: University of North Carolina Press, 1992.

Lombardo, Paul A. "Eugenic Sterilization in Virginia: Aubrey Strode and the Case of *Buck v. Bell*." Ph.D. diss., University of Virginia, 1982.

———. "Involuntary Sterilization in Virginia: From *Buck v. Bell* to *Poe v. Lynchburg*." *Developments in Mental Health Law* 3 (1983): 19.

———. "Miscegenation, Eugenics, and Racism: Historical Footnotes to *Loving v. Virginia*." *University of California at Davis Law Review* 21 (1988): 421–52.

Lutz, Francis Earle. *Richmond in World War II*. Richmond, Va.: Dietz, 1951.

Manning, Kenneth R. "Byrd, David Wellington." *Dictionary of Virginia Biography*, vol. 2, edited by Sara B. Bearss, John T. Kneebone, J. Jefferson Looney, Brent Tarter, and Sandra Gioia Treadway, 452–54. Richmond, Va.: Library of Virginia, 2001.

Martin-Perdue, Nancy J., and Charles L. Perdue Jr., eds. *Talk about Trouble: A New Deal Portrait of Virginians in the Great Depression*. Chapel Hill: University of North Carolina Press, 1996.

McArthur, Judith N. *Creating the New Woman: The Rise of Southern Women's Progressive Culture in Texas, 1893–1918*. Urbana: University of Illinois Press, 1998.

McCann, Carole R. *Birth Control Politics in the United States, 1916–1945*. Ithaca, N.Y.: Cornell University Press, 1994.

Meyer, Leisa. *Creating GI Jane: Sexuality and Power in the Women's Army Corps during World War II*. New York: Columbia University Press, 1996.

Mink, Gwendolyn. *The Wages of Motherhood: Inequality in the Welfare State, 1917–1942*. Ithaca, N.Y.: Cornell University Press, 1995.

Mumford, Kevin J. *Interzones: Black/White Sex Districts in Chicago and New York in the Early Twentieth Century*. New York: Columbia University Press, 1997.

Noll, Steven. *Feeble-Minded in Our Midst: Institutions for the Mentally Retarded in the South, 1900–1940*. Chapel Hill: University of North Carolina Press, 1995.

Odem, Mary E. *Delinquent Daughters: Protecting and Policing Adolescent Female Sexuality in the United States, 1885–1920*. Chapel Hill: University of North Carolina Press, 1995.

Ownby, Ted. *Subduing Satan: Religion, Recreation, and Manhood in the Rural South, 1865–1920*. Chapel Hill: University of North Carolina Press, 1990.

Parramore, Thomas C., with Peter C. Stewart and Tommy L. Bogger. *Norfolk: The First Four Centuries*. Charlottesville: University Press of Virginia, 1994.

Parran, Thomas, and R. A. Vonderlehr. *Plain Words about Venereal Disease*. New York: Reynal and Hitchcock, 1941.

Pascoe, Peggy. "Miscegenation Law, Court Cases, and Ideologies of 'Race' in Twentieth-Century America." *Journal of American History* 83 (June 1996): 44–69.

Peiss, Kathy. *Cheap Amusements: Working Women and Leisure in Turn-of-the-Century New York*. Philadelphia: Temple University Press, 1996.

Perman, Michael. *Struggle for Mastery: Disfranchisement in the South, 1888–1908*. Chapel Hill: University of North Carolina Press, 2001.

Pivar, David J. *Purity and Hygiene: Women, Prostitution, and the "American Plan," 1900–1930*. Westport, Conn.: Greenwood, 2002.

Piven, Frances Fox, and Richard A. Cloward. *Regulating the Poor: The Functions of Public Welfare*. New York: Random House, 1971.

Rabinowitz, Howard. *The First New South: 1865–1920*. Arlington Heights, Ill.: Harlan Davidson, 1992.

Rafter, Nicole Hahn. *Partial Justice: Women in State Prisons, 1800–1935*. Boston: Northeastern University Press, 1985.

Reagan, Leslie J. *When Abortion Was a Crime: Women, Medicine, and Law in the United States, 1867–1973*. Berkeley: University of California Press, 1997.

Reilly, Philip R. *The Surgical Solution: A History of Involuntary Sterilization in the United States*. Baltimore: Johns Hopkins University Press, 1991.

———. "The Virginia Racial Integrity Act Revisited: The Plecker-Laughlin Correspondence: 1928–1930." *American Journal of Medical Genetics* 16, no.4 (1983): 483–92.

Rise, Eric W. *The Martinsville Seven: Race, Rape, and Capital Punishment.* Charlottesville: University Press of Virginia, 1995.

Rodrique, Jessie. "The Black Community and the Birth Control Movement." In *Passion and Power: Sexuality in History*, edited by Kathy Peiss and Christina Simmons, 138–54. Philadelphia: Temple University Press, 1989.

Rosenbloom, Nancy J. "From Regulation to Censorship: Film and Political Culture in New York in the Early Twentieth Century." *Journal of the Gilded Age and Progressive Era* 3 (October 2004): 369–406.

Schlegel, Marvin W. *Conscripted City: Norfolk in World War II.* Norfolk, Va.: Norfolk War History Commission, 1951.

Schoen, Johanna. *Choice and Coercion: Birth Control, Sterilization, and Abortion in Public Health and Welfare.* Chapel Hill: University of North Carolina Press, 2005.

———. "Fighting for Child Health: Race, Birth Control, and the State in the Jim Crow South." *Social Politics* 4 (Spring 1997): 90–113.

Sherman, Richard B. "'The Last Stand': The Fight for Racial Integrity in Virginia in the 1920s." *Journal of Southern History* 54 (February 1988): 69–92.

Silver, Christopher. *Twentieth-Century Richmond: Planning, Politics, and Race.* Knoxville: University of Tennessee Press, 1984.

Sims, Anastasia. *The Power of Femininity in the New South: Women and Politics in North Carolina, 1883–1930.* Columbia: University of South Carolina Press, 1997.

Sklar, Robert. *Movie-Made America: A Cultural History of American Movies.* Revised edition. New York: Vintage Books, 1994.

Skowronek, Stephen. *Building a New American State: The Expansion of National Administrative Capacities, 1877–1920.* New York: Cambridge University Press.

Smith, Douglas L. *The New Deal in the Urban South.* Baton Rouge: Louisiana State University Press, 1988.

Smith, J. David. *The Eugenic Assault on America: Scenes in Red, White, and Black.* Fairfax, Va.: George Mason University Press, 1993.

Smith, J. David, and K. Ray Nelson. *The Sterilization of Carrie Buck.* Far Hills, N.J.: New Horizon, 1989.

Smith, J. Douglas. *Managing White Supremacy: Race, Politics, and Citizenship in Jim Crow Virginia.* Chapel Hill: University of North Carolina Press, 2002.

———. "Patrolling the Boundaries of Race: Motion Picture Censorship and Jim Crow in Virginia, 1922–1932." *Historical Journal of Film, Radio and Television* 21 (2001): 273–91.

Smith, Susan L. *Sick and Tired of Being Sick and Tired: Black Women's Health Activism in America, 1890–1950.* Philadelphia: University of Pennsylvania Press, 1995.

Solinger, Rickie. *Wake Up Little Suzie: Single Pregnancy and Race before Roe v. Wade.* New York: Routledge, 1992.

Somerville, Siobhan. *Queering the Color Line: Race and the Invention of Homosexuality in American Culture.* Durham, N.C.: Duke University Press, 2000.

Sosna, Morton. *In Search of the Silent South: Southern Liberals and the Race Issue*. New York: Columbia University Press, 1977.

Starr, Paul. *The Social Transformation of American Medicine: The Rise of a Sovereign Profession and the Making of a Vast Empire*. New York: Basic Books, 1982.

Stoler, Ann Laura. *Carnal Knowledge and Imperial Power: Race and the Intimate in Colonial Rule*. Berkeley: University of California Press, 2002.

Terry, Jennifer. *An American Obsession: Science, Medicine, and Homosexuality in Modern Society*. Chicago: University of Chicago Press, 1999.

Tindall, George. *The Emergence of the New South, 1913–1935*. Baton Rouge: Louisiana State University Press, 1967.

Tone, Andrea. *Devices and Desires: A History of Contraceptives in America*. New York: Hill and Wang, 2001.

Trent, James W. *Inventing the Feeble Mind: A History of Mental Retardation in the United States*. Berkeley: University of California Press, 1994.

Ullman, Sharon. *Sex Seen: The Emergence of Modern Sexuality in America*. Berkeley: University of California Press, 1997.

Wadlington, Walter. "The *Loving* Case: Virginia's Anti-Miscegenation Statute in Historical Perspective." *Virginia Law Review* 52 (1966): 1189–223.

Wailoo, Keith. *Dying in the City of the Blues: Sickle Cell Anemia and the Politics of Race and Health*. Chapel Hill: University of North Carolina Press, 2001.

Wallenstein, Peter. "Indian Foremothers: Race, Sex, Slavery, and Freedom in Early Virginia." In *The Devil's Lane: Sex and Race in the Early South*, edited by Catherine Clinton and Michele Gillespie, 57–73. New York: Oxford University Press, 1997.

———. "Race Marriage and the Law of Freedom: Alabama and Virginia, 1860s–1960s." *Chicago-Kent Law Review* 70 (1994): 371–437.

Welter, Barbara. "The Cult of True Womanhood, 1820–1860." *American Quarterly* 18 (1966): 151–74.

Wertenbaker, Thomas. *Norfolk: Historic Southern Port*. Durham, N.C.: Duke University Press, 1962.

White, Clare. *Roanoke: 1740–1982*. Roanoke, Va.: Roanoke Valley Historical Society, 1982.

White, Deborah Gray. *Ar'nt I a Woman?: Female Slaves in the Plantation South*. New York: Norton, 1985.

Wilkinson, J. Harvie, III. *Harry Byrd and the Changing Face of Virginia Politics, 1945–1966*. Charlottesville: University Press of Virginia, 1968.

Williamson, Joel. *New People: Miscegenation and Mulattoes in the United States*. New York: Free Press, 1980.

Winchell, Megan K. "Good Food, Good Fun, and Good Girls: USO Hostesses and World War Two." Ph.D. Diss., University of Arizona, 2003.

Woodside, Moya. *Sterilization in North Carolina: A Sociological and Psychological Study*. Chapel Hill: University of North Carolina Press, 1950.

Index